SAY HELLO TO MY LITTLE FRIEND
A CENTURY OF SCARFACE

SAY HELLO TO MY LITTLE FRIEND

A CENTURY OF SCARFACE

NAT SEGALOFF

Citadel Press
Kensington Publishing Corp.
www.kensingtonbooks.com

CITADEL PRESS BOOKS are published by

Kensington Publishing Corp.
119 West 40th Street
New York, NY 10018

All Kensington titles, imprints, and distributed lines are available at special quantity discounts for bulk purchases for sales promotions, premiums, fund-raising, educational, or institutional use. Special book excerpts or customized printings can also be created to fit specific needs. For details, write or phone the office of the Kensington sales manager: Kensington Publishing Corp., 119 West 40th Street, New York, NY 10018, attn: Sales Department; phone 1-800-221-2647.

ISBN: 978-0-8065-4296-6

First Citadel hardcover edition: November 2023

10   9   8   7   6   5   4   3   2   1

Printed in the United States of America

Library of Congress Control Number: 2023941472

ISBN: 978-0-8065-4298-0 (ebook)

To Roger L. Kohn and Kay Miranda Gilbert

The definition of friendship

A Note on Names

The spelling of Brian DePalma's name is as varied as his filmography. Over the years it has been written *DePalma*, *De Palma*, *de Palma*, and *dePalma*, with no consistency even on his own screen credits and in the many books and articles written about him. His 2015 film colloquy by Noah Baumbach and Jake Paltrow spells it *De* (half space) *Palma* in the title crawl and *De* (full space) *Palma* on the poster. IMDb says *De Palma*. The directorial credit on *Scarface*, however, spells it *DePalma,* so that is what this book will use.

The Motion Picture Association (MPA), as the American motion picture industry's trade organization is now called, was formed in 1922 as the Motion Picture Producers and Distributors of America (MPPDA) under Will H. Hays, at which time it was informally referred to as the Hays Office. From 1945 to 2019 it was known as the Motion Picture Association of America (MPAA). In 2019 its name was changed to the Motion Picture Association (MPA), reflecting the worldwide, multinational status of its member companies. One of its subdivisions is the Classification and Ratings Administration (CARA), successor to the Production Code Administration (PCA), informally referred to as, successively, the Hays Office, the Breen Office, the Shurlock Office, and the Valenti Office. Now it is simply referred to as the Ratings Board. Each use in this book is made in context.

Contents

Scarface and Me

by Steven Bauer

All of us who made *Scarface* knew that we'd caught lightning in a bottle. What we didn't know was that it would take the public ten years to open that bottle. Now, forty years later, it's rewarding to know that we've finally received that sense of gratification and acceptance and approval and respect for the things we fantasized about forty years ago.

If only we had known that at the time!

When you shoot a film, you enter a separate world: the world of the film. But the world outside goes on, and while we were making *Scarface* it was Al Pacino who kept me centered. It was my first big film, but Al was bringing twenty-five years of experience to the game and prepared me for what was to come. He was a sounding board who would tell me if I was off. He would not let me make a false move. We became a team: I taught Al how to be a Cuban, and he taught me how to be an actor.

A month into the shooting—we had done three-quarters of our work together—I asked him in confidence, "Don't you have some expectations? Nobody's ever seen anything like this before." We knew there was no way the film was going to go unnoticed, but Al told me to be prepared, because it might be more than fifty percent hating it.

Sadly, he was right. It became the fashion to reject *Scarface*, to blame it for establishing a frightening new trend of violence in American movies. But then I remembered that

Bonnie and Clyde got the same response sixteen years earlier, so *Scarface* was in good company.

Part of the audience that was first exposed to it had that response because of the subject matter. Al knew this. He said, "I told you not to read the reviews." When they came out, they were not good. I called him immediately. I couldn't wrap my head around it that the worst we thought could happen, had happened. I had been looking forward to a happy ending. But Al said, "At least *we* know that what we did was great." I went into a zombie state for days. Yet I always had the feeling that, maybe, one day, people would recognize our achievement.

In hindsight, some funny things happened. I was called to a meeting by some young hotshot producers. They wanted to meet me for their project. They started off saying, "We are such big fans." Then they said, "And you deserve credit because you're in that piece of shit movie." He said this to me while he was still shaking my hand! I wanted to say, "You have the balls to invite me here to insult what we did?" Needless to say, I didn't get the job, nor did I want it after that.

Universal and the producer, Marty Bregman, stood behind the picture. It opened in December 1983 (the day before my birthday), and it played in theaters through March 1984. But when it came out on home video and started appearing on cable TV, that's when things began to change. What we didn't expect was that it would happen in a bigger way than we could ever have imagined. It became iconic without the press declaring that it was iconic. People started hearing about it from each other, not from media sources. We started hearing voices of approval, not from the critics, but from people on the street. It hit me in waves, more and more every year. People went out of their way and crossed the street to tell me how much the film meant to them. By the late 1980s and early 1990s, the tide had turned. Instead of a slap in the face, I would get a pat on the back. When I would do signings, I would run into people who just wanted to meet me, to spend a few minutes with Manny. I tell them my stories and they tell me theirs. It's an honor for us to meet each other.

Scarface is now accepted as the important film we always knew it was. The good news that came from it is that whatever brought me to this place in my life, things are now better for me than they have been for the last thirty years. Better for me in terms of quality and joy. The fairy tale did happen, and those of us who are still around are able to enjoy this moment.

Since appearing in Scarface *in 1983, Steven Bauer has amassed nearly two hundred acting credits in feature films and on television. He is still active and lives in Miami, Florida, with his wife, Jennifer Brenon.*

INTRODUCTION

"I'm proud of that film and what we did!"

I had just finished a short, perfunctory television interview with Michele Pfeiffer for the film *Ladyhawke*. Warner Bros. had flown the usual gaggle of movie critics and entertainment reporters to Los Angeles for a press junket ahead of the film's April 12, 1985, opening, and I was one of them. My Sierra Club Engagement Calendar says it was February 10, 1985. I didn't much care for the film, but protocol dictated that I'd keep that to myself until I ran my review. Besides, why would I let my opinion lose me an opportunity to interview a director whose work I otherwise admired—Richard Donner—and the stars Rutger Hauer and Michelle Pfeiffer, who were relatively new to American films?

I was working for a TV station at the time, so I was given the usual ten minutes per person to ask whatever questions I could squeeze in. Junket interviews are an assembly line designed to keep the questions superficial and drive the stars batty. Imagine having to give the same sound bites over and over again to the same vapid questions as if a director had called for fifty takes of a scene with a new costar each time. As a cog on the press line, you do what you can to distinguish yourself: compliment them on an early film, say hello from anyone you know in common, and so forth. My trick was to tell them to pull down their jacket in back so they don't look hunched over. This not only makes them trust you, it makes them wonder why their publicist hadn't told them first. With Donner it was easy—he was as gripping

1

and energetic as his films, and garrulous beyond expectation. Great TV. I had been warned that Rutger Hauer could be testy, but not only had I seen his Dutch films, I knew his publicist and told him so, and we had a great ten minutes of tape time. (His jacket was fine.)

Michelle Pfeiffer posed a problem for me in those pre-IMDb days. I hadn't seen any of her episodic TV work and the only three movies she had made prior to *Ladyhawke* were *Grease 2*, which nobody saw, *Into the Night*, and *Scarface*. I like John Landis, who made *Into the Night*, in which Pfeiffer costarred with Jeff Goldblum in a pursuit mystery most notable for countless playful cameo appearances by directors. Of course, I had seen *Scarface*, but my mission was *Ladyhawke*. She was bright and articulate as well as heart-stoppingly beautiful, and we managed to keep the conversation flowing. The publicist called "time" just as I mentioned *Scarface*, specifically why it caught such grief from the press. Pfeiffer immediately became defensive. "That wasn't fair," she said. "I'm proud of that film and the work we did!" The crew had stopped tape by then, but I tried to assure her that I wasn't attacking *Scarface* and that, to the contrary, I loved Brian DePalma, I thought *Scarface* was brilliant, and I agreed with her. I don't think she heard me as the next interviewer arrived and I was handed my video-cassette as I left the room.

Time, of course, has proven both of us right. *Scarface* is not only celebrated as the film it always was, but it has taken on additional meanings as each generation has discovered and appreciated it. Although it barely turned a profit from ticket sales on its original 1983 release, according to more recent 2020 figures it has sold nearly four million DVD and Blu-ray discs, well outgrossing its theatrical revenue, and its popularity is still growing.[1]

Scarface is a phenomenon. It was about its time and yet was ahead of its time, and when the general public jumped on board twenty years later, the film was still relevant. This is because *Scarface* is not only about drugs, it's about two equally addictive and destructive substances: power and money. Brian DePalma, screenwriter Oliver Stone, and producers Martin Bregman, Peter Saphier, and Louis A. Stroller knew this going in. They painted a Boschian canvas with their 1983 film that hangs in a cinematic gallery that has many other rooms and masterpieces addressing the same subjects, among them *Citizen Kane*, *A Face in the Crowd*, *All the King's Men*, and *All the President's Men*. This book is not just about how *Scarface* went from victim to victor; it's about Hollywood's long-running infatuation with power, money, and organized crime, both illegal and legal, and on the screen as well as within its guarded, secretive studio walls.

This is less a chronicle about the making of *Scarface* (there are already a couple of those) than it is an exploration of its place in the history of Hollywood and America—not just the 1983 remake but its 1932 original. Each film was born of a time of social, economic, and political upheaval that only now, with the perspective of ninety years for one and forty years for the other, can we begin to find clarity.

I am indebted to the many people who offered their views and experiences to this adventure. In addition to those who are quoted in these pages, my appreciation goes to (alphabetically) Stacy Abrams, Donna Antsey (Yale University Press), Kari Campano, Nancy Down, David Feldman, Katie Feldman, Danny Goldberg, Lawrence Grobel, Cassandra Jaskulski, Aviva Kempner, April Kim, Barry Krost, Lisa Lieberman, Caroline Maguire, Kathy Manabat, Mayra Mendoza, David Morrell, Stan Rosenfeld, and Daniel Schweiger. The gang at Photofest New York were also helpful.

The enthusiasm and counsel of my editor James Abbate is especially appreciated, as is the support of Kensington's publisher Stephen Zacharius and his team of professionals. The staff of the Margaret Herrick Library of the Academy Foundation of the Academy of Motion Picture Arts and Sciences, as usual, came through, even during Covid, and I want to pay particular thanks to Elizabeth Youle, Genevieve Maxwell, and Howard Prouty. My agent, Lee Sobel, is the one who said, "Hey, *Scarface* has a fortieth anniversary coming up," and sent me on a mission to look at the film in different ways.

It will become clear as you keep reading that I am a fan of Brian DePalma and *Scarface*, but I have tried to keep my feet on the ground. I liked both of them from the first time we met on screen: DePalma with a double bill of *Greetings* and *Hi, Mom* at the Central Square Cinemas in Cambridge, Massachusetts, and *Scarface* when I caught it—and it caught me—at a critics' screening in Boston. Alas, at the time I was only a stringer for my newspaper, so their lead critic got to write the review instead of me. I never read what he wrote, so I have no idea what he said, but I hope, in the words that follow, to add to his praise if he bestowed it, or, conversely, to make up for any myopia on his part.

CHAPTER 1

"Get out of my way, Johnny, I'm gonna spit"

In a very large sense, the story of *Scarface* begins not with the movies, but in real life, on January 17, 1920, for that was the day that the Volstead Act went into effect. Named after Minnesota Republican Congressman Andrew J. Volstead, a teetotaler who chaired the House Judiciary Committee, it empowered the government to enforce the Eighteenth Amendment, better known as Prohibition. The Eighteenth Amendment had been ratified by Congress on January 19, 1919, and the Volstead Act was passed by that same sober body on October 28 of that year. "The Great Experiment," as Prohibition was also known, banned "the manufacture, sale, or transportation of intoxicating liquors within, the importation thereof into, or the exportation thereof from the United States and all territory subject to the jurisdiction thereof for beverage purposes."[1]

Like most attempts at legislating morality, Prohibition was contentious; even its passage was controversial: Congressman Volstead's Capitol Hill politicking had managed to wrangle a two-thirds majority vote to override President Woodrow Wilson's veto, and the partisan bitterness that grew out of the process lasted nearly as long as Prohibition itself. The Eighteenth Amendment remained law until December 5, 1933, when it was revoked by the Twenty-First Amendment. The intervening fourteen years saw one of the worst crime waves in American history; its effects compounded the widespread devastation of the Great Depression and the social schism of the Jazz Age. Not until the 1960s and '70s would so many otherwise moral people engage in willful yet risky violation of the law.

Every major city had speakeasies—secret clubs where patrons could buy illegal, or "bootleg," alcohol. The sources of illegal booze were broad. Some of it was from foreign distilleries and smuggled into the United States at great risk. Some of it was made in secret stills in America. Other hooch was fabricated from various dubious sources, including deadly wood grain/methyl alcohol that first made you blind drunk, then made you blind. Just as it would become with marijuana, LSD, cocaine, heroin, and other controlled substances in the 1960s through 1990s, having a reputable supplier who provided guaranteed quality was valued but expensive. And all of it was and is ultimately controlled by organized crime.

It wasn't always this way. Unlike what is generally recognized today as "organized crime," "the Syndicate," "Cosa Nostra," or "the Mob," the gangsters that appeared in America at the turn of the nineteenth into the twentieth century were mostly thugs and street hoodlums. The American Northeast, in particular, where the first cities sprouted just after the Revolutionary War, saw the formation of such groups.[2] But it was not until the massive wave of immigration in the late 1800s and early 1900s that the modern concept of gangs appeared. Crime was not their first calling; they were chiefly ethnic and were protecting their neighborhoods from the arrival of the next wave of immigrants. The Jewish Lennox Avenue Gang, the Dead Rabbits from Ireland, and their archrivals, the Bowery Boys (no, not *those* Bowery Boys), and gangs from Poland and Germany dominated the cities, especially New York. This changed in the 1920s, when one-quarter of New York City was Italian, and with this influx from the Mediterranean came the Black Hand and the Five Points Gang, the latter of which was led by Johnny Torrio and Paolo Antonio

Vaccarelli (aka. Paul Kelly).[3] With Torrio's organizing of the Five Points Gang, the American Mafia arrived.[4]

It took a while for the movies to catch on to this source of rich story material. The traditional, simplistic "good guy/bad guy" structure of literature and stage drama made the notion of a story with multiple villains seem foreign to audiences, especially unsophisticated nickelodeon customers of early silent movies. Filmmakers, however, were eager to explore this new dramatic possibility. The first to do so is claimed by many scholars to be D. W. Griffith. His 1912 two-reel drama *The Musketeers of Pig Alley* is cited as the first gangster film. Earlier examples may be the one-reel *The Moonshiners* (1904) unearthed by historian Tom Dirks, *A Desperate Encounter Between Burglars and Police* (Edwin S. Porter and Wallace McCutcheon, 1905), and *The Black Hand* (Wallace McCutcheon, 1906),[5] although precise release date documentation has been elusive.[6]

Because of Griffith's fame, *The Musketeers of Pig Alley* was given preference for preservation and has survived to represent that movie era's idea of street crime. Fittingly, it was shot in New York's Lower East Side, among real tenements and with actual gang members.[7] The story was basic: "Little Lady" (Griffith star Lillian Gish) and her husband (Walter Miller) are threatened by a gang leader "Snapper Kid" (Elmer Booth) after the husband's wallet is stolen, but they come to Snapper Kid's defense when another gangster threatens him. The seventeen-minute drama was written by Griffith and Anita Loos and can create chills even today from Griffith's pioneering use of close-ups and the casting of some truly threatening-looking performers.

Surprisingly few gangster movies seem to have been made in the silent era.

It was nearly ten years before the next major gangster film

appeared: *Underworld*,[8] written by Ben Hecht and directed by Josef von Sternberg (Jonas Sternberg) in 1927. The story of tough thief Bull Weed (George Bancroft)—who comes to suspect that the man he saved from the gutter, Rolls-Royce Wensel (Clive Owen), is after his woman friend "Feathers" McCoy (Evelyn Brent)—was considered a failure by both its makers and its studio (Paramount) until the day it opened, when it took off thanks to reviews and word of mouth.

Underworld was romantic but tough. Ben Hecht mined the stories and images he'd heard and covered as a Chicago journalist and, in so doing, is said to have laid the groundwork for all successive gangster films and even film noir: night-lit streets, deep shadows, drive-by machine gun killings, tough dames, and antiheroes. Breaking the good guy/bad guy tradition struck Hecht as an epiphany. "An idea came to me," he wrote of creating *Underworld*. "The thing to do was to skip the heroes and heroines, to write a movie containing only villains and bawds."[9] In doing so, he challenged accepted screen morality by giving his characters, all of whom were reprobates, a range of scruples. Audiences, he discovered, loved criminals. Five years later, Hecht would write *Scarface*.

The direct impetus for the 1932 *Scarface* was greater than a street gang's strong-arm larceny or a romantic love triangle. The drought of Prohibition and the public's relentless thirst created opportunities for those who were willing to quench it by breaking the law. Hollywood followed the headlines: Here were cops-and-robber stories based on real cops and real robbers made more vivid by the arrival of talking pictures. The first wave of Prohibition-inspired movie gangsters was the holy trinity of pre-Code[10] gangster films: *The Public Enemy*, *Little Caesar* (both 1931), and *Scarface* (1932). Unlike what organized criminals would become in the future, the tarnished yet romanticized heroes of these films were strictly into running beer and booze (and incidentally rubbing out anybody who got in their way). They avoided prostitution, drugs, protection, and other forms of vice that the Production Code wouldn't allow on the screen.

Warner Bros., in particular, was lucky enough to have three actors under contract who bore remarkable resemblances to real gangsters. Stocky Edward G. Robinson was their Al Capone type. Humphrey Bogart, though not yet a star, was easily John Dillinger's double. And James Cagney became Capone's Irish nemesis, Deanie O'Banion.

Little Caesar (released January 1931) and *The Public Enemy* (released May 1931) primed the public for *Scarface* (released April 1932). *Little Caesar*, in which Edward G. Robinson snarled his way to the top of the Mob only to be killed by police (whining "Mother of Mercy, is this the end of Rico?"), was brashly directed by Mervyn LeRoy from a book by W. R. Burnett, which was adapted by Francis Edward Faragoh and Robert N. Lee with uncredited contributions by Robert Lord and Warner Bros.' then production chief Darryl F. Zanuck. Zanuck was supposedly motivated to buy Burnett's book when a friend of his was killed by a bootlegger; likewise, Burnett found his writing inspiration after seeing the aftermath of the St. Valentine's Day Massacre in Chicago.[11] Soon the scrappy Warner Bros. studio would become known for making timely movies "torn from the morning's headlines." *Little Caesar* was one of the first and best.

Four months later, Warners released the even more galvanizing gangster film, William Wellman's *The Public Enemy*. Based on an unpublished novel by John Bright, it introduced James Cagney as Tom Powers, a homicidal killer who grows up around guns and vice and becomes a violent bootlegger until he is gunned down, admitting, "I ain't so tough."[12] Bright, Kubec Glasman, and Harvey F. Thew adapted it for

Edward Woods[13] to star and Cagney to support him.[14] On viewing the first rushes, however, Zanuck and Wellman saw that they couldn't take their eyes off Cagney, and the actors were told to switch roles. *The Public Enemy* was so electric and so offended Hollywood's chief censor Will H. Hays that he boldly predicted the public would reject it. He was wrong.

For all the fires that *Little Caesar* and *The Public Enemy* sparked at the box office, the rest of the industry was not eager to join the Warner Bros. gangster parade. Whodunnits, cops-and-robbers, and detective yarns were one thing, but pre-Code organized crime pictures were as rare as virtuous gun molls.

What held the moguls back? The Production Code.

Howard Hughes, who produced *Scarface*, among other controversial films, was not an ordinary mogul. For starters, his money didn't come from ticket sales, it came from an inherited tool corporation and real estate investments. Movies were for dallying and dabbling; he did the dallying with starlets, but the dabbling he reserved for picture making. Unbeholden to any studio (United Artists merely distributed his independently financed product), he called his own shots, and in 1930 the shots came from Armitage Trail's novel, *Scarface*.

The book was first published serially under the title *Gun Girl* in *Underworld* magazine, issues April through July 1929, and was reprinted as a standalone book, *Scarface*, on March 24, 1930, with the copyright belonging not to Trail but to the publisher, E.J. Clode.

Trail's novel is an unashamed roman-à-clef about Al Capone. Its central character, Tony Guarino (later the 1932 film's Tony Camonte), is a Chicago slum kid who rejects his likely life of anonymity and kills his way to the top of a crime syndicate. For him, gangsters are his boyhood heroes and cops are only there to bust you back to the gutter. Tony's first act is murdering crime boss Al Spingola (later the film's Louis Costillo) as the first step on a rise to having it all. At the end he is shot by his brother, who has chosen a career in law enforcement. (In actuality, one of Al Capone's brothers did become a policeman. Another, Frank Capone, was killed by the police.)

Unlike his power-driven creation, Trail himself was an enigma. Born Maurice R. Coons in Nebraska in 1902, he left school at age sixteen to become a writer. Although *Scarface* is his claim to literary fame, he is believed to have written under so many other pen names that his full bibliography may never be known. *Scarface* came to Howard Hughes's attention right after its publication, and he paid Coons/Trail $25,000 for the rights. This financed Trail's move to Los Angeles and apparently sent him off on a bender that lasted until his death of heart failure while at the Paramount Theatre two years later, at age twenty-eight, on October 10, 1930, before the film was released.[15]

In those days Hughes was not yet the bashful billionaire he became in his dotage and was a well-known bachelor-about-Hollywood. He and director Howard Hawks met and discovered that they shared a fierce independence that would come to fuel their collaboration. "We couldn't get a studio, and they wouldn't loan us anybody," Hawks told historian Joseph McBride for McBride's 1982 monograph, *Hawks on Hawks*. "They just didn't want independent pictures made in Hollywood. So we rented a little cobwebbed studio and opened it up and made the picture."[16] Hawks's recollections are as elliptical as his films; there was far more to it than that. For one thing, he needed a script, and the go-to man for *Scarface* was Ben Hecht, who had cracked the gangster genre with *Underworld*. Hecht was already working with Hughes on the screen adaptation of his play cowritten with Charles MacArthur, *The Front Page* (Lewis Milestone, 1931), but he was unsure about adapting another writer's work.

Hecht's agent, Leland Hayward, took credit for selling Hughes the idea of hiring Hecht. "I went back to Hughes," Hayward told historian Max Wilk, "and told him I'd been able to persuade Hecht to do the script; I told him Ben's terms—$1,000 per day—and Howard didn't blink an eye. He nodded and said, 'Okay, it's a deal. But you tell Hecht I want a real tough shoot-'em-up script that'll knock the audience out of its seats, okay?'

"So Ben went to work," Hayward continued. "He was a hell of a fast writer—sometimes too fast. I didn't even know how fast he could go. At the end of the first day, I went back to Ben's house. There he was, typing away. I said, 'Ben, please slow down.' Over the next few days, I couldn't slow the guy down."[17] Hayward was to collect an agent's 10 percent of the writer's fee, and if Hecht wrapped early, the money would stop.

According to Hayward's recollection, when he arrived at Hecht's home on the ninth day with Hughes's daily payment, Hecht was enjoying a highball and pointed to the manuscript: "Done!" Hughes loved it and showed it to Hawks, who loved it, too. Which is one version of the story.

A second version, which Hawks told McBride, is that it was *his* notion to pattern the script on the idea that the Borgias of Italy were living in present-day Chicago, and that Tony's policeman brother from Trail's novel would become his sister, and that Tony and his sister would be like Cesare and Lucrezia Borgia in an incestuous relationship.[18] It was after hearing that tantalizing (if forbidden) key that Hecht came aboard, and the two men immediately started working on the script, only it took eleven days, not nine, and it was a team effort.[19]

A third version is told by Hecht himself in his flashy

memoir, *A Child of the Century*. In his version his agent was Myron Selznick, not Leland Hayward, and Hecht told him he wanted $1,000 a day paid in cash by 6 p.m. in case Mr. Hughes didn't have any money. (Hecht was a master of irony, particularly in hindsight.) And he wrote the script alone.

The published writing credits are no help in untangling the Gordian knot of who did what. If Hawks and Hecht wrote the script in eleven days as both men have said (Hawks in the McBride monograph and Hecht in his memoir), what were Seton I. Miller, John Lee Mahin, W. R. Burnett (who received screen credit), and Fred Pasley (who did not) doing?[20]

At some point after he'd finished (Hecht is vague), Hecht was in his hotel room when he had a midnight visit from two guys armed with the usual explosive hardware as well as a copy of his eleven-day wonder that had somehow come into their possession. As he recalled in *A Child of the Century*:

> "You the guy that wrote this?" I said I was.
>
> "We read it." I inquired how they had liked it.
>
> "We wanna ask you some questions." I invited them to go ahead.
>
> "Is this stuff about Al Capone?"
>
> "God, no," I said. "I don't even know Al."
>
> "Never met him, huh?"
>
> I pointed out I had left Chicago just as Al was coming into prominence.
>
> "I knew Jim Colosimo pretty well," I said.
>
> "That so?"
>
> "I also knew Mossy Enright and Pete Gentleman."

"That so? Did you know Deanie?"

"Deanie O'Banion? Sure. I used to ride around with him in his flivver. I also knew Barney."

"Which Barney?"

"Barnie Grogan—Eighteenth Ward," I said.

A pause.

"O.K., then. We'll tell Al this stuff you wrote is about them other guys."

They started out and halted in the doorway, worried again.

"If this stuff ain't about Al Capone, why are you callin' it *Scarface*? Everybody'll think it's him."

"That's the reason," I said. "Al is one of the most famous and fascinating men of our time. If we call the movie *Scarface*, everybody will want to see it, figuring it's about Al. That's part of the racket we call showmanship."

My visitors pondered this, and then one of them finally said, "I'll tell Al." A pause. "Who's this fella Howard Hughes?"

"He's got nothing to do with anything," I said, speaking truthfully at last. "He's the sucker with the money."

"O.K. The hell with him."

My visitors left.[21]

Hawks also had encounters with mobsters. As he told McBride, when word got around that he was making a film about Capone, he would get visits from people who said they were connected with the Mob and wanted to offer information. Hawks would put them off long enough to contact a newspaper source in Chicago who would give him the skinny. He used the example of a man calling himself James White.

"So when he came in," Hawks continues, "I would say, 'Hello, Puggy,' 'How did you know my name?' I'd say, 'I know all about you.' He'd say, 'How do you know?' And I'd say, 'Oh, I know. I know you started as a bouncer and became a pimp, you ran a saloon, you carried a gun for so-and-so, did such-and-such a murder.' I'd get through it and he'd say, 'I wasn't no pimp' . . . and he told me quite a lot." Hawks also says he had an audience years later with Capone himself, who had obtained his own print of *Scarface* and enjoyed screening it.[22]

Between Hecht and Hawks, *Scarface* was infused with just enough authenticity to be real and just enough invention to be safe.

Refused studio loan-outs of established actors for their independent film, Hughes and Hawks sought new faces. Paul Muni was acting onstage in New York, where Hawks noticed him. He was not, as some have said, a new face; he had already been signed by the Fox Film Corporation as the star of *The Valiant* (1929) for which he was nominated for Best Actor at the second Academy Awards.[23] *Scarface* would be his third film, and he prepared to play Tony Camonte by assuming a hulking, apelike stance, adding lifts to his shoes, and adopting the mannerisms of a child finding joy in lawbreaking. ("A great many of the gangsters I met *were* pretty childish," said Hawks.)[24]

George Raft, who spent his career playing gangsters, actually was one;[25] he carried a gun for the gangs. Hawks said he met him at a prizefight and cast him as Guino Rinaldo, giving him the business of tossing a half dollar in the air, a trademark he kept for the rest of his career.[26]

Ann Dvorak was playing small roles at Metro, and Hawks was so impressed that he bought her contract for his own company, making her Tony's sister Cesca. Boris Karloff's breakthrough in *Frankenstein* had yet to be released when Hawks put him in as Gaffney, whose bowling alley murder became one of the film's memorable moments. Osgood Perkins, who had appeared as Walter Burns in *The Front Page* on Broadway, played Tony's mentor, the film's anxious Johnny Lovo. Karen Morley had languished at Fox until Hughes gave her the role of the vixen Poppy. The film's comedy relief was Vince Barnett, who made an off-screen career of being hired to play clumsy waiters at posh Hollywood dinner parties. (His scenes were praised at the time but are cringingly puerile for a director with Hawks's expertise at comedy.)

It's a long road from script to screen, and *Scarface* hit many an obstacle along the way, most of them from the censors to whom Hughes had to repeatedly submit the material for Hays Office approval. The first draft set the story in an unnamed city (Chicago is what appears in the final film) and features a state's attorney named Benson who, with one hand, makes public speeches against the gangs while the other hand is open to accepting payoffs from Johnny Lovo and Tony Camonte. Mrs. Camonte, Tony and Cesca's apparently widowed mother, silently accepts her son's gifts of money that she knows full well is tainted, whereas, in the finished film, she disapproves of her son's activities. And there is a tangential plot, noted by scholar Gerald Mast, in which Tony and Poppy throw a yacht party for Florida society doyens who revel in being close to a famous crime figure. The implication, Mast notes, is that organized crime could not exist without the complicity of powerful community leaders.[27]

On January 26, 1931, Colonel Jason Joy, director of studio

relations for the Hays Office (he would later be hired by Fox in a counterpart capacity), noted in his "resume" (diary) that Ben Hecht had been signed to write *Scarface*.[28] Following a March 7 meeting among Joy, Hawks, Hughes, and Fred Pasley (here spelled *Parsley*), who was Al Capone's biographer, Joy wrote to file, "Their story is startling, to say the least, but apparently deals with facts. We have not yet discussed to [*sic*] censorable difficulties choosing to wait until after the rough draft has been committed to paper." In the interim—February 1931—Hughes planted a story with columnist Eileen Percy that Arthur Rosson, known for writing Hoot Gibson westerns, was adapting the Armitage Trail book.[29]

Things began heating up on May 1 when Joy drafted a self-righteous letter to "My dear Mr. Hughes" that the motion picture industry should not make films about real people or stories, especially Al Capone, lest it glorify them. Moreover, Joy cautioned, "We doubt very much that any sort of picture dealing with the life of Capone could be made to satisfy the requirements of the Code."[30] Twenty-five days later, Hughes's production executive E. B. Dorr sent a draft of the then-current rewrite to Joy asking for a twenty-four-hour turnaround, adding that they had already cast the picture and were ready to shoot. Among Dorr's comments were that they would "get across by impression rather than by direct shot" their points and would not name Chicago, but only say "city."[31] Joy wrote back on June 3 referencing an analysis by one Carlton Simon that the script glorified violence and that showing Camonte as a "home loving man" made him appear all the more like Capone, who was married and presented a domestic image to the public.[32] He also wanted the final scene to show Camonte cringing like a coward at being captured.[33] Rather than make the changes, Hughes doubled down so that, by July 23, Joy had to memo

Will Hays, president of the AMPP (Association of Motion Picture Producers), that not only had Hughes not made the required changes, he had added incest to the mix.

The back-and-forth continued through a screening of the finished film for the AMPP on September 8, 1931. By that time Hughes had appended the prologue disclaimer, made the lawyer Epstein (Bert Starkey) appear less Jewish, had Cesca and Guino secretly married instead of living together, made Mama Camonte explain to her wayward son that he is bringing shame to the Italian race, and had Camonte not kill the arresting detective at the end but be captured and taken away by the authorities.

Hughes reluctantly agreed to reshoots to mitigate the picture's perceived offensiveness and to remind audiences that the authorities disapproved of crime. These (written by Fred Pasley and directed by Richard Rosson after Hawks had finished)[34] involved Edwin Maxwell as the detective chief pontificating about the responsibility of elected officials and individual citizens to resist mobster rule, and what can only be called a seminar between newspaper publisher Purnell Pratt and an office full of community leaders in which he exhorts them to lean on politicians to right the wrongs that a free press has the duty to uncover rather than hide.

But the greatest change came with a new ending. Originally, Tony was to pretend to surrender to Detective Guarino until he was close enough to fire his pistol into the policeman's face. By then, however, the gun is empty and all he can do is click the trigger, which he continues to do in his death throes as he dies in a fusillade of police bullets. That was changed to his making a break for it and running into the same fusillade, after which the camera tilts up to see the neon sign reading the now-ironic message, "The World is Yours." When even that wasn't enough to placate the Production Code, Hughes shot another ending (whose director is unknown),[35] in which Muni was not present, and in which a judge, played by William Burgess, lectures a convicted (and off-screen) Tony about the woes of crime before he sentences him to hang. This is followed by a stylized execution in which a black hood is placed over the camera to represent Tony's final view of life.[36]

The most objectionable element of *Scarface*—which is to say the thing that makes it so enjoyable—is Tony's sheer exuberance about his chosen profession. While not as psychotic as, say, James Cagney in *The Public Enemy* (and later in *White Heat*) or as methodical as Edward G. Robinson in *Littler Caesar*, Paul Muni's Tony is best seen as a perverse efficiency expert. He does what Johnny Lovo doesn't have the guts to do. Like Michael Corleone in the *Godfather* films forty years later, it's strictly business and yet, unlike the pragmatic Michael Corleone, Tony enjoys his work. In this way he is more depraved, which makes both him and *Scarface* among the most subversive creatures in screen history.

The new ending cost Hughes $25,000. He also added an anti-gun statement to reference a law that then New York governor Franklin Delano Roosevelt was supporting that would make civilian ownership of tommy guns illegal.[37] By October 2, 1931, all the changes had been made.

Yet in November, Will Hays announced that he was still not satisfied. He demanded that all sympathy for Camonte be bled from the film; that stronger propaganda against the purchase of guns be added; and that a new title be found. Hughes dug in on this last point, inspiring a frenzy of alternate titles to be registered with the MPPDA's Title Registration Bureau. Variations (note the differing punctuation) were *Scarface: Shame of the Nation*; *Scarface, The Shame of the Nation*; *Scarface: Shame of A Nation*; *Scarface: The Shame of the Nation*;

The Scar; *Scar-Face*; and *The Menace*.[38] Eventually all parties decided to call it *Scarface: The Shame of the Nation*, which was registered by distributor United Artists on December 4, 1931. On January 29, 1932, Lamar Trotti sent out wires to the press that the title should be appended henceforth.[39] On February 26, Hawks decided he was having none of that and got Joseph Schenck (who then headed United Artists, the film's distributor) to write Will Hays that there was nothing in *Scarface* that hadn't been in previous gangster films.[40]

All seemed well until Hays again held the film hostage for his approval. In late December 1931, he ordered removing a "reign of terror" montage leading up to the St. Valentine's Day massacre, cutting a scene where Tony slaps Cesca and then embraces her (Hays finally waking up to the incest intimations), and removing the scene on Camonte's yacht and Tony slugging Detective Guarino on their first meeting in the barbershop.

When even these changes did not pass New York state censors, whom Hays considered a bellwether, Hughes was outraged. He arranged a March 1932 private critics screening at Grauman's Chinese Theater in Hollywood and showed the press his complete, uncensored version.[41] Their reaction was positive, and they saw nothing censorable in the film. This gave Hughes the clout to lean on Schenck for a settlement: The company released the cut version in territories that had censorship boards and the full version everywhere else. Nevertheless, *Scarface* continued to face resistance throughout its theatrical release.

Despite this, or perhaps because of it, the picture was also voted one of the ten best of the year by *Film Daily,* and the National Board of Review nominated it as one of the best American films of 1932.

There exists today no known copy of Hawks and Hughes's

original cut that riled the censors, but the version that remains is still powerful. It begins with that written prologue that sanctimoniously states:

> This picture is an indictment of gang rule in America and of the callous indifference of the government to this constantly increasing menace to our safety and liberty. Every incident in this picture is a reproduction of an actual occurrence and the purpose of this picture is to demand of the government: "What are you going to do about it?" The government is your government. What are YOU going to do about it?

By throwing ultimate responsibility upon the viewer, the picture dodges its own culpability for glorifying the very violence it pretends to chastise. But then the only people who would see the message would already be in the theater, having bought tickets in anticipation of seeing the self-same violence.

Scarface is many things, but there are some things that it is not. Although its main characters are Italian, if not Sicilian, absolutely no mention is made of what today is called the Mafia, even though that organization's American origins have been, as shown, traced back to 1889 and flourished in the 1920s. The lack of public awareness of the Mafia might also be explained by the position staunchly held by J. Edgar Hoover (who had taken over the Department of Justice's Bureau of Investigation in 1924 and made it the FBI) that the Mafia didn't exist. To Hoover, the real threat to American democracy was the Communist Party, a group that was, and always has been, entirely legal in the U.S., as opposed to the Mafia, which never was. This may be due in part to the widely held belief that Hoover, a gay man, was being blackmailed into declaring the Syndicate nonexistent. It is not known whether the film's appended moral message was a sly move by Hughes to inspire public pressure to demand that Hoover leave his closet and go after the Mob.

Predictably, there was reaction to the film from the Italian-American community. A July 1932 telegram from Guido Orlando, executive secretary of the Italian-American Women's Club, demanded that Will Hays delete the Italian names attached to the characters, as it branded the picture as an "outrageous reflection upon [the] entire Italian race."[42] Worth N. Tippy of the Federal Council of the Churches of Christ in America didn't like the hanging at the end and would have preferred that Camonte die in the gutter.[43] But the ultimate blow came three years later from Joseph I. Breen, who had been hired in 1934 as the new head of the Production Code Administration, when Hughes tried to reissue the film in 1935. On April 19 of that year, Breen wrote that "this picture is not suitable screen material for general exhibition before mixed audiences in theaters."[44] After all the hoops through which Breen's predecessor had made Hughes et al. jump years earlier, the new sheriff was rendering all their efforts moot and refused to award it a Code seal, a license device he had implemented in 1934 to label those films deemed safe for public consumption. In anger and frustration, Hughes withdrew *Scarface* from circulation, imprisoned it in storage, and attempted to destroy all prints. Somehow, Howard Hawks—who claimed in 1982 that it was his favorite of all his films—got hold of the original negative[45] and preserved it, yet couldn't release it because it still belonged to Hughes's Summa Corporation through its production subsidiary, the Caddo Company, which held the copyright. In 1979, following Hughes's 1976 death, the rights to his films were sold to Universal Pictures (although several titles, such as *The Outlaw* and *The Front Page*, managed to slip into public domain), who made it available for booking. While it had been in Hughes's vault, the only way to see it had been in pirated 16mm prints circulated privately among collectors. It is ironic that a movie about bootlegging could only be seen as a bootleg, but that was how two generations of film scholars came to know and respect *Scarface*.[46]

When the idea was floated in the early 1980s to update and remake it, many of the same issues arose that had made the 1932 version both memorable and controversial. The remake, the story behind it, and the aftermath would also become epic.

SIDEBAR

Biography of Al Capone

It's hard to write anything new about Al Capone. Journalists, novelists, fantasists, historians, and district attorneys long ago filled the archives about him. There have been movies, television series, miniseries, documentaries, and somebody is probably composing an opera right now. One TV sensationalist even squeezed a live television special out of finding and opening Capone's abandoned office safe, which, like the two hours leading up to it, turned out to be empty.[47] Until John Gotti, the "Teflon Don" of the 1980s, who courted public attention while defying the law, Capone was easily the most feared and yet exciting crime figure America had ever known. From the time he rose to power in 1925 to his conviction on tax evasion charges in 1931, he was an expert in both politics and crime (before the two fields merged).

Alphonse Gabriel Capone was a native New Yorker born

January 17, 1899, to Gabriele and Teresa Capone of Brooklyn, but originally of Naples, Italy. He was one of nine siblings. Al and school didn't get along, and he left it at the age of fourteen, preferring the tutelage of gangster Johnny Torrio, who was in the process of organizing a Chicago crime syndicate that came to be called the Outfit (and later the Five Points Gang). When he turned nineteen, Capone married Mae Josephine Coughlin, who had just given birth to their son, Albert Francis, who was deaf. Remarkably, Al was loyal to both his family and Da Family, although, considering that he died with syphilis, he must have freelanced at some point.[48]

Capone worked his way up through the New York gangs: the Bowery Boys, the Brooklyn Rippers, the Five Points Gang, and finally went to work for Frankie Yale at the Harvard Inn in Coney Island. It was there that he had the left side of his face slashed by Frank Galluccio for insulting Galluccio's sister. Capone became as fond of the nickname "Scarface" as Benjamin Siegel was of being called "Bugsy"— which is to say not at all.

At age twenty, Capone joined Johnny Torrio (who became the 1932 film's Johnny Lovo) in Chicago as an enforcer for James "Big Jim" Colosimo (the prototype for Louie Costillo in *Scarface*) and, after Colosimo's murder in 1920, was considered the prime suspect. Capone and Torrio ran the South Side and supposedly tried to avoid conflict with the North Side Gang headed by Dion (sometimes Dean or Deanie) O'Banion (O'Hara in *Scarface*), but that truce ended in 1924 when Torrio had O'Banion killed in his own flower shop and headquarters, preceded by the handshake of death from Frankie Yale, who held him firm as his cohorts rained him with bullets. Whether in an attempt to deflect blame from himself or to jam it down the North Side Gang's throats, Capone even attended O'Banion's funeral and sent flowers—an ironic touch. Little good did it do; the hit on O'Banion fomented a gang war between Torrio and O'Banion's successors: Hymie Weiss, Bugs Moran, and Vincent Drucci. In 1925, assassins tried killing Capone but failed; shortly thereafter, they shot Torrio. Torrio recovered but was scared away from the business, handing control over to Capone. Capone immediately expanded his organization's illegal liquor operation, intimidating taverns into buying his brew and blowing up those who refused. In 1926, Weiss also went the way of the dodo bird, dying in a submachine gun volley outside of Schofield's Flowers, the same fitting location in which his predecessor had bought it.

The spectacle of violence intrigued rather than outraged the public. They reasoned that it was just one gangster killing another; that is, until children became collateral damage and community leaders started putting pressure on police and elected officials (many of whom were getting payoffs) to intervene. This placed Chicago Mayor William Hale "Big Bill" Thompson in a tight spot. The Republican had campaigned on a platform of reopening the speakeasies that the previous administration had raided. He won, in part, because polling places in districts favorable to his opponent, William Emmett Dever, had been mysteriously bombed. Naturally there were no witnesses.

Capone himself seemed to rise above these squalid deeds even though he was widely rumored to have been behind them. It was an era when *reputed* wasn't a pejorative. He nurtured his image by dressing nattily, wearing flashy jewelry, smoking good cigars, and enjoying attention from press and public alike (just like Tony Camonte). He swayed his fellow Chicagoans by giving generously to charities, buying milk for impoverished schoolchildren, and opening a soup kitchen for people driven to poverty by the Depression. He was applauded at his public appearances and counted community leaders among his supporters. His Chicago fame expanded to national coverage when he bought a palatial mansion in Palm Island, Florida, in 1928, where he flaunted his riches in the face of society.

His biggest misstep occurred on February 14, 1929, in a Lincoln Park garage at 2122 North Clark Street, when five members of Bugs Moran's gang and two unlucky bystanders were gunned down by men, some of whom were dressed as policemen, almost certainly sent there by Al Capone. The "St. Valentine's Day Massacre," as the mass killing immediately came to be known, soured the public on Capone and helped defeat the reelection of his crony Mayor Thompson in 1931.

Enough was enough. Following the massacre, the publisher of the *Chicago Daily News*, Walter A. Strong (in the 1932 *Scarface*, he is the publisher of the fictitious *Chicago Daily Record*), prevailed on President Herbert Hoover, who had just been inaugurated, to intervene. A federal task force of uncorruptible men led by Eliot Ness was soon empowered (a reporter called them the "Untouchables") and ultimately found that they could indict Capone, not for his illegal income, but for not paying taxes on it.[49]

Starting March 27, 1929, Capone underwent a series of government rousts and arrests akin to being nibbled to death by ducks. The feds were relentless: contempt of court, carrying a concealed weapon, vagrancy, perjury, and murder. After legal wrangling, he escaped prolonged imprisonment for all of them, although he did spend some time behind bars (in a well-appointed cell not unlike the one where Paulie Cicero and the boys languish in *Goodfellas*).

Eventually the income tax issue defeated him. On June 16, 1931, Capone entered a plea bargain to income tax evasion and violations of the Volstead Act. Part of the plea involved a letter that Capone had asked his lawyer to write outlining his tax position. The plea bargain, however, was vacated by presiding Judge James Herbert Wilkerson, who then went back and allowed into evidence Capone's lawyer's letter, which the jurist declared was a confession of tax evasion, before he tried Capone on taxes alone, dismissing the Volstead violations.

After appeals and negotiations, in May 1932 Capone was sent to Atlanta Penitentiary. His medical examination upon entry revealed that the thirty-three-year-old had both syphilis and gonorrhea. (He was still married to Mae.) Following threats by other inmates, Capone was transferred to Alcatraz in August 1934. In January 1936, he was moved again, this time to the Terminal Island, California, federal correctional facility to serve out a lingering contempt citation. With his venereal diseases advanced and incurable, he was given a medical parole on November 16, 1939, and released into the custodianship of his wife. Ensconced in his Florida mansion, he had a stroke on January 21, 1947, and on January 25 died following a heart attack. He was first buried at Mount Olivet Cemetery in Chicago, but, in 1950, his remains were moved to the Hillside, Illinois, Mount Carmel Cemetery.

Al Capone remains a riveting and divisive fixture in American criminal history. This might be due as much to Americans' sense of mischief in being able to vicariously get away with breaking laws they consider to be wrong, as to his sheer honesty about being dishonest. "I am just a businessman giving people what they want," he famously said, both justifying his bootlegging and tweaking the nose of the people behind Prohibition. "All I do is satisfy a public demand." What the public didn't know was that the web of vice and corruption that Capone created metastasized into the vast template for crime today, both the organized kind and the type that corporate

America and the government have institutionalized. There aren't many people who can keep changing history while no longer being a part of it.

The St. Valentine's Day Massacre

Al Capone knew that he had to get rid of the one man he feared (the last one surviving, at least), George "Bugs" Moran, who ran the North Side. He slipped word to Moran, through mutual trusted contacts, that a large shipment of Canadian whiskey would be arriving by truck. It was a setup. At around ten-thirty on the morning of February 14, 1929, five members of Moran's gang were awaiting delivery at Chicago's SMC Cartage Warehouse at 2122 North Clark Street: Albert Kachellek, Albert Weinshank, Adam Heyer, Frank Gusenberg, and George Gusenberg. John May and Reinhardt H. Schwimmer, who were not gang members, were also present.

They were soon met by four men—two were dressed like Chicago police and two wore long overcoats. All of them were armed. They lined the victims against the rear wall of the garage and shot them to pieces, literally and figuratively. Miraculously, Frank Gusenberg survived, despite having fourteen bullets in him. He crawled to the entrance of the garage, where police found him and took him to the hospital. When they asked him, "Who did this to you?" Gusenberg maintained his silence right to the end: "No one shot me," he replied, and died three hours later.

Moran escaped assassination only because he arrived late and saw Capone's men enter the building (in the 1932 *Scarface*, Gaffney, the Moran figure, is similarly delayed).

Thus the one reason Capone staged the massacre—rubbing out Moran—failed, and Capone thereafter lived in fear that Moran would come for him.

The police investigation, of course, uncovered little. Capone had been in Florida at the time and there were no surviving witnesses. Nevertheless, the massacre shocked Chicagoans into finally realizing that Capone was not the civic-minded hero they wanted him to be.

The 1932 movie takes off into its own storytelling territory after the massacre occurs forty-eight minutes in, but leading up to it, it's possible to closely compare Camonte's rise with that of the real Scarface, Al Capone.

SIDEBAR

Biography of Ben Hecht

Ben Hecht was one of the greatest screenwriters who ever lived. Too bad he hated the movies. Born in New York in 1894 and raised in Wisconsin when his Russian-Jewish immigrant family moved there, he fled to Chicago in 1910 as a teenager and fell in love with journalism. His first job was on the *Chicago Journal*, whose editor, Sherman Reilly Duffy, told him, "Socially a journalist fits in somewhere between a whore and a bartender, but spiritually he stands beside Galileo. He knows the world is round."[50] Hecht would name the city editor of the fictitious *Morning Post* after Duffy when he and Charles MacArthur wrote *The Front Page*.

Chicago was a journalist's dream in the 1910s; there was competition among the city's up to eleven newspapers (depending on what year in that decade), and their reporters engaged in combat on the streets. At first Hecht was made a "picture chaser," a job given to eager young men who could run fast. Picture chasers were journalism's version of a summons server, only in reverse—when the City Room got a call from police that there had been a murder, a picture chaser would rush to the dead man's home and tell his wife, who had not yet been informed that she was a widow, that her husband was being given some sort of civic honor, and ask if she had a photograph of him. Sometimes the picture chaser would barge into the house, grab a framed portrait from the mantelpiece, and escape out the back window when the police—or, worse, another paper's picture chaser—arrived at the front door. Hecht was constantly challenged, and sometimes beaten, by a competing picture chaser named Benzinger. It took him years to get his revenge, but he did; in *The Front Page* he named a character after him and made him effete, implying that he was gay.

When Hecht moved to the *Chicago Daily News*, he became a reporter and a columnist with his innovative feature *One Thousand and One Afternoons*, a chronicle, not of pols or punks, but of average people. It was the kind of blue collar writing that would distinguish Mike Royko, Jimmy Breslin, Pete Hamill, and Bob Green in later decades. But it left Hecht unsatisfied. He yearned to be a novelist, the one romantic notion left to people of letters in a changing world after World War I. Between 1921 and 1924, he published six books (one of which was a collection of his *Daily News* columns) and, in his spare time, wrote plays, first one-acters, and then, in 1922, the full-length *The Egotist*, which ran on Broadway for forty-eight performances. He was thrown off the staff of the *Daily News* when one of his books, the 1922 novel *Fantazius Mallare*, was seized by local bluenoses for obscenity.[51]

It was in Chicago that Hecht met fellow journalist Charles MacArthur. In 1924, both men moved to New York and quickly joined the wits at the Algonquin Round Table.

Deciding to try playwriting as a team, they wove their various Chicago journalism experiences into *The Front Page*, which opened on Broadway in 1928 and ran a respectable 281 performances.

The Algonquins were an eclectic group. Although they endlessly quoted each other in their own newspaper columns, they didn't seem particularly eager to help newcomers land a job on any of their rags. Hecht—who married Rose Caylor (née Libman) in 1925 after divorcing his first wife, Marie Armstrong—continued to write books, three or four during this lean period, until in spring 1925 he got a now-infamous telegram from former Algonquin member Herman J. Mankiewicz, who had gone to Hollywood and wanted intelligent company:

> WILL YOU ACCEPT THREE HUNDRED
> PER WEEK TO WORK FOR PARAMOUNT
> PICTURES. ALL EXPENSES PAID. THE
> THREE HUNDRED IS PEANUTS. MILLIONS
> ARE TO BE GRABBED OUT HERE AND
> YOUR ONLY COMPETITION IS IDIOTS.
> DON'T LET THIS GET AROUND.

Although talkies weren't yet on the horizon, the studios still needed fresh stories, and who better to write them than playwrights or journalists, and Hecht was both. His facility with dialogue would become an even greater gift once sound arrived, but first things first. Hecht was set to work at Paramount writing stories, and the first one he created was *Underworld*, a silent film that immediately confronted the prevailing morals (or lack of them) in Hollywood.

A series of scandals in the film community had brought a national outcry for film censorship, and the studios were terrified of government intrusion into their freewheeling industry. While the film companies were putting together what would become, the day before April Fool's Day 1930, the Motion Picture Production Code of Self-Censorship, the threatening atmosphere was pressuring filmmakers to clean up their act. This meant that every female character had to be pure and every male character virtuous, except for the villains, who had to get their comeuppance at the end. Hecht was vexed at this departure from reality until he realized that if he made all of his characters disreputable, he could let them do anything they wanted. The result was *Underworld*, which won Hecht one of the first Academy Awards for writing, in the category of Best Original Story.

He was on a journey that he didn't want to take that would lead him where he didn't want to go yet, handing him success he didn't like because it came too easily. The man who yearned to be a novelist became instead one of the most desired, fastest, highest-paid, and skillful screenwriters that Hollywood has ever known. His sense of story structure, characterization, and dialogue distinguished such films as *Notorious, Spellbound, Nothing Sacred, Gunga Din, Kiss of Death, Wuthering Heights*, and *Gone with the Wind*. He also wrote—or doctored without credit—*Angel Face, Hans Christian Andersen, Portrait of Jenny, Lifeboat, Roxy Hart, Duel in the Sun*, and *Twentieth Century*, among scores of others. It is estimated that Hecht was involved with nearly every major film made in Hollywood between 1930 and his death in 1964. He even worked on the kaleidoscopically bizarre James Bond picture *Casino Royale* released in 1967.

But by that time Hecht's reputation was in eclipse, largely because of his political activity. In 1941, concerned for the fate of European Jewry under Hitler, he had joined the Committee for a Jewish Army and raised rescue money through a series of benefits for which he called on his Hollywood contacts to appear.[52] He became a passionate Zionist, helping to fund the Zionist paramilitary organization the Irgun through writing the play *A Flag Is Born* (1946), which starred newcomer Marlon Brando on Broadway, and campaigning for the founding of the State of Israel. His attacks on the British partition of Palestine were so intense that business forces in England boycotted his films, a liability that was reflected in Hollywood by producers refusing to pay him his full working price. In 1954 he published his vastly entertaining memoir, *A Child of the Century*, and in 1963 a collection of Chicago reminiscences, *Gaily, Gaily*, some of which may involve a certain degree of embellishment and which inspired a 1969 film of the same name. Astonishingly, for a man whose books were so numerous and whose screenwriting was so respected, he was only once hired to turn any of his own novels into a film, the lightweight but charming wartime romance *Miracle in the Rain* (1956). No wonder he reviled the movies even as he cashed his Hollywood checks. Surely he recognized this irony and had the intelligence to direct it into the cynicism that makes much of his work enjoyable and enduring.

His keen ear and agile mind inspired him to write not merely dialogue but to craft epigrams. *Scarface* is enlivened throughout by such lines as "politicians with the gimmes" (bribes); "take a look at the goldfish" (drown someone); Tony leering at Poppy and calling her "expensive"; insulting someone by saying they were "right where the horses had been standing"; and, of course, firing a machine gun after saying, "Get outta my way, Johnny, I'm gonna spit!" People don't really talk like that, but you wish they did.

Hecht died on April 18, 1964, of a heart attack at home in New York City. His wife died in March 1979. Their daughter,

Jennie, had died in 1971. If there is a tragedy in Ben Hecht's life, it's that he spent all of it reaching for the brass ring and didn't appreciate all the gold rings that were placed at his feet.

The Family That Preys Together

In describing how to set *Scarface* apart from other gangster films of the era, Ben Hecht and Howard Hawks pitched Howard Hughes that Tony and Cesca would be like the Borgias, the notorious Italian-Spanish family of the Renaissance. Incredibly rich, influential, and, some say, perverse, the Borgias insinuated themselves into all areas of European culture, producing two popes (Calixtus III, 1455–1458 and Alexander VI, 1492–1503), the organizer of the Jesuits (Francis Borgia), several bishops, cardinals, poets, presidents, scholars, and a nun. But the Borgias that the world knows best are Cesare (1475–1507) and Lucrezia (1480–1519), the children of Rodrigo Borgia (1431–1503), who later became Pope Alexander VI after fathering a number of children, legitimate and not, including the aforementioned siblings.

According to legend, which vacillates between asserting and denying it, Cesare and Lucrezia were as close as Mississippi cousins, and so were Lucrezia and her father, the future pope. Whether they were actually incestuous or victims of the same kind of historical smear that turned Shakespeare's Richard III into a villain is open to conjecture, but it was enough to inspire Hecht to use it to legitimize (or, rather, delegitimize) the relationship between Tony and Francesca Camonte. Censors often yield to historical precedent.

Lucrezia, for example, continued to love Cesare even though he was responsible for killing her second husband,

Alfonso; likewise, Cesca ultimately forgives Tony despite his slaying of her husband, Guino. There is but one line in the Hecht screenplay that validates this theory. Because the Hays Office picked through every script like a monkey grooming for mites, it was cleverly placed at the end of an exchange so that it could be deleted if the censor caught it. When Cesca shows up at Tony's fortress to kill him and, in the process, leads the police there, he asks her why she didn't shoot him. She says, "I don't know, Tony. Maybe it's because . . . you and me . . . I love you. It's always been that way." Perhaps to head off the censor at the pass, Hecht then has Tony shrug and say, "What's da difference? Your fault, my fault? Just so's you're here, that's all that matters. Here, you load 'em, huh?"

Oliver Stone, on the other hand, stands his ground in the 1983 screenplay when he has Gina burst in on Tony Montana while he is under attack from Alejandro Sosa's men. Wearing the same panties and negligee she wore when Tony killed Manny Ribera, she shoots Tony in the leg with a Beretta and says, "I'm all yours, Tony, I'm all yours now." Stone writes, "She advances, offering her sex" as she fires rhythmically into his desk. "Come and get me, Tony, before it's too late," she spits, "come on, Tony, fuck me! Fuck me! Fuck me!"

Hearing that, Al Pacino's Tony reacts with bewilderment and then descends into cocaine-induced incoherence when Gina is shot to death. Is this the first time he has had to confront his desire?

The Camonte and Montana crime families are nowhere as well organized, entrenched, or genetically adventurous as the Corleone or the Soprano crime families. Knowing Hawks's and Hecht's penchant for spinning stories and their need to dignify the production to stave off censorship, they probably pulled the Borgias out of their politically astute Hollywood hats. Stone took it a step or three further.

X Marks the Shot

Among other things for which it is noted, the 1932 *Scarface* has fourteen deaths that are marked by an occurrence of the letter *X*. This is no accident; the gimmick is boldly announced by an *X* appearing under the main titles. Internally, however, there is neither consistency nor symbolism to be inferred from its appearances. Moreover, it stands as probably the most pretentious imagery in any of director Howard Hawks's refreshingly unpretentious body of work. Here are where *X* marks the deaths:

1. Louis Costillo's assassin casts a shadow on a frosted glass door that has a cross-shaped frame.

2. North Side crime boss Meehan is shot to death in his hospital bed as struts from the medical equipment cast an *X* shadow on the wall.

3. O'Hara's thugs roll a dead body out of a car as a warning to Tony Camonte, and it lands in front of an undertaker's storefront under an *X* shadow from a street sign.

4. A sedan crashes into a fire hydrant near where a lighted *X* is displayed on a building behind the wreck.

5–11. Seven men are slaughtered in the St. Valentine's Day Massacre under a ceiling with seven *X*-shaped support beams.

12. The contorted bodies at the St. Valentine's Day Massacre have a lighted *X* shining between two of them.

13. When Gaffney is shot to death while bowling, his previous frame score sheet shows an *X* because he got a strike.

14. After Tony shoots Guino, there is a lighted *X* visible behind Guino, looking almost like a halo.

SIDEBAR

Bending the Code

However much trouble Howard Hawks's 1932 *Scarface* ran into with the Hays Office, it wasn't alone in weathering the censor's disdain for gangster movies. There were so many of them in the early thirties that the Production Code Administration declared them to be their own genre—not that this cut the pictures any slack when it came to censoring them. When Howard Hughes entered the field, however, his productions seem to have warranted a higher level of scrutiny than the established studios received, and with it the amount of capitulation the PCA demanded from Hughes and not the others. Or perhaps it was just because Hughes's pictures went further than his competitors. A comparison of *Scarface* with four other equally famous crime films of the era shows that the PCA was ever vigilant in protecting moviegoers from the shock of reality by not allowing filmmakers to bend the Code. *Scarface*, in particular, appears to have been treated more harshly in 1932, presaging how its remake would fare in 1983. The files of the Hays Office offer incisive (and frequently entertaining) insight into how the Code worked.

The gangster films in question are *Little Caesar* and *The Public Enemy* (both 1931), *Manhattan Melodrama* (1934), and *The Petrified Forest* (1936). The first two are considered pre-Code (more properly pre–Code seal enforcement), and the second two were made after Joseph Breen arrived in 1934 and put his foot down. *The Public Enemy* and *Little Caesar* have been selected because they are contemporaries of *Scarface*. *Manhattan Melodrama* is a more-or-less routine gangster film representative of the era. *The Petrified Forest* appears because it was based on a highly regarded stage play whose pedigree was not enough to shield it from Hays Office scrutiny.

Little Caesar was summarized for the censors in a report on W. R. Burnett's novel by J. B. M. Fisher of the Production Code Administration, who called it "a corking story" but found the central character "drab and unspectacular."[53] When Warner Bros. announced they were going to film it, the Code took the opportunity to raise concerns about the property's portrayal of cards, chips, and poker; for showing how holdups were committed; and having a gangster die on church steps.[54]

Because of its ultimate moral stance and resolute ending, *Little Caesar* sailed through and got approved with minor changes. Unexpected opposition, however, came from New York's Congressman Fiorello H. La Guardia, who usually opposed censorship but said, in this instance, that the picture misrepresented Italian-Americans.[55] This drew a handwritten response to the file from Jason Joy, who opined, "My guess is La Guardia is sore because Little Caesar looks like him."[56] The film was eventually passed for New York, but with several cuts, mostly (nonsensical) dialogue deletions, but also any shots of gangsters brandishing guns, and images of Edward G. Robinson holding stolen cash.

Surprisingly, the real controversy over the film was not directed at *Little Caesar* but at the Code itself for permitting it to be made in the first place. Elaborate back-and-forth correspondence between the Hays office and various bureaucrats from Alberta and British Columbia show that Canada's watchdogs objected to any depiction at all of racketeering.

The Public Enemy was more violent than *Little Caesar*, primarily because of the energy generated by James Cagney. Even before the cameras rolled, caution was in the air. Cagney played Tom Powers, a neighborhood tough guy who, with his friend Matt Doyle (Edward Woods), rises in the bootlegging racket with a manic intensity from which no one is safe.

After warning Warner Bros. that some local censorship boards might object to showing machine guns in the hands of criminals, the PCA's R. E. Plummer praised it as "possibly the strongest gangster film yet produced" and commended it as "a more or less correct depiction of what transpired in Chicago recently and may be said to follow very carefully one of the more notorious characters of that city from his infancy to his last hour on earth."

But in the same letter he also had these reservations from the standpoint of the Code:

- A scene involving a "pansy [*sic*]" tailor
- Social drinking (come on, it *is* a story about bootlegging)
- The gruesome finale in which Tom is brought home dead
- Tom saying, "Jeez, I ain't so tough" (the "Jeez" was cut)
- A scene where it is presumed that Tom spent the night with Bess and he slaps her[57]

Other scenes made it through the Code's obstacle course: James Cagney slapping a tavern owner, a machine gun assassination attempt where Cagney escapes but Woods is killed, and Jean Harlow burying James Cagney's face in her bosom.

Upon the film's general release on May 15, 1931, the Code office received several expected complaints from localities such as conservative, old-line Pasadena, California, about the picture's content and the opinion that the ending did not teach a strong enough moral lesson. Such letters were politely dealt with.

When Breen took over the Production Code Administration in 1934, he decreed that all pre-Code films should be resubmitted for Code seals if they were to be rereleased. Warner Bros., eager to reissue *Little Caesar* and *The Public Enemy* as a double feature, blissfully did so and were surprised to learn that *Little Caesar* was approved because it was by then seen as a "period piece,"[58] but *The Public Enemy* could not be released abroad because "we might be playing directly and blindly into the hands of the Communists, offering them material which they could use to assault the American culture."[59] No attempt was made to reconcile those apparently disparate decisions. By then, Breen had also eliminated the specific genre of "gangster films."

Manhattan Melodrama (pre-production title *Three Men*) is a stock story of two boyhood friends who take different paths as they grow to adulthood—one, Blackie Gallagher (Clark Gable), becoming a racketeer, and the other, Jim Wade (William Powell), rising as a crusading district attorney. Directed by W. S. Van Dyke, with retakes by MGM contract directors George Cukor and Jack Conway,[60] the film is better known as the movie that John Dillinger had just seen at Chicago's Biograph Theater with the woman in red (Anna Sage, aka Ana Cumpănas) when he exited into an FBI ambush on July 2, 1934.

Writing directly to MGM's production chief Louis B. Mayer, the newly installed Joseph I. Breen showed initial enthusiasm for *Manhattan Melodrama* as "basically satisfactory under the Code," but added two and a half pages of suggested changes and deletions anyway. Among them were:

- A section of boys crawling under women's skirts
- Blackie slapping Eleanor (Myrna Loy) on the posterior
- Modifying the line "Do what he liked to me and make me take it"
- Not to make a bed in a bedroom look as if Eleanor has slept in it and remove the line, "on her back as usual"
- Omitting the line "I didn't ask you to feel me"
- Changing the reference to the pope[61]

Of interest is that, even though *Manhattan Melodrama* is a gangster film, there is no mention in the censor's notes of firearm violence. And that was just at the script stage. On viewing the nearly finished film, Breen made additional "suggestions," among them not showing Blackie wiping his hands on a towel to hide his fingerpints and Blackie playfully removing the "WO" from the women's powder room door sign,[62] and—in a separate letter from Hays himself—to be cautious about showing riots between police and public, as this might be inflammatory.[63] Mayer ordered retakes, which were presumably those that were handled by MGM contract directors Cukor and Conway. *Manhattan Melodrama* entered theaters on May 4, 1934, and entered history on July 2, 1934.[64]

The anomaly in this quartet is *The Petrified Forest*, the 1936 film adaptation of the highly honored 1935 play by

Robert E. Sherwood. Leslie Howard starred as Alan Squier in the Broadway production, and when Warner Bros. bought the film rights with him in the lead, he insisted that they hire his stage costar, Humphrey Bogart. Sherwood based the character of Duke Mantee, an escaped gangster who holds a diner full of people hostage and, in the end, kills one of them on request, on Dillinger. Bogart's likeness to the FBI's Public Enemy #1 was perfect casting, and Bogart was forever grateful to Howard for giving him a screen career.

The play's positive reviews and hit status didn't mean that the film would get an automatic pass by the Breen Office. Urbane New York theatergoers were one audience, but the Code was mindful of the sensibilities of people in the flyover states. An unsigned report on the play from the Code's New York office alerted the powers that be to several elements that might run afoul of the Code, such as profanity, frank sexual discussion, use of machine guns, satirizing the American Legion, and Howard's de facto suicide at Mantee's hands.[65]

By September 9, 1935, Joseph Breen had written Jack Warner that they had "read with considerable pleasure and every great interest" what he called the "temporary" script for *The Petrified Forest*, and called it "unacceptable." He then followed his compliments with seven single-spaced pages of things that would have to be changed in order to meet Code standards. These mixed signals covered three general categories: the frank discussion of sex, the favorable treatment of suicide, and the need to punish Mantee and his gang. The devilish details included prohibited or suggestive words such as *lousy, potbelly, gigolo, where's the ladies' room, punk,* and *holy mother of God.* The gunplay, however, was left intact.

After all of that, *The Petrified Forest* was cut as demanded and released nationwide on February 8, 1936, making Bogart a star and confirming the stardom of Leslie Howard and their costar, Bette Davis.

While the four films discussed above endured what was then a routine examination and scrubbing by the Code, *Scarface*'s violence and innuendo are undeniably greater than any of them. Nevertheless, the correspondence noted earlier suggests that the Production Code Administration came down harder on Howard Hughes than on other studios. Was this because he was an independent producer? Such inequity is a recurrent charge that is frequently made today against the Motion Picture Association by some independent producers who feel that their films are scrutinized more harshly than those from studios. Given that the MPA's expenses are paid by charging for Code seals, it is easy to speculate that they favor their own sponsors, who provide them with a steady source of films to rate, rather than independent companies who may have one film every few years. For the record, the MPA (formerly the MPAA) has consistently denied this dichotomy, and their position is maintained by the fact that there are no published, consistent criteria for what constitutes film ratings.

As much as Howard Hughes grumbled, he had to capitulate. Then he got even for the next forty-seven years.

SIDEBAR

Synopsis of *Scarface* (1932)

Chicago in the late 1920s is run by politicians elected by the public but controlled by gangsters, specifically by "Big Louis" Costillo (Harry J. Vejar). But Louis is losing control, and one night after a stag party he is shot to death by a shadowy, whistling figure who turns out to be his own bodyguard, Tony Camonte (Paul Muni).

The managing editor of the *Chicago Daily Record* (Tully Marshall) salivates over the prospect of a gang war that would be good for the paper's circulation. "This town is up for grabs," he tells his city editor. "You put that in the lede: war, gang war."

Detective Guarino (C. Henry Gordon) visits Pietro's (Henry Armetta) barbershop. Tony Camonte's ever-observant minion Guino Rinaldo (George Raft) shows him that Tony is under a hot towel about to get a shave. Guarino tells Tony that the chief wants to see him. Tony strikes a match on Guarino's badge to light his cigar, and the detective slugs him. Tony dares not return the slug. At the station, the chief (Edwin Maxwell) recites Tony's rap sheet and indirectly accuses him of killing Costillo and hanging around with Johnny Lovo, who is known to have coveted Costillo's power. Tony wisely keeps his mouth shut. Then Tony and Guino's lawyer (Bert Starkey) arrives with a writ of habeas corpus (which Tony refers to as a writ of "hocus pocus"), and they all leave.

Three rings of the buzzer at the apartment of Johnny Lovo (Osgood Perkins) alerts him and his moll, Poppy (Karen Morley), that it's safe to open the door for Tony. Johnny introduces Poppy to Tony. She is not impressed. Tony keeps remarking how expensive everything is in Johnny's apartment, including Poppy. When she alludes to his scar, he claims he got it in the war, but Lovo says he got it "with a blonde in a Brooklyn speakeasy." Lovo tells Tony that they are moving in on the South Side and to stay out of the North Side so as not to buck O'Hara, the boss who runs it.

Riding with Guino after meeting with Lovo, Tony reasons that Lovo is soft and that the North is ready for takeover because they didn't kill Costillo first. "There's only one law you gotta follow to keep outta trouble," Tony says, miming shooting with a pistol, "do it first, do it yourself, and keep on doin' it."

At the Camonte home, Tony's widowed mother (Inez Palange) serves him dinner. When his sister Francesca, called Cesca (Ann Dvorak), returns from a date and Tony sees her kissing a man (Douglas Walton), he chases the suitor off and is notably possessive of her. Then he gives her money, which mollifies her, much to the concern of their mother, who suspects its illegal origins. She advises Cesca that Tony is up to no good and doesn't really like her as he says he does. From her bedroom window Cesca tosses a quarter to an organ grinder, but the ever-watchful Guino catches it, pockets it, and gives his half dollar to the monkey (after flipping it, of course). Thus do Guino and Cesca make first contact.

At Louis Costillo's First Ward offices, Tony announces his and Lovo's arrival by throwing a spittoon through the glass door. When any of "the boys" objects to Lovo taking over, Tony roughs him up. Lovo tells them that Prohibition is making the town thirsty and he wants to run their operation like a business, with Tony Camonte as the salesman along with Guino and moon-faced Angelo (Vince Barnett), whom he refers to as Stupe, a contemporary pejorative for "stupid."

Tony and his men shake down bar after bar for large orders, except for one owned by their brewing rival Zeigler, so they bomb it instead. Then they shoot up the Shamrock Tavern. Later they report their sales figures to Johnny Lovo, telling him that competitors Meehan and Berdini have "retired." When there's a newspaper report that Meehan has survived being "retired," Tony goes to the hospital and finishes him off.

By August, Tony is cock of the walk and Poppy's resistance starts to melt. He invites her to visit him at his new house, unbeknownst to her sugar daddy, Lovo. Tony's brazenness angers Lovo, who berates him for entering O'Hara's North Side and selling beer at one of his joints. Tony senses that Lovo is afraid of O'Hara. As the men leave the office, a car drives up and tosses out an unidentified body. Pinned to it is a note: "Keep out of the North Side."

Angelo becomes Tony's incompetent secretary in an ongoing comic relief routine in which he never understands how to properly answer the office phone. Guino arrives to inform Tony that he did a job. Poppy arrives and says that O'Hara was killed in his flower shop. She also says that she is here on her own, not at Lovo's orders. Tony shows Poppy around his digs, his wardrobe, his gaudy appointments, and bulletproof shutters. He is proudest of his view overlooking a neon Cook's Tours sign that proclaims, "The World is Yours." He puts moves on her. When police arrive, Tony shows Poppy out by a back exit.

Across town, Tom Gaffney (Boris Karloff), one of O'Hara's capos, prepares to do battle with Tony using newly arrived Thompson submachine guns, which, unlike the maxim guns used in the recent war, can be hand-carried. An informant within the police force, McGill, tells Gaffney that Tony is on the way to a café.

Tony and his bodyguards meet Poppy at the Columbia Café. Gaffney's men drive by and shoot up the place. Guino kills one of the gunmen and retrieves a tommy gun. Tony is inspired by these new weapons and races to Lovo's headquarters, which he discovers has also been shot up. Lovo is angry at Tony for having O'Hara hit. Tony, showing off the tommy gun, takes charge: "Some little typewriter, huh? I'm gonna write my name all over this town with it, in big letters! Get outta my way, Johnny, I'm gonna spit!" and he fires. Then he goes on a shooting spree, peppering O'Hara's flower shop and a tavern.

The detective chief notes the hypocrisy that it's legal to bring machine guns into the state but not to use them.

Tony's shooting campaign continues. It includes beer trucks, speakeasies, and a man whose body is dropped off at an undertaker's parlor in the cross of a lamppost's shadows. Lastly Tony and his boys assassinate seven men in a garage as a Valentine's Day present. Gaffney, who arrives late, is shown the massacre by police. He fears for his life as the only member of O'Hara's gang left alive, and goes into hiding.

The police can't find Gaffney. The chief lectures a detective that these gangsters are a menace to society. Furthermore, a citizen's group complains to newspaper publisher Garston (Purnell Pratt) to stop covering the gang war. Garston grandstands to them that the government needs to pass laws against what the gangs do and that these (you) citizens are the government.

Tony, Guino, and the boys attend a performance of the play *Rain*. During intermission Tony learns that Gaffney is at a local bowling alley. Although he wants to find out the ending of the play, Tony takes his boys off to execute Gaffney. Gaffney is shot just as he scores a strike.

Tony sees Lovo and Poppy at the Paradise Club. Both are cold to him. Cesca is also at the club, dressed to do the town. Guino takes her aside and cautions her about her revealing outfit. She gyrates seductively, trying to get him to dance with her, but he refuses, so she goes off with another man. Tony asks Poppy to dance, and she agrees. While on the dance floor, Tony sees Cesca, decks her partner (Warner Richmond), and drags her home. Cesca is in tears, and her mother tries to comfort her by saying that Tony hurts everybody. As Tony drives away, a car full of gunmen try to assassinate him, but he runs them off the road with his bulletproof sedan. He goes off the road, too, but survives and makes it to Pietro's barbershop, where he calls around town for Guino to meet him there. He has a plan and tells the barber to phone Johnny Lovo at exactly 2:10 and say that Tony got away from an attempt on his life.

Tony and Guino show up at Lovo's when Pietro's call comes in, and from Lovo's jitters, Tony knows that his boss tried to have him bumped off. Lovo begs Tony not to kill him, so, instead of killing Lovo himself, he has Guino do it.

Poppy moves into Tony's house, but Tony flees to Florida to hide out till the heat's off.[66] While he's away, Cesca makes moves on Guino.

Reporters talk about how the town is changing in Tony's absence and that he's not going to like it when he gets back. Tony returns from Florida, to his mother's apartment, and learns that Cesca has moved into her own place. Their mother gives him the address. Tony and his boys head there and find Guino and Cesca shacked up. Enraged and jealous, Tony kills Guino, only to learn from a hysterical Cesca that she and Guino have just been married and wanted to surprise him with the news.

A warrant is issued for Tony's arrest. Arriving at his home fortress in shock, he barricades himself against an onslaught by rival gangsters. Angelo is shot in the gunplay and dies answering the phone, ironically finally getting the secretarial job right. It's Poppy calling. The chief sends cops over to get Tony.

Meanwhile, Cesca arrives intending to kill her brother, but she cannot, and instead, she confesses that she loves him. The siblings fight off the police, but Cesca is killed by one of their bullets. The police lob tear gas into the house. Tony tries to flee by the back stairs, but the police are waiting for him. He begs for his life, then tries to escape but is mowed down by police bullets. As he dies, the camera tilts up to see the neon sign, "The World is Yours."[67]

Alternate Ending

When censorship orders threatened to shelve the picture, Hughes shot the sermonizing interior scenes with the chief and an alternate ending in which Muni did not participate. Written by Fred Pasley and directed by Richard Rosson (neither of whom is credited), the alternate ending runs about two-and-a-half minutes. It shows Tony (a stand-in) being led away alive by the police as in the original film, which then fades out before he flees into gunfire. Instead, a judge sternly sentences an off-screen Tony to death by hanging and moralizes, "You are ruthless, immoral, and vicious. There is no place in this country for your type." In the prison yard in a high-angle long shot, Tony is led to the gallows, a sack is placed over his head (covering the camera's POV), and prison guards cut lines that release the trapdoor.

The date given for his hanging is December 10, 1931.[68]

SIDEBAR

Synopsis of the Novel *Scarface* and Comparison with the 1932 Film

Scarface *by Armitage Trail was published in 1930 by A. L. Burt, although publisher E. J. Clode was also involved in undetermined ways. It is an early attempt at what became known as "hardboiled" crime fiction in which the language of telling the story is as colorful as the things that the characters say and do. Alas, Trail was not Hammett, Chandler, Ellroy, or Spillane; his prose is simplistic and not as colorful as the genre would become, but it does the job. A detailed synopsis is helpful in illustrating the many differences between what Trail wrote and what Ben Hecht chose to use in his script. There will be comparison comments at the end.*

Tony Guarino is an eighteen-year-old living with his big brother, Ben, a policeman. Tony long ago realized that, in his world, the only difference between cops and gangsters is a badge, but he honors Ben's desire for him to keep his nose clean, for fear it would hurt his brother at work if he didn't. Tony and his friends hang out at Klondike O'Hara's pool hall, which is a front for illegal activities. The Guarinos—Tony, Ben, sister Rosie, their mother Carlotta, and six other kids— live above the family's grocery store.

Tony spends his $200 life savings dating Vyvyan Lovejoy, renting a car and taking her to an expensive restaurant that has no trouble getting real champagne despite Prohibition. There is danger involved because Vyvyan is the moll of gagster Al Spingola. This doesn't scare the brash Tony, who shoots and kills Spingola. Word gets around town, and soon Tony is picked up for questioning by the police. He's bluffing his way through the interrogation when a lawyer, sent by O'Hara, shows up with a writ of habeas corpus to release him. Tony joins O'Hara's gang—the Italian-Irish rivalry be damned—and is prized for his organizing abilities and pragmatism ("I ain't riskin' a pinch for a coupla bucks"). He also inherits Vyvyan.

Tony and Vyvyan are at Bloom's supper club when Tony spots the attractive Jane Conley, known as a "gun girl," that is, a woman who holds on to a killer's pistol so he can be clean if the cops shake him down. Tony decks the man with whom she's dancing, only to learn that he was the brutal chief of detectives, Captain Flanagan. While he's escorting

Vyvyan home, a car drives past them and fires. Neither Tony nor Vyvyan is hurt.

Flanagan leans so heavily on Tony that Klondike O'Hara lays him off (promising to give him his share of the jobs he has set up) because he's bringing too much heat on the gang. Spingola's mob is after him, too, but Tony survives an assassination attempt by shooting first. He decides to join the army to fight in the war and, not coincidentally, get out of town so Spingola's guys can't kill him. He makes arrangements with O'Hara to give his cut to Vyvyan and his mother.

In the army, Tony is cool under fire and becomes a hero, suffers a facial injury, protects his colonel, and takes command of his leaderless troops. After the Armistice he returns home (to an unnamed Chicago) and collects $6,000 O'Hara was holding for him. "He had come home with a new face and a lot of ideas, ideas that were going to be profitable for him but detrimental to the community in which he put them into practice," Trail writes, indicating that Tony is unrecognizable even to those who knew him. He finds Vyvyan with another man and kills her for two-timing him despite her protests that she'd heard he had been reported dead in combat. The man he killed was "Frog" Merlin of the North Side. The detective assigned to solve the murder is Tony's brother Ben Guarino.

Tony visits his old haunts and quickly realizes that the illicit booze business is making people rich, but that more could be made if the bootlegging was better organized. He seeks Johnny Lovo, a bootlegger operating out of Cicero, who knows how to run a business. Tony joins with Lovo and becomes "a real modern gangster" (his term) selling protection to South Side speakeasies and angering the North Side gangs whom he is forcing out of the area. Soon he is warned by two of the North Side men that he will be "taken for a ride" if he doesn't stop strong-arming their customers.

Johnny Lovo tells Tony to take his girlfriend, Jane Conley, to the Embassy Club and kill Jerry Hoffman, the leader of the North Side mob. Jane will be his gun girl. At the club, when the lights go off, Tony shoots Hoffman, and he and Jane escape without incident—except that, once they're in the limo heading away, he kisses her.

Tony rises in Lovo's gang and also pursues Jane, who likes him but won't commit to move in with him. Tony accompanies Johnny to see the DA, who tells him that the North Side's Schemer Bruno will stop the gang war if Johnny will, too; conveniently, the DA is collecting bribes from both. The truce lasts six months, until somebody tries killing Johnny with a new invention, a tommy gun. Tony procures one and shoots up the flower shop above which the North Side Gang has its headquarters, evening the score.

Jane agrees to move in with Tony for a trial month. Johnny chastises Tony for having shot up the flower shop; he doesn't want an all-out gang war. In fact, he wants to retire and turn the gang over to Tony if Tony will send him money in retirement and work with Steve Libati. Right from the start, Tony and Libati don't get along. Neither do he and Captain Flanagan, who arrives for his monthly payoff of $500. Flanagan doesn't recognize Tony from when he was a troublemaking kid, and Tony sets him straight, demanding more help from the cops and warning Flanagan by patting his automatic weapon, indicating that he can settle any dispute.

Charlie Martino's truck is hijacked and he is shot, setting off the feared gang war with the North Side. A newspaper story breaks in which Flanagan takes credit for chasing Lovo out of town and refers to a kid named Tony Camonte (the first time "Camonte" is used), who has taken over for Lovo.

Tony summons Mike Rinaldo, chief of Lovo's gunmen. District Attorney Crowder calls Tony to confirm that the payoffs will continue. Katherine Merton of the *Examiner* wangles an interview with Tony. He is impressed with her but becomes suspicious that she knows more about the women in his life than he thinks she should. After she leaves, he phones the *Examiner* to speak with her. The paper has no one working there by that name.

Mike Rinaldi and his backup goons bring Benny Peluso of the North Side Gang to see Tony. Under threat of torture versus a promise of $15,000, Peluso spills on the North Side Gang, and Tony sets the wheels in motion. Libati suggests knocking off Peluso anyway and saving the dough, but Tony says it's a point of honor to make good on his promise. He sends Steve to kill Schemer Bruno.

Taking Jane to the Embassy Club where he had shot Hoffman, Tony sees Katherine Merton, the supposed reporter, but Jane becomes uneasy and wants to leave the club. Tony also learns that Steve did not kill Bruno, but only wounded him. This means big trouble. After dropping Jane back home, he takes off in his armored sedan and is ambushed by another car and run off the road. He comes to consciousness inside a car with Jerry Hoffman's brother. Tony attacks the driver and crashes, escaping through the intervention of a stranger.

The gang war rages. Tony banishes Steve from the mob, for blowing the Bruno killing, and hires bodyguards. He then finds Jane and confronts her over why she left the Embassy Club in such a hurry. She admits that Katherine Merton is Schemer Bruno's gun girl and that he was with her. Tony orders Jane to help him get Bruno. Meanwhile, he pays Benny the $15,000 ("I always keep my word, good or bad," he says) and has Rinaldi and a couple of the guys escort him to the train station, only to have Benny assassinated on the way. Tony suspects Rinaldi bumped off Benny, but at least he, Tony, kept his word.

Tony is taken by cops to a hotel meeting where the DA walks him in a room with Bruno and other gang leaders, telling them "this killing must stop." The DA then hands each of them a map on which he has divided their territories fairly and tells them to stop fighting. They all agree, but Tony now knows what Bruno looks like.

Bruno's men break the truce and take shots at Tony. One of Bruno's men is killed: Steve, who must have turned. Tony and his men plan to ambush Bruno when he comes out of court but fail when the police shake them down.

Jane learns that Bruno will attend a masked ball at Woodland Casino and tells Tony that's where they can get him. What Tony doesn't know is that he is walking into a trap. He canvasses the room and sees Katherine Merton. He suspects that the man standing beside her dressed as Satan is Bruno. As he and Jane escape, he asks her how she got so much information from Merton. "She's my sister," Jane says.

After a year, things have become routine. Tony's father has died, brother Ben has been promoted on the police force, and neither knows that Scarface Tony Camonte is their own Tony Guarino. Easterners move in and try to scare Tony off by shooting at him. It doesn't work. One night he sees Rinaldi entering the hotel with Tony's sister Rosie. He goes to their room, finds Rinaldi with Rosie, and kills him. Not only is Rosie angry with him, she thought Tony had died in the war. Not long after, he is pulled in by Assistant District Attorney Moran, from whom he learns that Rinaldi and Rosie had been married. He also learns that, by giving all the gangs their own territories, the DA rendered any individual gang powerless against the police. Tried for murder, Tony gets off and announces that he is going to retire like Johnny Lovo.

Vowing revenge on Flanagan and Moran, Tony is side-tracked when his boys don't want him to retire for fear that their income will stop. Tony kills Flanagan. Ben is made the new police captain. Tony meets Rosie for dinner at his hotel. She puts poison in his soup, but he finds out and accuses her of attempting to murder him. She won't forgive him for killing Rinaldi. Preparing for the final outcome, Tony puts his little black book of payoffs in an envelope addressed to one of the town's newspapers. He guns down Moran and sets out to get the DA.

Believing he has two-timed her, Jane calls Tony to meet her at Jake's, a supposedly neutral club place. It's a trap, and Tony dies in a hail of bullets, but the one that finishes him is fired by his brother Ben.

The broad strokes are here, but Hecht's inventions focus the story. From the book we learn that Tony got his scar in the Great War, but it is never realistically explained that he has become so disfigured that nobody can recognize him, including his own family, except some people still can. The brother-sister relationship is minimal, Tony's brother serves an ironic function, and the other Guarino children didn't make it into the movie. Although it becomes clear that Tony wants to protect his family from shame by changing his name to Camonte, Trail just changes it from one page to another without comment. There is no St. Valentine's Day Massacre (which, occurring on February 14, 1929, presumably happened while Trail was writing his book). Tony has a sense of honor (of sorts), and is portrayed as more subtle, brighter, and aware of others than the 1932 Tony, but these are traits that can be effortlessly expressed in the narrative of a novel, whereas thought processes are largely invisible in a screen characterization.

In short, by bringing his script for Scarface *closer to Al*

Capone than Armitage Trail drew in his novel, Ben Hecht gave the story urgency and leanness that Howard Hawks honed to perfection and, fifty years later, Oliver Stone and Brian DePalma polished like a neon sign reading "The World is Yours."

CHAPTER 2

The Moguls and the Mob

As much as audiences crave watching gangster movies, whether the stylish street-wise films of Martin Scorsese, the blue collar HBO adventures of David Chase's *The Sopranos*, or Francis Ford Coppola's epic *Godfather*s, the genre pales in comparison to Hollywood's actual infatuation with gangsters. It is a history that might even be called professional courtesy. Both business models make their money by giving the public what it wants; their power is transient, highly competitive, and must be constantly defended, and the rewards for those at the top are astronomical. Both also have a huge cash flow that they keep track of in Byzantine ways, and operate in constant fear of government intervention.

They started off as enemies. Early filmmakers fled Fort Lee, New Jersey, which was the heart of the movie industry in the early 1900s, because they refused to pay royalties to Thomas Edison's patents syndicate. When they headed west, settling in Hollywood (which was only a short hop away from the Mexican border to escape Edison's subpoena servers), they were pursued by thugs who beat them, shot holes in their equipment, and threatened their actors. In response, some of the independent producers took to hiring their own thugs in case Edison's showed up. In many cases, they even put them in their movies as extras to save money. When Edison's Patents Trust was outlawed in 1915,[1] the industry completed its relocation to Hollywood, where the founding moguls designed their own vertically integrated monopoly that the government stepped in to correct in 1948.[2]

Historically, the relationship between the moguls and the Mob has been informal and personal. Entertainment has long been a favored investment for organized crime, who used performers as attractions to draw spenders into their clubs, casinos, and restaurants. Each side had a kind of glamor and knew its place, except perhaps for the time that Columbia Pictures president Harry Cohn took out a contract on Sammy Davis, Jr., because Davis was dating Columbia's biggest star, Kim Novak.[3]

There was a time, however, when the Mob moved in on the movies and the movies were happy to have them; in fact, the studio heads were poised to turn over control to them in order to avoid bowing to unions.

In the 1920s, the studios were flush with income. They had consolidated their production-distribution-exhibition cartel and were making a fortune serving the dreams of a public that was intoxicated with the Jazz Age. But the intoxication didn't trickle down to the crews who did all the heavy lifting. Even the stars were exhausted from working six-day weeks for the benefit of the studio moguls. They wanted fairness. They began to get it on November 29, 1926, when nine major studios and six unions concluded the Studio Basic Agreement that set forth the terms and conditions for union employment. The unions were the IATSE (International Alliance of Theatrical Stage Employees, the industry's basic craft union); the Moving Picture Machine Operators (projectionists); the United Brotherhood of Carpenters and Joiners; the IBEW (International Brotherhood of Electrical Workers); the International Brotherhood of Painters and Paper Hangers; and the AFM (American Federation of Musicians).[4] In 1935, the federal Wagner Act was passed, guaranteeing workers the right to unionize.

One man who had been upset at the growing union activity in 1926 was Louis B. Mayer, head of the then-recently (1924) merged Metro-Goldwyn-Mayer. Mayer wanted to erect a beach house on his property in Santa Monica and even had studio art director Cedric Gibbons design it, but his own studio laborers refused to build it because they insisted they worked for MGM, not him. Not only did Mayer suspect that their resistance was caused by Communist infiltration (the Palmer Raids had occurred only six years earlier, supposedly purging Reds from America), but he considered his employees to be family and took their spurn personally. In order to drive a wedge between his newly unionized crews and the department heads who managed them, he spearheaded the creation of the Academy of Motion Picture Arts and Sciences, whose first task was breaking the unions by setting laborers against their bosses by conferring Oscars upon the department heads while the underlings who did the actual work watched from afar.[5]

Regardless, labor organizing continued throughout Hollywood. Even when the Great Depression arrived in 1929, the film industry seemed immune; tickets only cost two bits, a cheap price for several hours of escapism. Nevertheless, the film companies cried poverty and persuaded their employees to take salary cuts—some of them by as much as 50 percent—to "do their bit" to save the studio. When the Depression began to lift, management conveniently forgot to restore their workers' wages, while returning their executives' salaries to pre-Depression levels. By May 1, 1937, some people had had enough; seventy-five set decorators broke away from the IATSE to form their own union and negotiate an independent contract with the producers. They were one of some fifteen other groups who walked off their jobs in protest actions both of the studios and their own union.[6]

What had happened in the intervening years?

The answer was George Browne and Willie Bioff.

When Prohibition was repealed in 1933, bootlegging became superfluous and the Mob had to find new sources of income. Al Capone had been in the pokey since October 1931, and the new guy running Chicago was Frank "The Enforcer" Nitti. When he realized that Hollywood was still making money despite the Depression, he turned his eyes to Tinseltown. Nitti tested the waters by moving in on the Chicago local of the Motion Picture Machine Operator's Union (the projectionists), whose president, Tom Maloy, owed him a favor. Nitti was able to collect a percentage of the members' dues and shake down theater owners who didn't want their screens to go dark.[7] They first hit Barney Balaban, who was then the head of the Balaban and Katz chain, and demanded $50,000 to guarantee that his projectionists would not want raises and would keep labor peace. Balaban—who would later head Paramount Pictures, where he would institute tight budgets—negotiated Nitti and Maloy down to $20,000.

But that was local and Nitti wanted to go national. He called upon one of Capone's men, Willie Bioff, to look into getting into the movies, not as a performer but as a player. Bioff discovered George Browne, who was a member of the Chicago IATSE, after Browne lost an election against William C. Elliot for general president of the Union. Impressed with Browne, Bioff engineered Browne's election as national head of the IATSE in 1933. The pair lost no time shaking down the local projectionists for a percentage of their dues, and the Chicago theaters to insure them against strikes. Browne then appointed Bioff the union's West Coast representative and, with Nitti's blessing, relocated to Los Angeles.[8]

Their plan in LA was more ambitious than it had been in Chicago. They were assisted by Mob enforcer John "Handsome

Johnny" Rosselli and another thug, Nick Circella. At a secret meeting in April 1936 in the New York office of Loew's Incorporated's president Nick Schenck, they demanded that each of the studios pay protection money to prevent strikes among the IATSE employees they were supposed to be representing.[9] This included the theaters belonging to the studios. (Not all of them did. Columbia, for example, did not own theaters.) Their price was a cool $2 million. When Schenck argued that that amount wasn't possible all at once, he and Bioff worked out an installment plan whereby the major studios would pay $50,000 a year and the minor ones would ante up $25,000 a year. The moguls were eager to cooperate with the Mob because it was cheaper than a strike and more efficient (not to mention predictable) than negotiating with the unions.[10]

Bioff also kept his hand in the projectionists union by going to New York and demanding that theaters keep two projectionists in each booth instead of one. The exhibitors complained that this would hurt them financially, so Bioff arranged to cut his own projectionists' pay to compensate.[11]

It didn't always work. In 1933, the engineers of Sound Local 695 struck Columbia Pictures and the studio's combative boss Harry Cohn locked them out. Other studios followed suit, dropping the IATSE from the Basic Studio Agreement and hiring IBEW members to replace them. The strike died and so, almost, did the IATSE.[12]

Bioff and Browne went public with their scheme on July 15, 1935, wielding their control of projectionists against studios that owned theater chains. A strike against RKO theaters was canceled when RKO gave the pair $87,000. The mobsters then selected brothers Nicholas and Joseph Schenck for extortion. Nick Schenck headed Loew's Incorporated, which owned MGM; Joe had just started Twentieth Century-Fox. Both men came out of New York City, where they were in the beer, movie theater, and vaudeville business, so they were not naïfs when it came to dealing with guys who carried loaded violin cases. Nick quickly settled for a $143,000 payoff. Soon Paramount paid $138,000 and Warner Bros. $91,000, all to keep their theater chains from being shut by the projectionists union that was, by then, under the control of Nick Circella.

The IATSE rank and file knew they were being sold out when Bioff swaggered through their ranks at a meeting and announced that he was taking over and would be appointing new officers. Along with those new officers came a huge financial surcharge for members. Soon the press began running articles questioning what was happening. Actor Robert Montgomery, former head of the Screen Actors Guild, hired an ex-FBI agent as a private detective to investigate Bioff. The former G-man uncovered a pandering charge against Bioff from 1922 in Chicago. According to the IATSE's own website, Montgomery gave the information to national columnist Westbrook Pegler, who began a crusade against Bioff (and would win a Pulitzer Prize for his reports). On January 10, 1940, Bioff was indicted and extradited to Chicago.

But the feds were already at work on him after Joseph Schenck, chairman of Fox, tried to deduct his company's $100,000 payoff from his 1937 income taxes as a business expense. This was uncovered in an audit by the National Labor Relations Board at IATSE's request. The investigation also revealed that the IATSE locals were to be turned into house unions and that collective bargaining would be pro forma only. The IRS brought up Schenck on tax evasion charges; he was tried and sentenced to a year and a day, which was reduced when he agreed to testify against Bioff.

Bioff's 1943 indictment for a panoply of crimes (tax evasion, extortion, racketeering) inspired him to turn state's evidence against his former associates, including Johnny

Rosselli and Frank Nitti, for which he received a reduced sentence. Not long after Bioff's testimony incriminated him, Nitti committed suicide sitting against a wall, somehow putting three slugs in his own head.

On his release from prison, Bioff moved to Arizona, took the identity "William Nelson," and reportedly became friends with Senator Barry Goldwater. He soon drifted into the casino business, which, at the time, was still Mob-controlled.

On November 4, 1955, Bioff got into his truck in his home driveway, turned the ignition, and exploded all over the neighborhood. "We're certain it was a revenge killing," said sheriff's captain Vernon Le More. "We are trying to determine whether any known gangsters were here at the time of the killing, but it's a pretty tough job."[13] Bioff's assassins were never found.[14]

But by then the Hollywood moguls had long since forgotten their flirtation with the Mob and were deep into blacklisting suspected Communists. It never bothered them that membership in the Communist Party was legal in America while membership in the Mob was not. Maybe because it was just strictly business.

Bioff and Browne would not be the Mob's sole incursion into the movies. By the 1970s both industries—crime and filmmaking—had become highly corporatized. It's been established that the only reason *The Godfather* could shoot in New York was because of certain agreements and understandings that producer Albert S. Ruddy made with New York syndicate head Joe Colombo.[15] But there's another story to which director Francis Ford Coppola alluded when he made an obscure reference in the end credits of *The Godfather Part III*: "Dedicated to Charlie Bluhdorn, who inspired it." It seems that, at the time that the original *Godfather* was being shot in 1971, Charles Bluhdorn, the excitable founder of Gulf +Western Industries, which had acquired a struggling Paramount Pictures in 1966, was quietly fending off a Wall Street takeover attempt by the Italian firm Societa Generale Immobiliare International (SGI).[16] At some point Bluhdorn confided this to Coppola who, with Mario Puzo, later used it as the basis for *The Godfather Part III*, in which the Immobiliare corporation has bought into the Vatican Bank, and the scoundrel in charge of allowing the investments asks Michael Corleone for help getting free of them.

More recently, Coppola's 1984 movie *The Cotton Club* became soaked in scandal when the production's first financial backer, Roy Radin, was murdered execution-style before the start of filming. In the investigation, it developed that most of the film's $60 million budget came from Las Vegas casino and hotel owners the brothers Eddie and Freddie Doumani, who were alleged to have Mob ties. Neither Coppola nor producer Robert Evans was implicated, but the sordid story (which could make its own separate movie) played out on the news pages as well as the movie pages.[17]

Whether it's life versus art or art versus life, the symbiosis between the Mob and the movies is almost like chicken and egg. As long as audiences hunger for movies and TV shows where the bad guys are the heroes, there will always be entertainment offers that are too good to refuse.

SIDEBAR

The Irony of the Blacklist

Four years after Willie Bioff was indicted for his shakedown of the studios, the film industry was again awash in scandal, this time from the House Un-American Activities Committee that went looking for Communists in Hollywood. The politicians on the Committee could have investigated other businesses, but they were after two things besides Reds: publicity and Jews, both of which the movies offered in abundance.[18] Unlike bootlegging and extortion, Communism was (and remains) legal in the United States, but that didn't stop Congressman J. Parnell Thomas (R-NJ) from holding HUAC hearings looking for them. One of his youngest committee members was Richard M. Nixon (R-CA). From October 20 to 30, 1947, a parade of witnesses, some friendly and some unfriendly, testified or dodged before the Thomas committee. Ten of them who refused to name names or admit whether they were Communists were indicted for contempt of Congress and eventually went to prison. These men became known as the Hollywood Ten.

A month after the HUAC hearings—on November 24 and 25, 1947—forty-eight studio heads, lawyers, and other executives gathered at New York's Waldorf-Astoria Hotel to decide how to deflect the U.S. government from further scrutiny of the movie business. It was a secret meeting. Nobody kept notes. No transcripts were ever released.

The moguls met in panic. They knew that the U.S. Department of Justice was about to bring antitrust action against them for their monopolistic practices of making and distributing movies and then exhibiting them in their own theaters. The case, *U.S. v. Paramount et al.*, brought in 1940, would result, in 1948, in a consent decree divorcing theater chains from their studio owners.

But there were other cards on the table. Television had been invented and ticket sales were plunging. The Wall Street investors demanded that Hollywood make money again. Foreign countries, under pressure from the U.S. State Department, were refusing to show movies made in any way by suspected Communists. The strain of anti-Semitism was also apparent when, on November 24, Congressman John Rankin (D-MI) ranted on the floor of Congress against Jews in the film industry.[19]

The Waldorf Conference, as the confab later came to be called, was already tempting the antitrust laws by allowing all of Hollywood's key people to meet together in secret to discuss business, although they were ostensibly chaperoned by James F. Byrnes, the esteemed secretary of state and former U.S. Supreme Court justice. After two days of deliberation, the moguls issued a statement on November 25 vowing to banish anyone suspected of Communism and never hire others like them again. The two-page press release was dubbed the Waldorf Peace Pact, and it was the beginning of the Hollywood Blacklist.

What is ironic is that most of the executives in the room had eagerly acquiesced to Willie Bioff and George Browne's extortion only ten years earlier. They had practically, if not specifically, invited the Mob to take over the unions. Now they were accusing Communists of doing the same thing. The moguls had forced wage cuts, blocked unions, and engaged in restraint of trade to the point where the U.S. Supreme Court would hold it against them. None of the studios was ever punished for collusion.

In other words, the Mob was okay, but Reds were not.[20]

CHAPTER 3

A Few Lines About Cocaine

Much changed in the American landscape in the fifty years between 1932 when the first *Scarface* was released and 1982 when the second one went into production. The repeal of Prohibition made bootleggers obsolete, so, good capitalists that they were, the Syndicate found other forms of commerce: protection, prostitution, gambling, infiltrating other businesses, and, of course, drugs, which remained under statutory, rather than constitutional, prohibition. Although heroin was the constant over the decades, cocaine, because it was popularly believed to be less addictive, rose to general acceptance in the 1970s. The five decades between *Scarface*s reflect this shift in details but not the machinations behind it.

There is a reason that the 1983 *Scarface* dwells solely on powdered cocaine, and it's purely a matter of lucky timing, not intent: When it was planned and made between 1979 and 1983, crack—that is, purified rock cocaine—had not yet invaded the streets of America. It would do so the next year, 1984, in New York, Philadelphia, Baltimore, Los Angeles, San Francisco, Washington, DC, and Miami, among other urban centers, and primarily in the impoverished areas of those cities where people of color lived. None of this applied to Tony Montana, or would have concerned him if it had. In a sense, the filmmakers dodged the racial crack bullet by a year (although they faced others with their portrayal of Cubans, but that's a story for another chapter).

Cocaine is a Schedule II controlled substance that is

traditionally ingested by several means: intranasally, inhalation, intravenously, or orally. Intranasal use (snorting) is the most common.[1]

Users sniff finely ground powder into their noses, where the semipermeable membrane of the septum is thinner and the capillaries are closer to the surface, allowing the drug to be quickly infused into the bloodstream, then to the brain. Users can also dissolve the cocaine in water and inject it, achieving an intense rush or "buzz." When cocaine is smoked (see "crack" or "freebase"), the smoke carries the intoxicant into the lungs for a similar high. If it's used orally—that is, rubbed on the gums—a sensation of local dullness is achieved without euphoria; for this reason, a suspension of cocaine in oil (for some reason usually banana- or cherry-flavored) is favored by dentists as a topical anesthetic to dull the pain of gum scaling or injecting Novocain. Some people may also use it to dull the sensitivity of their genitals to prolong coitus.

The issue of powdered versus rock cocaine is controversial and racially significant. Powdered cocaine was traditionally treated differently by the enforcement and legal system than was rock, or crack, cocaine. Therein lay the hypocrisy of the drug war, which favored prosecution over treatment. Did it have more to do with the color of the user than the color of the substance? Was that, in fact, the unspoken rule?

The history of cocaine in America is far more complex than can be summarized here, but for Tony Montana's purposes, a few things need to be established. The substance widely and popularly known as cocaine is chemically called *cocaine hydrochloride*, a purified version of a liquid called *Erythroxylon coca* that is extracted from the leaves of the coca plant indigenous to South America, particularly Colombia, Peru, and Bolivia (but mostly Colombia). For centuries, Incas and others chewed on the leaves as a stimulant and brewed it as a tea for digestive purposes. There was not enough of the intoxicating chemical in leaves to produce a high, nor was that apparently the purpose of chewing it.

Cocaine became part of American culture in the late 1800s as doctors desperately sought a painkiller for surgery. One of the first to experiment with it in that way was William Stewart Halsted (1852–1922). Hearing that ophthalmologists had used it to numb their patients' eyes during procedures, Halsted searched for other applications—unfortunately becoming addicted to it along the way. The liabilities, however, were ignored as cocaine worked its way into American society. Part of that came from John Pemberton (1831–1888). A Civil War veteran who experimented with tonics and curatives, he hit on the idea of adding cocaine to a sugared wine beverage he was making called Pemberton's French Wine Coca when temperance laws forbade the use of alcohol and he was forced to use it to replace the wine component. He marketed the concoction as an aphrodisiac and headache remedy to be sold by pharmacists.[2] Later he added carbonated water and served it as a fountain beverage. Eventually, Pemberton sold his formula to what became the Coca-Cola Company, and several iterations and inventor interventions later, it became the world's favorite soft drink. But that was long after any trace of cocaine had been eliminated, if there was ever a significant amount of the real thing present anyway.[3]

And yet the medicinal popularity of cocaine began what pundits called a "cocaine honeymoon" in America at the turn of the twentieth century.[4] Only when its downside became well known (including Sigmund Freud's repudiation of its benefits) was it held to any real scrutiny. Yet by the early 1900s, it was still popular in American society for recreation as well as an anesthetic. This changed in 1914 when the U.S.

Congress passed the Harrison Narcotics Act designating cocaine and opiates as illegal substances. Today cocaine's status as a Schedule II drug means that a doctor can use it for legitimate medical purposes but nonmedical (i.e., recreational) use is prohibited.

Good luck with that.

Cocaine is not a new character in American popular culture. Cole Porter said that he got no kick from it, Sherlock Holmes famously injected a seven percent solution when he was bored, and stage star Talullah Bankhead wrote in her memoirs that she used both cocaine and marijuana and that cocaine made her ill. (She also supposedly insisted that it wasn't addictive, "because I've been using it for thirty years and I should know.") The wisest advice might be that of Robin Williams, a self-confessed user, who said, "Cocaine is God's way of telling you you're too rich." In the late 1800s, Robert Louis Stevenson supposedly used it to inspire him to write *The Strange Case of Dr. Jekyll and Mr. Hyde*. And, of course, a more recent roster of celebrity abusers is practically a roll call of Oprah Winfrey's talk show guests.

During its heyday in the 1980s, good quality cocaine was selling for between $47,000 to $70,000 per kilogram (2.2 pounds).[5] On the way to hitting the street, dealers would "step on it," that is, cut or dilute it with an inert substance, such as mannitol (a plant-based sweetener that also has mild laxative properties), and divide it into grams for street sale at between $80 and $135 depending on the quality of the drug and the affluence of the buyer.[6] Bargain hunters would buy an "eight-ball," that is, one-eighth of an ounce (3.5 grams), for $325 to $350.[7] It may be coincidental, but when the price of cocaine rose during a shortage in the early 1980s, the ATM machines in some cities raised their daily withdrawal limit from $300 to

$350. Rocks of cocaine, or crack, weighed from one-tenth to one-half of a gram and sold for as high as $50.[8]

One of the risks of the cocaine trade so vividly displayed in *Scarface* is a seller becoming addicted to his own product, or as Tony is admonished, "Don't get high on your own supply." Use of the "head stash," as it was also called, was an obvious liability, as one can see demonstrated so vividly in the film.

Without going into the hypocrisy behind the government's criminalization of some substances (cannabis, amphetamines, opium, heroin) and not others (tobacco, alcohol, "snake oil"), a look at the cocaine laws raise a particularly obvious yet stunning judicial issue the more one analyzes them—specifically crack.

"Crack," or *methyl (1R,2R,3S,5S)-3- (benzoyloxy)-8-methyl-8-azabicyclo [3.2.1] octane-2-carboxylate*, is a refined form of cocaine hydrochloride produced by the addition of water and baking soda (sodium bicarbonate) and dried until it forms small rocks. It can be smoked in a small pipe or hidden in a tobacco cigarette. At one time it even had to be heated in a glass flask using a blowtorch to extract the vapors. Crack is stronger than powdered cocaine and is considered more addictive. If the results are any guide, lawmakers determined crack to be more dangerous to society than powder because it can be hidden easily, sold promiscuously, is easier to store in quantity, is more intoxicating, and can be purchased on a scale of lower prices, like fast food. What the facts also say, but lawmakers don't, is that the reason penalties are more harsh for crack is that it is more frequently used by people of color.

According to the United States Sentencing Commission,[9] the penalties for powdered cocaine differ markedly from the penalties for rock cocaine. Their figures from 2009 (the most recent available at this writing) cover 5,669 people convicted and sentenced for crack possession:

- 79 percent were Black.
- 10 percent were White.
- 10 percent were Hispanic.

On the other hand, sentences for powdered cocaine show a contrast:

- 28 percent were Black.
- 17 percent were White.
- 53 percent were Hispanic.

All told, Black Americans were sent to prison at a rate six times that of white Americans who were convicted for similar use, and they served longer sentences. People convicted for powder averaged 87 months; for crack, 115 months. Moreover, it took twenty-eight grams of crack to bring on conviction but five hundred grams of powder to trigger the same result. In calling this hypocrisy to the public and Congress's attention, the American Civil Liberties Union argued that the concept of "mandatory minimums" was levied more often against Blacks than whites, causing "vast racial disparities."[10] Moreover, the ACLU noted, Black Americans served more time in general for nonviolent offenses than white Americans did for violent crimes. In other words, drugs were not the only form of racial imbalance.

This race-based discrepancy was addressed in 2010 by Senator Dick Durbin (D-IL), who introduced the Fair Sentencing Act, which was signed by President Barack Obama. Further, the United States Sentencing Commission voted to apply the law retroactively to people already incarcerated, allowing some twelve thousand individuals serving time to have their sentences reviewed by a judge. (No, it didn't release them all at once.) Eighty-five percent of these inmates were Black.

On December 16, 2022, U.S. Attorney General Merrick Garland admitted the discrepancy in sentencing and announced plans to change Department of Justice policy to equate penalties for rock and powder. "The crack/powder disparity in sentencing has no basis in science," he said through spokesperson Aryele Bradford, "furthers no law enforcement purposes, and drives unwarranted racial disparities in our criminal justice system." He further noted that prosecutors would reserve harsher sentence requests for violent offenders or those who have "significant ties" to gangs. The changes were to take place by mid-January 2023.[11] How this improved the Fair Sentencing Act of 2010 was not explained.

And then there's the ongoing question of whether the U.S. government is behind the drug trade, starting with Air America.

Secretly established by the Central Intelligence Agency in 1946 to support covert operations in Southeast Asia, by the 1960s the airline transport system known as Air America was allegedly being used to support drug trafficking in Laos. To be fair, it has never been established whether Air America actually supplied the drugs or was only involved in protecting those who did. But there is the suggestion that the CIA used its light planes to carry opium poppies from the growing fields of the Plain of Jars to military headquarters in Long Tieng. As writer Alfred McCoy held, "In most cases, the CIA's role involved various forms of complicity, tolerance, or studied ignorance about the trade, not any direct culpability in the actual trafficking. . . . The CIA did not handle heroin, but it did provide its drug lord allies with transport, arms, and political protection."[12]

In 1969, President Richard M. Nixon clamped down on the South American marijuana cartels, who had risen to power in the 1960s and early 1970s, by instituting "Operation Intercept" and tightening the U.S. border against smuggling. As with Prohibition in the 1920s, this simply made purveyors shift from pot to another commodity, in this case toot, unleashing a blizzard of cocaine and, worse, heroin into a United States market that had hitherto been content with grass. It is, of course, the rise of the South American drug cartels that forms the backstory for the 1983 version of *Scarface*.

Here is where the CIA reappears. In 1996, reporter Gary Webb of the *San Jose Mercury News* broke a highly controversial investigative series called "Dark Alliance: The Story Behind the Crack Explosion."[13] In three parts running between August 18 and 20 of that year, Webb detailed how the Nicaraguan Contras, whom the Reagan administration had supported to overthrow the democratically elected socialist government of Nicaragua, created the crack trade to finance their actions when the U.S. Congress cut off military funding in 1982. (This was in addition to the Reagan administration's illegal sale of arms to Iran from 1981 to 1986 for the same purpose, also called the "Iran-Contra Scandal."[14]) Although Webb's articles never conclusively proved direct CIA involvement targeting inner city people of color, especially in Los Angeles, the inference was that the CIA looked the other way as the cartels plied their trade, because it benefited the Contras. Webb was attacked across the media spectrum for flaws in his reporting, rather than the essence of his story being examined. Resigning from the *Mercury-News* in November 1997 and unable to find steady work, Webb died by his own hand on December 10, 2004.[15]

This is what producer Martin Bregman objected to when politics were raised by Sidney Lumet while they were in talks to make *Scarface*. Lumet wanted to include the U.S. government's hypocrisy in the drug trade and Bregman was against it.[16] The only vestige of that idea exists in a brief scene in the final film where a shady government contact, "Charles Goodson from Washington," is strangely present in the scene at Sosa's compound where Tony is tasked with killing the Bolivian journalist. Yet its specter is omnipresent through the diligence of Stone, who scrupulously credits, in an early draft, those advisors whose names he could safely disclose (and he had the good sense not to name the cartel members he surveyed):

"I wish to express my thanks to those people for their generous assistance in writing this screenplay," Stone begins, listing Atlee Wampler III, United States Attorney for the Southern District of Florida; Martin Raskin, Assistant United States Attorney, Chief of the Criminal Division, and Joel Rosenthal, U.S. Attorney; Captain Nick Navarro, Commander, Organized Crime Division, Broward County, Florida, and Rafael Hernandez, Jr., OCD Broward County; Sergeant Juan Caydo and Sergeant Bob Fernandez, Metro Dade County Narcotics Division; Arthur Neahbass, Organized Crime Bureau, Metro Dade County; Peter Scrocca, Drug Enforcement Agency, Dade County, Florida; Welton Merry, Special Agent, Federal Bureau of Investigation; Sergeant Mike Gonzalez, Homicide Unit, City of Miami Police Department; Jay Hoyan and Neil Sonnet, Defense Attorneys; and Vic Jamal, Ralph Rennick, and Mel Dick of Miami.

Although cocaine and crack have been pushed out of the headlines with the rise of opioids, hallucinogens, methedrine, and a panoply of other substances—natural and designer— they remain a danger to society not only in and of themselves but for the shadow economy fueled by their production and sale.

CHAPTER 4

"I Want to Be Paul Muni"

"The difference between an actor and a star," said Warren Beatty, who was both, "is that an actor works because he has to, but a star works when he wants to."[1]

There are very few stars in Hollywood—that is, someone who can get a movie greenlighted just by saying he'll do it. Most of them are men, and one of them for over four decades has been Alfredo James Pacino.

Although perhaps most widely known for his three appearances as the coolly malevolent Michael Corleone in the *Godfather* trilogy, Pacino has chosen an enviable range of other projects to enable. From his first major role—a heroin addict in 1971's *The Panic in Needle Park*—to his quirky street person "Lion" in 1973's *Scarecrow*, his troubled undercover detective in *Cruising* (1980), the malignant Roy Cohn in *Angels in America* (2003), and the flamboyant blind army officer in *Scent of a Woman* (1992), and beyond, he both inhabits his roles and burnishes them with his personality. Even for his roles in projects that did not, for various reasons, achieve wide release, such as his brilliant Shylock in 2004's *The Merchant of Venice* or the aging rock star in *Danny Collins* (2015), he fully commits. He will even accept supporting roles if they are interesting enough, such as Big Boy Caprice in *Dick Tracy* (1990). And this isn't even mentioning his legacy performances in *Serpico, Heat, Carlito's Way, The Devil's Advocate, The Insider,* and a dozen more. It is because of this star power that, when he called producer Martin Bregman and said he wanted to do a remake of *Scarface*, it took Bregman only "four phone calls" to set it up.[2]

There is some playful dispute as to whose idea it actually was. Pacino has stated that he caught a revival showing of the Hawks original at what was then the Tiffany theater, a repertory house on LA's Sunset Strip. He had earlier acted in Bertolt Brecht's 1941 parable of the ascendency of Adolf Hitler, *The Resistible Rise of Arturo Ui*, and wanted to further explore the gangster genre. During rehearsals for that play, the cast even watched old gangster movies—with the unfortunate exception of *Scarface* because it was not then available.

When he finally saw it, Pacino was transfixed. "I just was stunned by it, the story, and completely taken by Paul Muni's performance. After I saw it, I thought, 'I want to be him, I wanted to be Paul Muni, I wanted to act like that," he said.[3] "I didn't want to do a copy of it, I was looking for a style. You see, what Muni had done was a base for me to start from; he gave such a solid foundation to the role, it was like a canvas. I knew it was a characterization I wanted to continue."[4]

Unlike the narrative structure of most Hollywood films, the backstories of how they get made are seldom linear, and the tributaries that flowed together to make the 1983 *Scarface* came from many sources. For Pacino, *Scarface* was a passion project. As an actor, he is led by his passions, and one of them is the stage, which figures into the genesis of *Scarface*. Indeed, when *The Godfather* opened across America on March 24, 1972, Pacino wasn't in New York or Los Angeles basking in his newfound film stardom. He was in Massachusetts appearing in David Rabe's *The Basic Training of Pavlo Hummel* at the Theater Company of Boston. The play had first opened in 1971 at Joseph Papp's New York Shakespeare Festival's Public Theater (hold that thought). A hallucinogenic drama about an army private whose wounding in a Vietnamese brothel triggers a series of flashbacks, it allows the actor to go from bravado to fear to anxiety to truth. Reviewing its Broadway mounting five years later, Clive Barnes of the *New York Times* wrote that Pacino "is acting in two voices, at two pressures. He is constantly alternating between intense and the casual, the comic and the deeper than comic. The voice at one moment will have the flip descant of the streets to it, and soon after it will be calling a different statement, with a slightly different tone. Mr. Pacino has lost nothing in his absence from the stage. He is still a skeleton hand in a shabby velvet glove, he still moves like a boxer, and addresses the audience directly with the daring impudence of an Olivier."[5]

Pacino's hangdog, nervous, sensitive Pavlo Hummel was in shocking contrast to the catlike precision of Michael Corleone. The actor used his small stature to ingratiate himself and draw compassion, then let loose with his inner power. More importantly, he was a generous actor who allowed his fellow cast members to have their moments by purposely upstaging himself and directing audience attention to them.[6] *Pavlo Hummel* was the second in David Rabe's Vietnam trilogy, the first being *Sticks and Bones* (1971) and the third being *Streamers* (1976). Pacino would later ask Rabe to write the screenplay for *Scarface*.

But first, in 1971, Pacino was cast in the small role of Mario, a bicycle racer brought from Italy by the New York Mob as a ringer in the film version of Jimmy Breslin's comic 1969 novel *The Gang That Couldn't Shoot Straight*. It was a big break for the thirty-one-year-old actor who had been struggling to survive. Naturally, just before filming started in New York in the summer of 1971, he landed the role for which he had been endlessly auditioning and for which the film's director was holding out against studio opposition: Michael Corleone. Pacino regretfully informed MGM, who was shooting

Gang, that he had to break his contract. MGM, not in the least regretful, sued him for $25,000, his entire *Godfather* salary.[7] Then they had to recast the role of Mario. They wound up giving it to another young New York actor who had just made three independent pictures titled *Greetings*, *The Wedding Party*, and *Hi Mom!* for a rising director named Brian DePalma. The actor's name was Robert De Niro.

Despite Pacino's insistence that *Scarface* 1983 was born after catching that screening of *Scarface* 1932 (a claim he repeated on *Inside the Actors Studio* and in an *E! True Hollywood Story*), producer Martin Bregman said that the idea started with his catching the film on a late-night television airing.[8] Bregman also told Ken Tucker, author of *Scarface Nation*, that the idea was his: "The concept was to do a film about the rise and fall of an American gangster, or the rise and fall of an American businessman, or somebody with power."[9]

Either way, and knowing that Universal Pictures owned *Scarface*, Bregman called them to make a deal, and the machine was set in motion even before both parties' phone handsets hit the cradle.

Bregman immediately thought of two directors who had done well by his former client and current partner. Bregman had been Pacino's business manager before turning to producing *Serpico* (1973) and *Dog Day Afternoon* (1975). Both of them were hits directed by Sidney Lumet. Brian DePalma at that time was in postproduction on *Blow Out*, a thriller in which a movie sound man accidentally records a political murder. DePalma had originally wanted Al Pacino to star in *Blow Out* but, when he was unavailable, had cast John Travolta, whom he had used in *Carrie* (1976).[10] Even though they didn't work together on that film, Pacino was impressed enough with DePalma to send him a videocassette of the 1932 *Scarface*.[11] In return, during *Blow Out*, Travolta tried to interest DePalma in his dream project, *Mr. Hughes*, about Howard Hughes (the producer of the 1932 *Scarface*).

At any given time, every filmmaker has multiple projects in the Hollywood pipeline, any one of which must be ready to go at the first spark of financial interest. For some time DePalma had been shopping *Act of Vengeance*, based on Trevor Armbrister's 1975 book about the 1969 killing of United Mine Workers of America dissident Joseph Albert "Jock" Yablonski, who had opposed the UMW's president, William Anthony "Tough Tony" Boyle, and was later murdered with his family. As good a film as *Blow Out* is now recognized as being, its cost overruns and financial failure at the time made DePalma a Hollywood pariah, and *Act of Vengeance* lost traction. Then Martin Bregman called with *Scarface*. Eager, if not desperate, to leave his horror movie reputation behind, DePalma bit.

DePalma enters the *Scarface* odyssey twice. At the time, the notion was to keep *Scarface* set in its original world of 1930s Prohibition (an era DePalma would finally visit in 1987 with *The Untouchables*, in which De Niro played Capone). He began working on a script with playwright David Rabe. Along with *Act of Vengeance*, which he had scripted with Scott Spencer, DePalma had also, with David Rabe, been developing *Prince of the City* from Bob Daley's book about New York cop Bob Leuci who goes undercover against his own kind. DePalma spent a year-and-a-half with Leuci and then, working with Rabe, developed the *Prince* script.

Things did not go well for DePalma and Rabe on *Prince* and they were taken off the project for what were said to be budgetary reasons but had more to do with studio politics.[12] Luckily for Bregman and Pacino, this freed the writer and director to start on *Scarface*. But not for long, because the two men couldn't lick *Scarface*'s period plot.[13] They also had personal issues with Bregman. According to DePalma, after a year working together, he and Rabe took on *Scarface* with one demand: for unnamed reasons, Rabe said he would not work with Bregman or Pacino. When Pacino got a look at some of the pages, he was not pleased and alerted Bregman, who called DePalma and wanted a meeting. DePalma told Bregman that this would make Rabe quit. Bregman was insistent. DePalma called Rabe and told him about the meeting. As promised, Rabe quit, and DePalma, who was raised in the era where "the director went down with the writer,"[14] also quit the project because, he said later, he had trouble working out his relationship with Pacino and Bregman. At that point, Bregman went to Sidney Lumet.

Lumet and Bregman were old friends; Lumet had directed the first two films Bregman produced, *Serpico* and *Dog Day Afternoon*, both of which starred Pacino. Lumet's astute observation was to take *Scarface* out of 1920s Chicago (the setting that had vexed DePalma and Rabe) and update the story, reasoning, "Liquor is no longer outlawed, there's no such thing as Prohibition, and why don't you look into the cocaine world?"[15] This inspired Bregman to bring in Oliver Stone, whose Oscar for writing *Midnight Express* (1978) had positioned him to begin making his own films, but whose first directing effort, *Seizure* (1974), had gone awry.[16]

Bregman already knew Stone's work. In 1977, when *Platoon* was just a dream, he had been impressed with Stone's screenplay and optioned it, hoping to set it up at Columbia. But Francis Coppola's *Apocalypse Now* was also in production at that time, and the stories of delays, cost overruns, and monsoons scared the studio away from making a Vietnam War film.[17] Also in the ether was Vietnam veteran Ron Kovic's passionate 1976 political memoir *Born on the Fourth of July*, which Stone was adapting for Al Pacino to star in and William Friedkin (who had made *The French Connection*, 1971, and *The Exorcist*, 1973) to direct. But funding for *Born*, in which Pacino would play the wheelchair-bound Kovic, was not easy to find, and when Jane Fonda and Jon Voight announced *Coming Home* (1978), which also involved a Vietnam vet in a wheelchair, Friedkin bowed out. Instead, he and Pacino made *Cruising* (1980), after which their association dissolved for reasons neither man has ever publicly discussed.[18]

Meanwhile, Stone had managed to get money from Warner Bros. to shoot his thriller *The Hand* (1981), starring Michael Caine as a comic book artist whose severed hand goes rogue. This was during Caine's self-confessed "payday" period (which included *The Swarm*, *Beyond the Poseidon Adventure*, and *Jaws: The Revenge*), and its failure, despite a modest budget, drove Stone back to the typewriter, where he turned out *Conan the Barbarian* (1981) for director John Milius. It was at this point that Bregman asked him to tackle *Scarface*. Astonishingly, Stone passed. "I didn't want to do another Italian Mafia film," he says flatly. "I had no interest in that. Frankly, there's too much of it and I was burned out on that stuff. However, Sidney Lumet came back with Bregman about two weeks later after I passed and said, 'Would you consider doing it with a change of scenery, being about the Cuban, Colombian, and Dominican connection to Miami' that, at that time, was happening, and that interested me."[19]

Stone's process in researching and writing his script became an escapade in itself. (See Sidebar: "The Adventures of Oliver Stone.") Then came an impasse. Although Stone is one of the industry's most political filmmakers, in his early drafts he downplayed the politics and stressed the violence that his research told him was omnipresent in the cocaine trade. This turned Lumet off.

"Lumet wanted to make it more political," Stone says, "[and] Bregman didn't want to go political at all. I compromised and I have a very important scene where I show the drug connection and the United States' possible involvement in the cocaine trade in Bolivia."[20]

Stone's take stuck with Pacino and Bregman even when Lumet himself did not. Then one of those things happened that only could occur in the movie business: When DePalma and Rabe departed *Prince of the City*, the studio offered it to Sidney Lumet (or Lumet got the studio to take it away from DePalma). Lumet took on the project, rejecting Rabe's *Prince* script and adapting it himself with Jay Presson Allen. The nature and swiftness of the swap angered DePalma, who said on at least two occasions that Lumet "stole" the project away.[21] The irony is that, without *Prince of the City* to occupy him, DePalma was free to direct *Scarface*, which, by this time, had a script by Oliver Stone—an element that attracted the director.

At the same time, DePalma had a competing glimmer when Paramount Pictures suddenly expressed interest in *Act of Vengeance*. He was waiting for the green light when they told him they wanted him to direct another picture first, one they had been developing with hitmakers Don Simpson and Jerry Bruckheimer about a female welder who moonlights as an exotic dancer while she waits to get into ballet school. DePalma lasted two weeks on *Flashdance* before he realized he didn't have the necessary directorial flux. This is when Bregman lured him back to *Scarface* with Stone's script as enticement. DePalma usually wrote his own films. This time he was a hireling (albeit a highly credentialed one), and he made the most of it.

"*Scarface* is a new way of working for me," he said at the time. "Here I've got a very strong script, an actor who knows what he wants, and a producer who is in on every detail. This is more like a collaboration."[22]

The *Scarface* remake hit the trades. On January 8, 1981, the *Hollywood Reporter* carried an item that Al Pacino was going to "pick up for Paul Muni" in *Scarface*, and a week later the *Film Journal* confirmed that the new production was a remake of the 1932 original. By February 18, the *Hollywood Reporter* said that Pacino had been locked in "firm" to star and that he wanted Meryl Streep to play his "ever lovin' moll."[23]

John Travolta's name entered the mix on April 20 when Hank Grant, writing as the Rambling Reporter for the *Hollywood Reporter*, said the star was under consideration to play the George Raft role in the *Scarface* remake. The part would eventually go to Steven Bauer.

Universal was in a bragging mood in summer 1981 with an announcement that, for the spring of 1982, the studio was about to spend $125 million "of its own money"[24] on ten pictures during the rest of the year, but that those ten would be only one-third of the company's output. Steven Grossberg's article in *Variety* did not mention the sleight-of-hand by which the venerable studio was able to commit what was then a huge sum to production. During 1981, Universal had released twenty-five films, some of which were modest hits, like *The Four Seasons* and *Bustin' Loose*, but many of which were disasters, like *The Legend of the Lone Ranger*, *Honky Tonk Freeway*, *Endless Love*, and *Heartbeeps*. But the company's clever president, Sid Sheinberg, had arranged to be only the distributor for ten of the twenty-five and not the financing production company, and those ten were the ones that had flopped. Since a film's distributor collects the first money that comes in and charges a hefty percentage as its handling fee, Universal suffered minimal losses. Among the pictures announced for the next year were "a Neil Simon comedy" that became *The Lonely Guy*, John Carpenter's *Firestarter*, *Psycho 2*, *Halloween III*,[25] a film from Alan Alda (*Sweet Liberty*, 1986), a film from the Pythons (*Monty Python's The Meaning of Life*, 1983), and Mark Rydell's *Nuts* (which Barbra Streisand took to Warner Bros. and replaced Rydell with Martin Ritt in 1983). The next day Universal's production VP Ned Tanen announced that *Scarface* would be added to that list—with Pacino.[26]

"I felt good when he [DePalma] was involved," Pacino said, "because, first of all, he responded to the script in such a passionate and positive way. This idea he had of making this thing larger than life, a little bit more heightened reality, really appealed to me." Echoed DePalma, "The most defining experience on *Scarface* was the opportunity to work with a truly great actor. It makes you better to work with a great actor because you've got to be driven to find ways to deal with the input they give you."[27] It may have sounded press-releasey, but it was true—the mutual admiration society would continue throughout filming.

On May 24, executive producer Lou Stroller in "Just for *Variety*" confirmed that *Scarface* was a go at Universal with Pacino starring, DePalma directing, Stone writing, and Bregman producing.[28] Not until August 6, 1982 did it appear in the *Hollywood Reporter*, which quoted Martin Bregman that the budget would be $10 million.

Filming was announced to start on October 4, 1982, in Florida. That date turned out to be optimistic when, on August 22, Miami city commissioner Demetrio Perez, Jr., announced plans to introduce a resolution to block the permits that DePalma's crew would need in order to shoot in that city. His resolution, which he touted in the pages of *Libre*, a bilingual community newspaper that he owned, would forbid the "use of any city facility to any productions in which any minority is portrayed in a bad light and contributes to disharmony between ethnic groups."[29]

"They just assumed the movie would be anti-Cuban, pro-crime, or both," Bregman told writer Colin Dangaard. "It angered me that nobody asked to see the script before they made judgments. When Perez attacked me for making *Serpico*, which he said was an offensive film, well, that did it. Way later, when they did ask [for a script], I told them to go to hell."[30] (In 2002 Perez would plead guilty to defrauding three elderly tenants in his low-income Little Havana apartments. He would also draw criticism when he received a $110 million bond from the Miami-Dade Commission to help his private charter school business.)[31]

With the next city commission meeting not scheduled to happen until September, Lou Stroller said that the company wouldn't hang around that long. "If you ask me right now," he said, "I'd say I'm 70–80 percent in favor of moving to Los Angeles."[32]

The next day Miami film coordinator Marylee Lander chimed in. Although production officials had met with members of the city's Cuban community and "calmed some worries," according to Stroller, the Perez measure threatened to rend the tentative truce. Stroller, after confabs with the Spanish-American League Against Discrimination, the Cuban National Planning Counsel, and the Dade County (Miami) Manager's Office, agreed to put a disclaimer "either in the body of the film or during the opening or closing credits." The overriding concern was that the Cuban community feared that viewers would get the impression from the film that all of the Castro refugees were criminals.[33]

Stroller had to make a decision. In addition to expensive delays in production, the relocation itself would cost between

$100,000 and $200,000. It would also mean that the company would have to abandon the $250,000 worth of set construction that they had already built in Miami.[34]

Councilmember Perez was not mollified by the promised disclaimer and said that he would keep his measure "active" until he was certain no offense to the Cuban community was in the movie.[35]

He needn't have bothered. On August 31, Universal decided to move the now-$15-million-budget *Scarface* to Los Angeles, citing two negative *Miami Herald* editorial columns that had run on August 28.[36] Ten days later, however, Bregman reversed himself and announced that the sides had conferred and production would resume in Miami with Perez agreeing to wait until seeing the finished film before deciding whether to act. He added that he and Miami mayor Maurice Ferré would look at the finished film and decide whether a disclaimer would be needed.[37] A new start date of November 22 was announced[38] and Al Pacino would start taking Cuban dialect lessons from well-known linguistic coach Robert Easton.[39]

While Miami was simmering, Steven Bauer, an actor of Cuban descent, was cast as Manny[40] and was drawn into the Miami fray by his fellow Cubans. "When people started to ask me," he said, "I just told them all that [Perez] was a fool, and that it's not about them, it's about a specific type of individual that was of a specific event: the Mariel boatlift, [and] along with those who had been waiting to leave Castro's Cuba, Castro threw in all the human refuse from prisons, the hardened criminals, along with other undesirables to the revolution. I emphasized that to equate one generation with another was just plain dumb, and they would do themselves a favor to stop thinking about that, and ignore this guy so that you can see the movie open-minded when it comes out."[41]

The casting continued. On December 2, 1982, Michelle Pfeiffer, not Meryl Streep, was given the role of Tony's mistress Elvira.[42] Her audition was an ordeal, she told *Tonight Show* host Jimmy Fallon. "[Pacino] didn't particularly want me for the part," she recalled. "My last credit before that was *Grease 2*. Can you blame him?" The process took two or three months, "and I was terrified. Brian was really rooting for me, but he said, 'You're really bad now. What's going on?'" Nevertheless, a month later they called her for a screen test. Feeling she had no shot at the job relaxed her. They improvised a marital snit predictive of the restaurant scene where Elvira leaves Tony, and when it was over, she said, "there was blood everywhere. I look over and Al is bleeding. I cut Al Pacino! And that's how I got the part."[43]

After that, however, DePalma's protectiveness toward her was over. "I was objectified," Pfeiffer says. "If there was one hair out of place, he could see an imperfection."[44] Soon she realized that DePalma was regarding her from Tony's domineering point of view. "Sometimes, by playing an object, you can actually say more about objectifying women than if you play somebody of strength. Elvira was a hood ornament, like another Rolls-Royce or something for both of the men that she was with. I felt that my playing something that mirrors someone's life in that way, I could make a kind of feminist statement."[45] She succeeded; in *Scarface Nation*, Ken Tucker posits that Pfeiffer is one of the few women in a DePalma film to take charge of her own life.[46]

The same might be said of Gina, played by Mary Elizabeth Mastrantonio, who rebels against her brother and confronts the elephant in their emotional room. Mastrantonio would make her feature debut as Gina, according to *Daily Variety* of December 12, 1982. Harris Yulin (Detective Bernstein) was announced on March 21, 1983; Paul Shenar (Alejandro Sosa) on February 10, 1983; Miriam Colon (Tony's mother) on January 19, 1983; and Robert Loggia (Frank Lopez) postponed his December wedding to his personal manager Audrey O'Brien to the 27th so he could appear in the film.[47]

This series of castings, announcements, leavings, and switches is de rigueur for what had become and remains the current glacial process for getting movies made, and *Scarface* is an example of the fast track. Before the studio system collapsed in the early 1960s, the head of production—say, Jack L. Warner—would approve a script, take out a list of contract players from his desk drawer and see who was available to appear in it, send the script to one of his contract directors, and tell everybody to show up first thing Monday morning to make the picture. In this way, each studio turned out an average of one film a week over the course of nearly four decades. The delay, waste, and soul-shattering ego games of what Hollywood has become since then caused, for example, director Milos Forman (*Amadeus*, *One Flew Over the Cuckoo's Nest*), who was a successful survivor, to say, "So much energy is spent here on things that never appear on the screen at all. The film . . . is not proof of your talent but evidence of your ability as a promoter. So much time and work is spent on negotiations, contracts, money, talking with agents, producers, companies, lawyers, and unions that there is no energy left for what WILL appear on the screen. You can see this in the vast quantity of boring and mediocre American films that come all the time from the major studios."[48]

With that baggage, *Scarface* finally got rolling on December 23, 1982.

The Miami Cubans

The Cuban revolution of 1953–1958 resulted, on January 1, 1959, in the ascension of Fidel Castro as prime minister, replacing the country's president Fulgencio Batista.[49] The wave of populism that swept the oppressed proletariat of the Caribbean island was not shared by the moneyed class who had supported Batista, and tens of thousands of them began migrating to America, principally to Florida, aided first by the Eisenhower and then by the Kennedy administration in the United States. Over the next twenty years a million or more Cubans joined this first wave; many of them were displaced professionals, political exiles, and businesspeople who distrusted Castro's intentions or were afraid of being fingered as collaborators. From April 17 to 21, 1961, twelve hundred Cubans invested hope and participated in what became an ill-fated CIA-backed attempt to reclaim Cuba by invasion at the Bay of Pigs.[50] The Cuban Missile Crisis of October 16 to 28, 1962 further chilled relations between the U.S. and the Cuban government when Castro allowed the USSR to construct missile bases ninety miles from U.S. shores and President Kennedy sent the navy to turn away Soviet ships heading to the island with a payload of nuclear warheads. Thereafter, sanctions were put in place against Cuba, restricting U.S. trade and travel, a policy that found fervent support within the exiled Miami Cuban community.

By October of 1965, Castro had fully embraced Marxist-Leninist Communism, and a second wave of Cuban exiles headed to Florida. These were not only those whose businesses Castro had nationalized but even more who were fleeing appalling living and financial conditions.[51] These

"Freedom Flights" lasted until 1973 and expanded Florida's anti-Castro Cuban community by over a quarter of a million people.[52]

The Eisenhower, Kennedy, and Johnson administrations facilitated the credentialing process for the Cuban émigrés, arranging green cards and other work and entry documents for them. Not only did the exiles become a successful economic force in Miami and other Floridian cities, they became a powerful lobbying ally, primarily in support of conservative politicians who vowed to uphold the Cuban blockade. At the same time, there was tension between the African American community and the newly arrived Cubans whom the African Americans felt were taking their jobs and undoing the gains they had made during the civil rights struggle of the 1960s and '70s.

The third wave of immigration is the one reflected in *Scarface*: the Mariel boatlift of 1980 in which 125,000 Cubans departed the port of El Mariel. The background was violence at the Peruvian embassy to which a frustrated Castro reacted by vowing, in essence, "Cuba: love it or leave it." Tens of thousands of dissatisfied Cubans did the latter, overwhelming Miami and bringing to the States not only those disaffected with Castro's regime but malcontents and criminals whom Castro was eager to be rid of.[53] Of the 125,000 immigrants, only 2,746 were deemed unacceptable and were denied automatic citizenship. (The 25,000 mentioned in the film's opening title card are others who were allowed in, presumably by subterfuge.) The influx was terminated in September 1980, but Mariel Harbor stayed open until October 31 in an agreement between the U.S. and Cuba, and tensions remained.

Finally, the collapse of the Soviet Union in 1991 cut off the financial lifeline that had supported Cuba, and once again, Castro decreed that anyone who wanted to leave

Cuba could do so. This time, however, there were no open arms in America. Scores of people arrived in boats, rafts, inner tubes, and by any floating means possible, many of them dying en route. An agreement between the Castro regime and the George H. W. Bush administration limited the number of emigres to 20,000 a year. In recent years, however, tens of thousands of Cubans have been entering the U.S. via Mexico, confounding quotas.

The Cuban community in Miami remains a singularly powerful and emphatically conservative lobbying force, generally favoring the Republican Party. They are vehemently opposed to even a hint of normalized relations with Cuba, as President Barack Obama discovered in December 2014, when he announced he had spoken to Fidel Castro, the first communication between the nations' two leaders in over fifty years. He was immediately chastised by the GOP's congressional bloc, who later supported, with no trace of irony, the anti-immigration stance of the Trump Administration.[54]

They are also a poised powder keg toward outsiders, as Oliver Stone discovered when he ventured to Miami to research writing *Scarface*. "The Cuban right wing is a very scary group," he said. "Honestly, even to talk about them is dangerous, they may be the single most dangerous group of guys I have ever met. It's the whole group from the Bay of Pigs. A few of them are drug dealers and use drug moneys to keep their political work going. A lot of these guys have disguised drug dealing as legitimate anti-Castro political activities, and that is mentioned in the movie."[55]

Their influence, above and below the surface, was to affect *Scarface* as cameras rolled—and then didn't.

SIDEBAR

The Adventures of Oliver Stone

In his 2014 book, *Five Came Back: A Story of Hollywood and the Second World War*, Mark Harris writes movingly of five top Hollywood directors whose military service forever changed them and the kind of films they made.[56] Their postwar movies, he writes, reflected reality instead of escapism and brought a maturity to the screen that audiences of the time not only appreciated but shared.

Contrast this with the filmmaking generation that came of draft age during the Vietnam War. Rather than serve, most of them were safe in college with 2-S student deferments or had contrived other means of avoiding conscription. Their knowledge of the hell of battle came secondhand through television news and friends who weren't as lucky to escape service. There were only a tiny number of mainstream Hollywood movies made about Vietnam while America was in the thick of it. Other than John Wayne's hawkish *The Green Berets* for Warner Bros. in 1968 and Elia Kazan's little seen 1972 drama *The Visitor* for United Artists, no mainstream American studio committed to making a Vietnam film during the ongoing conflict. [57] Thus the films they made when they took hold of Hollywood reflects these war experiences, or lack of them.[58]

Except, notably, for Oliver Stone.

Stone's boots-on-the-ground war film trilogy (*Platoon*, 1987; *Born on the Fourth of July*, 1989; *Heaven and Earth*, 1994) are the work of a seasoned, scarred combatant. More to the point, Stone's survival in country from 1967 to 1968 (he was with the 2nd Platoon, Bravo Company, 3rd Battalion, 25th Infantry, stationed along the Cambodian border, and earned a Bronze Star) gave him the chops to walk the halls of any agency or studio in town. It might be said that, after 'Nam, Hollywood was a breeze.

Stone's involvement in *Scarface* was not accidental. As has been noted, he and Martin Bregman had attempted in the early 1970s to set up what was then titled *The Platoon*. When Stone was enlisted to write *Scarface*, he made a fresh start from the DePalma-Rabe collaboration. The fly in the ointment was his self-confessed drug problem. But it also turned out to be a solution.

"I was a cocaine addict for about two and a half years prior to writing *Scarface*," Stone confessed in 2015. "I knew that world, the drug world of the early '80s very well. Cocaine had screwed me so much. It had taken so much of my money that now I needed to take my revenge and so I wrote *Scarface*."[59]

It was a daring exorcism. When first pitched on the project, Stone had no desire to remake the 1932 *Scarface*, holding no fascination with gangster films, and passed. But when Bregman called him again several months later with Sidney Lumet's idea about updating it to the Florida cocaine wars triggered by the human detritus of the Mariel boatlift, the writer saw broader possibilities in updating bootlegging into the drug trades.

"There's a prohibition against drugs that's created the same criminal class as [prohibition of alcohol] created the Mafia," he told David Konow in a remarkably frank interview. "The Marielitos at the time had gained a lot of publicity for their open brazenness. They were deported by Castro in 1981 to America. At the time, it was perceived he was dumping all the criminals into the American system. According to the police enforcement in Miami Beach, they were the poorest people, the roughest people in the prisons who would kill for a dollar. How could you get this outlandish, operatic character inside an American, contemporary framework?" This would be the milieu he would dramatize.

It involved taking a deep dive into the belly of the beast. "I researched it thoroughly in Florida and the Caribbean. I had been in South America recently and did some research there. So I saw quite a bit of the drug trade from the legal point of view as well as from the gangster point of view. Not many people would talk; it's a very closed world.

"I was exposed to certain situations on both sides of the law," he continued. "I went to the Caribbean, there's no law down there, they'll just shoot you in your hotel room. It got hairy. It gave me all this color. They were rough, the Colombians played rough." The threat became real when, while hanging out with big-time drug merchants, Stone disregarded his own mantra ("Never get high on your own supply") and got so buzzed that he joined their boasting and revealed that he was a Hollywood screenwriter. "They thought I was an informer because I dropped the name of a guy who . . . had previously busted one of these three guys as a prosecutor. So at four in the morning that gets dangerous! Two of them went into the bathroom and I thought they were gonna come out and blow me away. But you know, the truth of the matter is, I got out by bullshit, by the skin of my teeth. I was nervous the whole night, nervous beyond belief. That never could have happened to me if I had been straight. And they never would have taken me to any conference, nor would I have the necessary élan to approach them. I would have been totally out of sorts.

"It was a scary moment and it was good for me to get back in touch with the fear that I had felt so often in Vietnam," he explained. "Because that fear is the essence of what *Scarface* is about. Those moments of fear and the concept of not knowing what's going to happen next, that violence can come at any time."[60]

Having ended his research, Stone then ended his addiction. Accepting a $300,000 stipend from Bregman to start work on a script,[61] he began his research in the States, but after a year moved to Paris with his then-wife Elizabeth to finish the job—as he described to Konow—"totally fucking cold sober." He would also get $250,000 for his script if the picture was made.[62] At the time he was writing *Scarface* in 1981–1982, he had directed only two features and two shorts, neither of which had set the world—or his career—on fire. He had won the Oscar for writing *Midnight Express* (1978) but his riveting war drama *Salvador* (1986), which established him as a filmmaker, was still four years off.

Having followed the cocaine trail to the Colombian, Jamaican, and Dominican connections who were winning domination over the Italian Mob, Stone was then sent by Bregman to law enforcement authorities in Florida who were being swamped by the illegal drug trade. "It was Vietnam redux," Stone would write, "navy, army, air force, and marines, and do you think they ever really talked to one another? Hardly. It was impossible to stop the flow of a substance in popular demand."[63] He culled much information from DEA, FBI, and Justice Department contacts. A frightening number of the stories he heard were sworn as real, including the chainsaw murder, although he made it more dramatic(!) for the film.

At this stage, DePalma rejoined the project (sans Rabe) and understood the violent approach to megalomania that Stone had taken. He shared Bregman's and Stone's fascination, and the result is on the screen.[64]

But only so far. It was Bregman who reined in the politics that Stone had injected into early drafts. He and Pacino wanted to stick to Tony Montana's power trip. In adjusting his gaze to power and the corruption wrought by money, Stone crafted what some people accused of being a Hollywood parable disguised as a gangster film. On a more personal level, he used Tony's aggressiveness as a means to articulate his own frustration at his career obstacles.

"One of the things that's bugged me, I think a lot of writers will agree with this, is we spend money on our vices and we pay through the nose for our mistakes," he said. "I'll admit that coke kicked my ass. It's one of the things that beat me in life. As a result, getting even, getting paid to make a movie about it and making it a good one on top of it, there's nothing better."[65]

But not completely. There were disagreements between Stone and DePalma—the nascent director and the established one—during production.

"Oliver had directed one movie," DePalma recalled in his eponymous 2015 biographical documentary, "and he felt that I wasn't doing the movie the way he wanted to do it, and I ultimately had to have him taken off the set because he was talking to the actors. You can't have an actor getting two different points of view from two different people; it confuses them. They need a single voice."[66]

The schism continued even after DePalma delivered his first cut, which Bregman screened privately for Stone after cautioning him not to discuss his reaction with Pacino. When Pacino learned of Bregman's clandestine preview, he summoned Stone to his apartment in New York to hear his notes. What Bregman apparently didn't know was that Pacino had bonded with Stone back in 1978 when they spent a year trying to get Born on the Fourth of July made. Now they realized that Bregman and DePalma had set them against each other. Feeling that the air between them was now clear, Stone presented Pacino with a list of recommendations. "This, as it turned out, was a big mistake," Stone writes in his memoir *Chasing the Light*. "It was Al who'd asked me to step in as co-counsel in this dispute. Yet Al failed to defend me when Marty came down on me for betraying him. . . . I was cut out as the friend. . . . I wouldn't see or talk to Bregman until *Born on the Fourth of July* surprisingly came around again six years later. And then the tables would be turned."[67]

When *Scarface* opened to the public on December 9, 1983, Stone saw it in a packed theater on Broadway with a paying audience, mostly Black and Latino, he recounts. He said that those people knew that the film had cred. He further knew it when he began to hear his dialogue repeated on the subway, on the streets, and in playgrounds.

Despite this, *Scarface* did not boost Stone's fortunes. "Nothing came of it," he now says. "I was on the outs. Bregman had fallen out. He bad-mouthed me at Universal, and all that stuff. I guess I was a force in the sense that I was independent, and people perhaps resented that. It didn't help my career at all. Except Michael Cimino came to me to write *Year of the Dragon* (1985) but that was a different kind of story."[68]

When Universal began to make money with the unexpected interest in *Scarface* from the hip-hop community, however, they offered Stone the chance to make a sequel. "I could've made a great deal of money by accepting a sequel," he wrote, "but my 'gangster' thoughts were ready to explode into the new milieu of *Wall Street* (1987)."[69]

Because Stone has developed a reputation as a political filmmaker and documentarian (particularly through his and Peter Kuznick's 2012 Showtime series, *The Untold History of the United States*), it's tempting to see his work on *Scarface* as a stepping stone to loftier goals. But he threw himself wholly into the world of Tony Montana, stopping just short of going over the edge himself. That commitment is what gave

DePalma, his crew, and his actors the stuff that nightmares are made of. *Scarface* is what the collaborative medium of movies is supposed to be about.

CHAPTER 5

The DePalma Dilemma

Brian DePalma is one of the best-reviewed directors, and one of the worst-reviewed. His films are daringly original but are sometimes (wrongly) called derivative. He began his career with impertinent low-budget comedies yet became one of the cinema's most accomplished directors of big-budget dramas. His films have been heavily criticized for victimizing women, yet it's nearly impossible to find a bad performance by any actress who has worked under his direction. About the only thing that is at all predictable about Brian DePalma is that he is unpredictable—that and the khaki safari jacket he consistently wears to interviews.

He also has the reputation of being grumpy and distant on his sets, to which he readily confesses, but explains that it's the result of being totally focused on what he is doing, where to place the camera, and using his energy to make the film because, if he fails to do so, he will have to live with it for the rest of his life.[1]

DePalma is one of the most interviewed and written about directors of the Hollywood "New Age," that cadre of filmmakers who entered the business as the studio system was crumbling in the late 1960s and early 1970s. These filmmakers, who included Steven Spielberg, George Lucas, Martin Scorsese, Paul Schrader, and Francis Coppola as well as DePalma, redefined, for good or ill, American cinema. With the possible exception of William Friedkin, DePalma has been uniquely open to being examined by critics and historians; not only has he subjected himself to countless interviews and a career documentary (*DePalma*, directed by Noah Baumbach and Jake Paltrow, 2015), but he was brave enough to allow a *Wall Street Journal* reporter, Julie Salamon, to shadow what became his disastrous 1990 movie *Bonfire of the Vanities*. The resulting book, *The Devil's Candy* (New York: Houghton-Mifflin Co., 1991), is the most astute "making of" journal since Lillian Ross's devastating *Picture* (New York: Rinehart & Co., 1952) about John Huston's equally ill-fated 1951 *The Red Badge of Courage*.

The reception to many of DePalma's pictures varies from the beatific (*The Untouchables, Carrie, Dressed to Kill, Mission: Impossible, Carlito's Way*) to the execrable (*Bonfire of the Vanities, Blow Out, Wise Guys, Mission to Mars*). If the list looks skewed, it's because some of his films that were received coolly when they were new (*Blow Out, Obsession, Sisters, Body Double* being notable) have increased in respect not so much as they have aged, but as the critics have become younger. This is literally the definition of a filmmaker being ahead of his time, and the title that most clearly limns this revisionism is *Scarface*.

What led Brian DePalma to *Scarface*? Not the Hollywood dealmaking behind it, which is covered elsewhere, but the personal and directorial sensibilities that prepared him to make it at that moment in time?

Brian Russell DePalma was born in Garden City, New Jersey on September 11, 1940, to Vivienne (née Muti) and Anthony DePalma. He has two older bothers, Barton and Bruce, and the three of them are second generation Americans, their grandparents having hailed from Alberona, Foggia, in Apulia, Italy. Anthony DePalma was a successful orthopedic surgeon, which meant that the family lived in reasonable comfort. They moved to Philadelphia when Brian was five.

DePalma's home life was both unsettled and unsettling. His mother, who was charming but judgmental, made no secret of the fact that his birth was unintentional and that she preferred the firstborn brother Bruce to both Brian and Barton. In his teens, when he learned that his father was having an affair, Brian took to spying on him (much as the Keith Gordon character does in *Home Movies*, 1979, and in *Dressed to Kill*, 1980), recording his phone conversations and even going so far as to break into his medical office and stalk him at night with a knife.[2] "I actually approached it as a comedy," DePalma told *Business Insider*'s Jason Guerrasio. "A bizarre comedy. It all happened, but by the time I made the movie I saw the absurd aspects to it.

"We're all a product of our upbringing to some extent," he continues. "But my older brother [presumably Bruce] was very influential too because he sort of represents that egomaniac that appears in many of my movies. Whatever happened between [my father] and my mother by the time I was born, they were at odds with each other and just hung in there until I went to college, basically. So it's interesting, the times I spent with my father I can count on one hand. I remember going to see a John Wayne Western with him, *The Horse Soldiers* (1959)."[3]

The stalking also firmly established in young DePalma the realization that cinema was a voyeuristic experience with a vocabulary of involving as well as alienating effects that could be summoned in service of emotion, information, or a combination. His growing fluency in this language defines his growth as a filmmaker and a manipulator.

Like Gordon's character in *Dressed to Kill*, DePalma was a computer nerd working on a science fair project and, in fact, won a second place award for computer design in a regional science fair in the mid-1950s. This propelled him to enter Columbia University as a physics and math major, also studying Russian, but traditional academics went by the boards when he encountered Hitchcock's *Vertigo* first-run at the Radio City Music Hall in 1958 and switched to New York University to study film. There he met fellow student Martin Scorsese and, in class, the stylistically diverse films of Welles, Hitchcock, Antonioni, Warhol, and the Maysles Brothers. He also attended screenings at Amos Vogel's avant-garde Cinema 16, where young filmmakers were showing their underground work. Graduate studies at Sarah Lawrence College led him to the tutelage of resident drama teacher Wilford Leach, who directed him as an actor in class exercises. DePalma learned directing on his own. He quickly realized that movies were at their best when they told their stories visually, and that films of suspense and action, above other genres, best utilized those elements of cinema. This, he said, was why those wordless sequences in Hitchcock's films remain so memorable: Hitchcock was a visual storyteller.

When DePalma decided to start making his own movies, he hocked his science fair awards and equipment (a frequency generator and oscilloscope) and bought a Bolex 16mm silent camera. From this (and rented sound cameras) came the shorts *Icarus* (1960), *660124: The Story of an IBM Card* (1961), and *Woton's Wake* (1963). His other short films of this period include *Jennifer* (1964), a sponsored film for the Museum of Modern Art called *The Responsive Eye* (1965), and *Show Me a Strong Town and I'll Show You a Strong Bank* (1966), which can only be described as a Chamber of Commerce pitch. Two features, *Murder à la Mod* and *Greetings*, came out in 1968, but were made much earlier.[4]

In 1964, he made his first feature, *The Wedding Party*, codirected with Leach and financed to the tune of $100,000 by his fellow student Cynthia Munroe, who shares a "film by" credit. Leach directed the actors and DePalma headed the photographic and editing teams, but during production he disagreed with Leach's flat staging and took over blocking for the camera rather than the stage. His cast included fellow students Jill Clayburgh, Jennifer Salt, and Robert De Niro. The film wasn't released until 1969, after *Greetings* drew notice. It was inspired by the wedding of his Columbia roommate Jered Martin for which he and William Finley had been groomsmen.

De Niro at the time was barely twenty and had to have his mother sign his acting contract. He was also painfully shy. DePalma has said that when he and Leach were holding auditions, De Niro was the last person they saw. He said hello and then left the room after telling them that he had prepared something. Twenty minutes passed and DePalma thought De Niro had gone home, but then the young actor burst into the room and did a monologue from Clifford Odets's *Strike* and blew everyone away.[5] He got the part.

DePalma's second film was more assured and, at the same time, more disturbing. *Murder à la Mod* was a mystery told from three points of view, not as Kurosawa might have shown it in *Rashomon*, but as if Hitchcock, Godard, and a soap opera director had each done a segment. Like *The Wedding Party*, it, too, had trouble finding distribution, and the $25,000 "horror comedy," as it has been called, had to wait until 1968 to be seen.

Hovering over everyone's head as *The Wedding Party* and *Murder à la Mod* were finished and shelved was the Indochina war. President Kennedy had committed "advisors" to Laos and was propping up the government of South Vietnam. Following JFK's assassination in 1963, President Lyndon Johnson escalated the war and DePalma's coming-of-age generation was expecting to be drafted to fight it.

Young men of eighteen, the prime draft age, were desperate to find ways to be disqualified from military service. Out of that exploration came *Greetings* (the widely feared vocative on Selective Service draft notices), written by DePalma and Charles Hirsch. In the sardonic comedy, Jonathan Warden, Gerrit Graham, and Robert De Niro scheme to dodge the draft and consider such an adventurous range of techniques that the film earned one of the Motion Picture Association's earliest X ratings.[6] It would be the first of many showdowns DePalma would have with the regulatory body.

DePalma would use De Niro again in his even more confrontational comedy, *Hi, Mom!* (1970), before losing him to Martin Scorsese and their fabled collaboration.

DePalma had earned his comedy chops—not just standard comedy but a particularly brutal satirical humor—and it winds through all his work, often combined with grotesquerie (just like Hitchcock). As for De Niro, strangely, in 1975, he was cast in Neil Simon's romantic comedy *Bogart Slept Here* for Mike Nichols, but had so much trouble getting a grip on the character (he had just wrapped *Taxi Driver* and Travis Bickle must have lingered in the dedicated actor's soul) that Nichols shut down the production in August and fired him, claiming that he wasn't funny.[7] Later, of course, De Niro scored in *Meet the Parents* (2000) and other comedies. What did DePalma and the others see that Nichols didn't?

Between *Greetings* and *Hi, Mom!* DePalma directed *Dionysus in '69* (shot in 1968 and released in 1970) as a filmization of Euripides's *The Bacchae* presented at Richard Schechter's Performance Group. In that film, DePalma experimented with split screen, a technique he would perfect in *Carrie* (1976) and apply to subsequent works, providing the audience with two points of view by which they could construct their own narrative without being forced by traditional cutting to see it a fixed editorial way.

DePalma's momentum stopped with *Get to Know Your Rabbit*, a 1970 comedy about a tap-dancing magician that was not released until 1972 (delay in releasing his films was becoming a tradition). *Rabbit*, for Warner Bros., was his first studio job and was intended as a breakthrough into mainstream filmmaking. Instead, it was recut by the studio and disowned by its star, Tom Smothers. Although DePalma's apparent rebellion against a studio made him welcome among his filmmaking peers, its failure sent him back to square one. Then he found independent producer (and scion of a wealthy family) Edward Pressman to make *Sisters* (1972). This was DePalma's first formal suspense film, and his use of the camera to tell his story visually earned him the reputation as a Hitchcock imitator even though both it and *Obsession* (1976) were clearly intended as homages.[8]

It isn't necessary to scroll through the seven motion pictures in DePalma's filmography between *Sisters* and *Scarface* to chart his accruing skills.[9] What is important is that, by the time DePalma finished *Blow Out* (which was undeservedly trashed by the critics), he was at a creative crossroads. Having written as well as directed most of his films, he seemed unsure that his taste was what the public wanted. He took *Scarface* solely as a director. "I got tired of making these 'Brian DePalma movies,'" he admitted. "You get tired of your own obsessions, the betrayal, the voyeurism, the twisted sexuality."[10] That did not mean that he wouldn't make changes—the auteurist cannot divorce himself from the art—only that the project was ready and waiting for him, and he came aboard.

Pacino was eager to have him. "DePalma had a different vision, a way I hadn't thought about it at all," the actor says, contrasting DePalma with Lumet. "I thought he was an interesting choice. He brought a definite style to it, almost Brechtian in a way. He knew what he wanted to do with it right from the start. Brian approaches things—situations, sensibilities, relationships—from another angle, another place than me. We both understood that, and so we were able to get along."[11] The Brechtian reference is an allusion to *Arturo Ui.*

But why *Scarface*? In addition to the excitement of Oliver Stone's script, DePalma has said that he has always had a fascination with megalomania and people living in isolated universes who are insulated from reality. Surely *Scarface* fits that description. So do *The Bonfire of the Vanities* (1990, privileged stockbroker), *The Untouchables* (1987, Al Capone versus the Bureau of Investigation), *Carlito's Way* (1993, a parolee's return to crime), and, in its way, *Mission: Impossible* (1996, spy vs. spy). Like Howard Hawks, who was celebrated for his films about professionals acting professionally within their professions, DePalma likes exploring systems as well as the people who are either caught in them or rebel against them. Even his first modest hit, *Carrie*, is about a bullied girl who rebels against her high school and über-religious mother, and what could insulate her further from reality than by being telekinetic? Similarly, *The Fury* (1978) has a psychic girl taking on the pseudo-governmental system that is exploiting her. Even *Casualties of War* (1993) shows a soldier going up against a system that is protecting other soldiers who committed a war crime when the system itself is engaged in a greater war crime.

This is the stuff of drama and it is not specific to DePalma. What makes DePalma's treatment of the subjects so noteworthy is his ability to both show the action and comment on it at the same time by use of his camera. He can make a shot from an unusual angle that can, as he puts it, "pop" the audience out of a picture (and it doesn't bother him) while still telling the story. The device is either self-conscious or Brechtian, depending on one's interpretation.

By that measure, the universe of *Scarface* has its own rules and behaviors just like society, only more so. It is a flamboyant extrapolation of capitalism—literally capitalism on drugs. He has even said that it is a kind of fantasy world, and because it is driven by drugs, it's even more of a fantasy. *Scarface* is all about excess and it gets more insane as it goes along.

There are even moments when one cannot be sure whether it is a drama or a comedy. The film's most quoted line, "Say hello to my little friend," is at once sarcastic, desperate, and horrendously sanguine. It is also completely in character, which is a testament to Pacino's ability to act organically and DePalma's skill in making the film's over-the-top climax appear within the realm of its own reality. A distorted reality, to be sure, but nevertheless consistent and frighteningly real.

It's interesting to chart DePalma's maturation over the years and films. While he has worked in any number of genres, the broad strokes are that he started in comedies, went into thrillers, entered gangster films, returned to thrillers, and confidently mixed elements as he went along. It was a creative career decision that, when he felt he was getting typed as a comedy director, he went to thrillers. When thrillers began to dominate his filmography, he switched back to comedies. His later films are dramas.

He is not a slave to any genre. If comedy is called for in a thriller, he uses it; if a tense moment serves a comedy, he puts it in. The trick is matching the style to the material and sidestepping notes from studio people who don't understand that storytelling demands a balance, just as meals cannot be all one flavor. DePalma worked for years to achieve the power to say no.

What drew him to *Scarface* beyond its megalomaniacal central character? He confessed that he was never a great fan of the Howard Hawks original because it looked mired in its period (something he and Rabe could not surmount) but that Stone's script and the concept of setting it in Miami's cocaine world gave it new life. Before production, Stone took DePalma around Miami's Cuban community, and DePalma was impressed with the canvas, the vibrancy, and the promise of setting Tony Montana's perversion of the American Dream in South Florida's sunny streets, pastel hovels, and shadowy nightspots. The idea that someone could come out of a Cuban prison, brave turbulent ocean straits sailing to the USA, and then become a billionaire was a seductive pitch.[12]

It was also an opportunity to once again change genres, moving from suspense films to what he called more character-driven pieces. An additional attraction was that the script was already written. "I always liked working with other people's materials," he told Charlie Rose in a 1992 interview. "It got me away from the particular ideas that I had so they could mature and maybe I'd get a better idea, but I worked with some great writers who did terrific screenplays. It's good to go out and just direct."[13]

He may have been a hireling, but he was a powerful one who shaped the film to his vision. He worked closely with art director Edward Richardson, visual consultant Ferdinando Scarfiotti (there is no credited production designer), and director of photography John A. Alonzo to stress the contrast between pastel exterior colors and bright interior colors, to underscore the fantasy of the mega-drug culture. "Give me the most beautiful pictures you can," DePalma told Alonzo. "I'm going to place violence inside of them."[14] Giorgio Moroder's mixture of throbbing acoustic and electronic music punctuated with percussion that suggests gunshots further drove *Scarface* toward its operatic footings.

At the same time that DePalma asserted his visual philosophy, he was perceptive about his actors' duties. He was mindful that actors operate not only intellectually but emotionally, and are sometimes incapable of articulating their difficulties with a scene. He was constantly alert for such obstacles. More importantly, he knew how to resolve them. When, for example, he saw that Pacino was unable to play the scene in Lopez's Cadillac dealership boardroom in which several other actors were sitting around a table, DePalma called for another rehearsal and summoned Stone to the trailer for a dialogue rewrite. But DePalma realized that the problem wasn't the lines, it was the set; Pacino didn't have enough physical space to move. The solution was simple: shoot another scene elsewhere while carpenters increased the size of the boardroom set.[15]

DePalma's skill with actors had begun at Sarah Lawrence, where he acted for Wilford Leach in addition to directing scenes on his own. There he learned the acting vocabulary and empathy for his performers. In addition to Jill Clayburgh, Jennifer Salt, and Robert De Niro, the Sarah Lawrence community included, at various times, Gerrit Graham, William Finley, Diane Keaton, Gregg Henry, and Betty Buckley.

His association with fellow directors is also celebrated, although the bonds may have slipped over the years. DePalma and Scorsese were the standouts among New York filmmakers of the era, although the city had a vibrant network of so-called "underground" filmmakers including Shirley Clarke (*The Connection*, 1961), Jack Smith ("Flaming Creatures," 1963), Adolfas Mekas (*Hallelujah, the Hills*, 1963), Robert Downey, Sr. (a prince) (*Chafed Elbows*, 1966),

Ken Jacobs ("Little Stabs at Happiness," 1960), and Bruce Conner ("A Movie," 1958) among many others. When the filmmaking craze went west late in the sixties and settled in universities, the first wave included Steven Spielberg, George and Marcia Lucas, John Milius, Francis Ford Coppola, and essentially everyone in the table of contents of Peter Biskind's lurid book about the New Hollywood, *Easy Riders, Raging Bulls* (New York: Simon & Schuster, 1999).

If DePalma is considered a maverick, it's only because he abandoned Hollywood to return to New York and, later, when financing opportunities were extended overseas, Europe. In the late 1970s, he said something prescient to Michael Pye and Lynda Myles for their book *The Movie Brats*: "Never, never live in Hollywood. I hate this insulated universe where film is the most important thing. The more powerful you become, the more you have to avoid insulating yourself. That is the problem in Los Angeles all the time."[16]

Brian DePalma has kept his word for the last fifty years; he stills lives in New York. Despite the expensive failure of *Mission to Mars* in 2000, he has still managed to keep up his schedule of turning out a new film every two or three years. He made *Femme Fatale* (2002); the 2006 murder mystery *The Black Dahlia*, from the James Ellroy novel; the war drama *Redacted* (2007), as a moral extension of *Casualties of War*; a thriller set in the business world, *Passion* (2012); and a little-seen crime drama set in Denmark, *Domino* (2019).

DePalma also cowrote a mystery novel with Susan Lehman, *Are Snakes Necessary?* (New York: Hard Case Crime, 2020). He still eschews Hollywood, and unless he makes hits for them, Hollywood returns the disfavor. There is a disconnect; the Internet Movie Database (IMDb) continues to identify him in their search engine as the director of *Body Double* when, as its huge fan base shows, he should be known for *Scarface*—even if neither he nor the studio had a clue at the time.

SIDEBAR

The Maestro and Me

We all have previous lives. Mine was as a movie publicist. Among my duties was arranging press tours for celebrities to visit various cities and hype their soon-to-open new films by talking with print and broadcast journalists. This was well before social media made credentialed critics irrelevant.

For the Boston opening of Brian DePalma's 1973 film *Sisters*, the distributor, American-International Pictures, flew Brian to town from New York and asked me to set up meetings with the press. It was a thrill for me because I was fresh out of college and had seen two of his early films, *Greetings* and *Hi, Mom!*, and thought them outrageously funny and politically astute. I had not seen his then-unreleased *Get to Know Your Rabbit* (1972), which was famously his first studio project (Warner Bros.) and had been just as famously derailed by its star and recut.[17]

Boston was considered an important city because it contained a million-plus college students and was the home office of four then-powerful theater chains: General Cinema, National Amusements, Hoyt's, and Sack/USA Cinemas.

Sisters was the first straightforward DePalma thriller. The story of conjoined twins (Margot Kidder and Margot Kidder) separated at birth into one who was sane and one who was homicidal, it was quirky as well as visionary. There were moments of bizarre humor, highly discomfiting tension, and sudden violence, all shot by Gregory Sandor, edited by Paul Hirsch, and scored by Hitchcock veteran Bernard

Herrmann. Despite its parsimonious budget ($500,000), it was a consummate job, using what would become known as DePalma's inventive camera moves and split-screen narrative and consistently effective performances.

"I showed my film to Bennie Herrmann," DePalma told me, recalling how it begins with a slow, building, non-dialogue sequence designed to create tension. "What's that?" DePalma quoted Herrmann as saying when he screened it. "I wanted to start off slowly," DePalma said he replied. "It's like the first part of Hitchcock's *Psycho*. Let the audience wait."

"For Hitchcock, they'll wait," Herrmann barked. "For you, they won't wait. You need music."

"And then," DePalma said, "he composed a minute and a half of title music that scared the hell out of me."[18]

Those stories made for one of my more interesting press tours, brief as it was. It began when DePalma stepped off the plane from New York at Boston's Logan Airport wearing what would soon become his trademark safari jacket. He carried with his luggage the script and storyboards for his next film, *The Phantom of the Fillmore* (later changed to *The Phantom of the Paradise* in the USA while retaining *Fillmore* internationally). He showed them to me and I was impressed; I had never seen real storyboards before, and these were so well drawn that it was easy to see the kind of film he wanted to make (and did). The press, however, was less enthusiastic and had little interest in them.

Brian was confident and glib. He explained why *Get to Know Your Rabbit* had turned out the way it did and described working with Orson Welles, who played a huckster magic teacher. "Orson is a whore," he said when asked the expected question "What was it like working with Orson Welles?" and went on to explain that Welles refused to learn his lines, even with cue cards placed about the set, so DePalma made him do take after take until he couldn't help but memorize them.

We did have one special adventure that I am proud I arranged. In the afternoon, after the press luncheon (where vying reporters fired questions at him, a process not unlike trying to follow a TV show while the kids are fighting over the remote), I took him to the Beacon Hill apartment of Marjory Adams. Marjory was the doyen of Boston critics, even though she had just been retired from her fifty-two-year tenure at the *Boston Globe* (though Marjory insisted on saying she had been fired) and was writing a celebrity interview column for a string of suburban newspapers. I considered Marjory a friend, but many did not; as benign as she was in print and to me in person, competing with her during a group interview was war. Marjory sat on the sofa in her Revere Street flat taking notes while Brian poised himself uncomfortably on an olive-colored ottoman a few feet across from her. Marjory, who was in her late seventies, had hurt her knee and was confined to her home, where she had her leg propped up on another ottoman, and if you weren't careful where you looked you could see all the way to Poughkeepsie.

Brian had to explain as many answers as he gave, but he was deferential and polite. After an hour I whisked him away to catch a plane home. I'm not sure if Marjory's interview benefitted the film, but I like to think Brian got something out of the experience that he could use in his continuing career, if only to buff his aplomb at dealing with cantankerous press.

Throughout our day, he was cordial with me but guarded. The last thing he said as I saw him off on the plane home was "Get rid of that necktie."

I don't know how many encounters Brian had had with out-of-town journalists before ours, but I'm sure it left a mark, or perhaps it was a scar; the Boston critics were chilly-to-negative

"The Musketeers of Pig Alley,"
D.W. Griffith, 1912.
This seventeen-minute drama
is considered the first American
gangster film. Frame enlargement.

Ben Hecht publicity photo.
He was twenty-five at the time.
Culver Pictures.
Wikimedia Commons.

Josef von Sternberg, director of *Underworld*.
Studio publicity photo.
Wikimedia Commons.

Underworld Lobby Card.
Wikimedia Commons.

George Bancroft in *Underworld*.
Studio publicity photo.

Scarface (1932) main title.
Frame enlargement.

HOWARD HUGHES

PRESENTS

SCARFACE

FROM THE BOOK
BY
ARMITAGE TRAIL

COPYRIGHT MCMXXXII BY THE CADDO COMPANY, INC.

Book cover, *Scarface* reprint.
Author's library.

SCARFACE

THE NOVEL. THE LEGEND.

ARMITAGE TRAIL

Howard Hawks, director of *Scarface* (1932).
Studio publicity shot.
Wikimedia Commons.

Publicity shot of Paul Muni as
Tony Camonte in *Scarface* (1932).
Studio publicity photo.
Wikimedia Commons.

Tony taunts the police
to come for him. They do.
Wikimedia Commons.

Al Capone summoned to
Chicago's FBI office for questioning.
*Photo by Chicago FBI Bureau/
Wide World Photos.
Wikimedia Commons.*

Al Capone photographed around 1935.
*Photo by Chicago FBI Bureau.
Wikimedia Commons.*

Willie Bioff, the Mob's
designated hitter, who came
to Hollywood in the 1930s
to take over the unions
and shake down the studios.
Photofest.

The classic image from *Scarface*.
Paul Muni (CENTER)
with Vince Barnett (LEFT).
Wikimedia Commons.

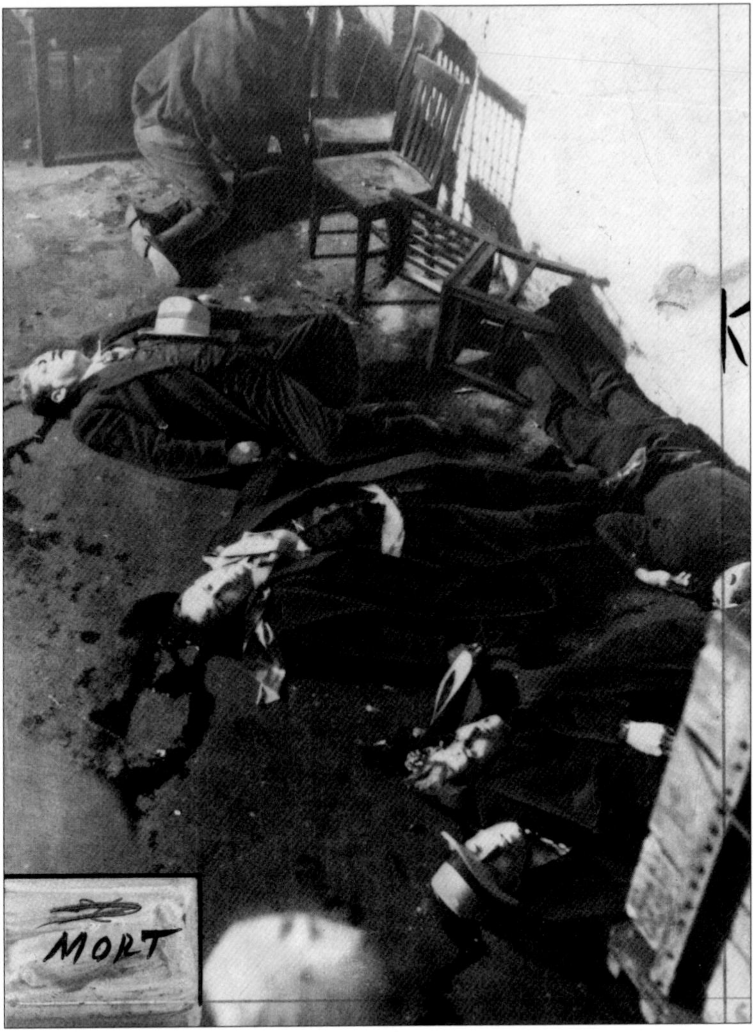

St. Valentine's Day Massacre, 1929.

Caption for St. Valentine's Day Massacre photo.

(Caption on photo of St. Valentine's Day Massacre 1929):

47915 WATCH YOUR CREDIT…INTERNATIONAL NEWS PHOTO
SLUG. . .(MASSACRE VICTIMS)

PRISONER TELLS STORY OF ST. VALENTINE'S DAY MASSACRE.

CHICAGO, ILL:. . GANGLAND'S GHASTLIEST CRIME, THE GRIM ST. VALENTINE'S DAY MASSACRE OF 1929, WHEN SEVEN WERE MOWED DOWN BY MACHINE GUNS IN A NORTH CLARK STREET GARAGE, MAY BE SOLVED BY THE STORY OF BYRON BOLTON, NOW A FEDERAL PRISONER.
ACCORDING TO A COPYRIGHTED STORY IN THE CHICAGO AMERICAN, BOLTON TELLS THE STORY OF THE MASSACRE AND NAMES FIVE OTHERS AND HIMSELF AS THE PERPETRATORS OF THE CRIME. ACCORDING TO HIS STORY FRED GOETZ, WHO HAS SINCE BEEN KILLED BY RIVAL GANGSTERS, AND FRED "KILLER" BURKE, NOW SERVING A LIFE SENTENCE IN MICGIGAN, STOOD GUARD WITH SAWED-OFF SHOTGUNS AS BOLTON, CLAUDE MADDOX, MURRAY HUMPHREYS. AND GUS WINKLER MOWED DOWN THE VICTIMS WITH MACHIME GUNS.

K-1-23-35 455 (SEE WIRE STORY)

PHOT RASN JANUARY 25, 1935.

Paul Muni and Ann Dvorak as the Camonte siblings in *Scarface*. *Wikimedia Commons.*

Paul Muni and his wife Bella at the 1937 Academy Awards. *Photo by Los Angeles Daily News. Wikimedia Commons.*

Scarface (1932) 22 x 28 poster.
Wikimedia Commons.

Scarface (1932) insert poster.
Wikimedia Commons.

Oliver Stone, screenwriter
of *Scarface* (1983),
when he served in Vietnam.
*Photo by Press Service of
the President of Russia.
Wikimedia Commons.*

Oliver Stone, screenwriter
of *Scarface* (1983).
*Photo by Oliver Stone
via Towpilot.
Wikimedia Commons.*

Director Brian DePalma
at Venice Film Festival, 2007.
*Photo by John Rubin,
Flickr. Wikimedia Commons.*

Director Brian DePalma at
Guadalajara Film Festival, 2008.
*Photo by Festival Internacional
de Cine en Guadalajara.
Wikimedia Commons.*

Director Brian DePalma at
Guadalajara Film Festival, 2008.
*Photo by Festival Internacional
de Cine en Guadalajara.
Wikimedia Commons.*

Giorgio Moroder, composer
for *Scarface* (1983).
Photofest.

Cuban refugees escape Castro on the Mariel Boat Lift. *Photo by Robert L. Scheina, U.S. Department of Homeland Security. Wikimedia Commons.*

Steven Bauer, who played Manny in *Scarface* (1983), today. *Photo by Romina Espinosa, Wikimedia Commons.*

Angel Salazar (Chi Chi in *Scarface* [1983]) and Dennis Plaksin, partners in the Scarface Store. *Photo courtesy of Dennis Plaksin, The Scarface Store.*

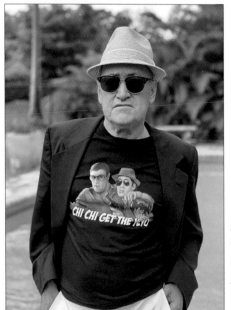

Angel Salazar (Chi Chi in Scarface [1983]) models the most popular shirt in the Scarface Store, "Chi Chi get the Yeyo." *Photo courtesy of Dennis Plaksin, The Scarface Store.*

LEFT TO RIGHT: Producers Martin Bregman and Louis Stroller confer with flack-jacketed director Brian DePalma on the sidelines of Scarface. *Photofest.*

Al Pacino, as Tony Montana, about to get even with Frank Lopez in Scarface (1983). *Photo accredited to Al Pacino. Wikimedia Commons.*

Al Pacino and Steve Bauer check out the sights on Miami Beach and discuss their future. *Photofest.*

Steven Bauer plays Manolo (Manny) Ribera, "Scarface" Tony Montana's best friend. *Photofest.*

Mary Elizabeth Mastrantonio, as Gina Montana, dances with a fella, to the disdain of her overprotective brother, Tony. *Photofest*.

The duplicitous Omar (F. Murray Abraham, LEFT) and his menschy boss Frank Lopez (Robert Loggia, RIGHT). *Photofest*.

Brian DePalma directs
Michelle Pfeiffer, who plays Elvira,
Tony Montana's trophy wife.
Photofest.

Tony Montana (Al Pacino)
marries Elvira (Michelle Pfeiffer)
as Manny (Steven Bauer) and
Gina's (Mary Elizabeth Mastrantonio)
romance blooms under their
cocaine-dusted noses.
Photofest.

Michelle Pfeiffer as Elvira,
the stylish woman who finally realizes
enough is enough.
Photofest.

Tony Montana (Al Pacino) introduces Sosa's invading army to his "little friend." *Photofest*.

Tony Montana's (Al Pacino) last stand against the invasion by his drug overlord enemy's army.
Photofest.

on *Sisters*. Unlike audiences since then, they didn't get it. Worse (for me), I had to call Brian at home the next day and read him the reviews. He was not thrilled. But he said something to me in frustration that I kept in mind after I ditched publicity a few years later and became a critic myself.

He said, "Why can't they review the film I made instead of the film they wanted to see?"

That advice has never left me, nor has the memory of working with a talented young filmmaker at a time in his career when it seemed that only Pauline Kael and I knew how good he was.

SIDEBAR

Scarface in Love

If any filmmaker has been more often accused of sexism and misogyny in his films, it would be news to Brian DePalma. For a man who has said many times that he likes women (as three marriages testify), his films appear to speak otherwise. The slashing murder of Angie Dickinson in *Dressed to Kill* (1980) was so revolting that not only was he forced to make cuts to the film, it still drew intense criticism from the activist group Women Against Violence Against Women (WAVAW), which cautioned that what appears as art can influence life. And that was nothing compared with the oversized drill bit murder in *Body Double* and the killing whose scream forms a horrifically poignant ending to *Blow Out*.

"I don't think women are beaten or raped because the rapist has been affected by the entertainment industry," DePalma responded. "If there were statistics to prove that, they'd be on the front page of every newspaper in the country." Furthermore, he insisted, "Women in peril are inherently more dramatic than men in peril because they're more vulnerable. It's just a convention of the genre."[19] When *Body Double* (1984) drew criticism because it showed a woman being killed with a nearly two-foot-long drill bit, DePalma stated the obvious: that the drill bit had to be that long to make it through the ceiling of the floor below for the effect to work. In other words, DePalma was criticized because he did a good job.

Oliver Stone disagrees with the label but ascribes it to "the one with Angie Dickinson, *Dressed to Kill*. The concept of killing women, the reputation, a horror film director. That's probably where it comes from. And Brian is a cold fish. He doesn't interview as the friendliest guy in the world, that's for sure. *Carrie* is a film about female empowerment, so I don't understand. But he does like to murder women so you could say there's a horror film aspect to that. Brian is not Mister Nice Guy, but he doesn't strike me as a misogynist. He has a sarcastic sense of humor. I can't say it's a benevolent one."[20]

Given these and other charges of sexism in his films, it is useful to look at DePalma's portrayal of women in *Scarface* and compare it with Howard Hawks's treatment of women in his version of the story. Hawks first.

In this regard, Hawks's *Scarface* is an anomaly. He is famously known for casting strong actresses to play strong female characters, frequently throwing them into an environment (newspapers, military service, high society, the Old West, big business, etc.) where they need to be the equal of the men. Hawks deals in insular worlds, but within these worlds the battle of the sexes is secondary to the battle between professionals.

Yet Hawks's *Scarface* has three women who don't fit what would become his mold. Tony Camonte's mother (Inez Palange) disapproves of her son's way of life and refuses his cash stipends even though she needs them. His sister, Cesca (Francesca) (Ann Dvorak), however, eagerly accepts his largesse and uses it to stand up against him and Mama Camonte—until Tony catches her doing it. Then there's Poppy (Karen Morley), Johnny Lovo's girl, who follows the cash and, in the end, has nothing to do with Tony's downfall. Mama and Poppy are stereotypes, but Hawks brings Cesca alive through her rebellion and subtle intimations of incest (albeit expressed more overtly by Tony than her). Even when Poppy is tapped as a gun moll, she does her job quietly and professionally.

DePalma gives two of these three roles more due. Mama Montana (Miriam Colon) is more emphatic about ordering her daughter, Gina (Mary Elizabeth Mastrantonio), to reject Tony's flamboyant gift of $1,000. One of her first lines on seeing him again is why he didn't send a postcard from jail, and she excoriates him for giving Cubans a bad name and ultimately disowns him in an exchange that cuts to the bone. In a line that is barely audible we learn that Tony blames his father's desertion on his mother's lack of love. For her part, Gina accepts a silver charm necklace ("To Gina from Tony, Always"). Only when Tony and Gina are out of the house and away from their mother's hearing does he press into her hand the $1,000 that their mother rejected, telling her to give some of it to their mother from time to time. Gina will also use it to buy some independence, including to date a man that Tony chases away (as in the Hawks film). Only Manny (Steven Bauer) later makes headway with Gina, and this leads to tragedy.

Elvira (Michelle Pfeiffer) emerges as a winner, even though she is rightly criticized by Tony for her cocaine dependency. She knows when to throw in the towel and leaves Tony in a public display of rejection. Unlike Poppy, who simply disappears from the narrative (aside from a contrived cut-away to resolve a plot point), Elvira gets to leave with her head held high and on her own terms. One hopes that, absent Tony's influence, she will seek recovery.

Their relationship prior to this was Hawksian. Pfeiffer's Elvira Hancock, named Elvira Snodgrass in an earlier script,[21] is the perfect trophy girlfriend, but her gold veneer is genuine. "It's an old name," she tells Tony in that script, as they step onto the dance floor at the Mutiny Club (later called the Babylon Club). "It's a Rhode Island name. My ancestors came here in 1640 on one of those sailing ships from England." (In the film she comes from Baltimore and does not speak of a pedigree.) By adding the veneer of aristocracy to Poppy's earlier hard-edged gold digger, Michelle Pfeiffer has more to work with than Karen Morley, even in an abbreviated role that became even more abbreviated from script to screen. She is not only classier than Tony, she is socially well above Frank Lopez (Robert Loggia). In other circumstances this would make her a gold digger like Poppy, but her blue blood makes her something even more fickle: a dilettante. She is a flirt with Tony, rejecting him while at the same time fascinating him. She also drops her guard (it isn't clear whether it's Elvira or Michelle who does this), corpsing at Pacino when he puts on her white hat at the car dealership. She is a completely self-assured woman.

Gina (Mary Elizabeth Mastrantonio, called "M.E." by the crew) is similarly cut from more textured cloth than Hecht and Hawks's Cesca. Her enthusiasm at seeing Tony after five years' separation is genuine, but the viewer has been deprived of the fact that Tony had the opportunity to see her and their mother when he arrived at Freedom Town, only he chose not to contact them until he had "made it." The film is vague about these five lost years as Tony rises to the top.

At age nineteen when she makes her first appearance, she is, like Ann Dvorak, eager to break her parental bonds, but M.E. shows a richer characterization, a girl on the cusp of womanhood, about to blossom—something Tony both resents and desires.

The film's unrestrained sexual character is Manolo (Manny) (Steven Bauer), whose strutting, priapic persona Tony ridicules early on at a Miami seaside park. Although Bauer is easily the best-looking man in the film, he has only one bedroom liaison (with Miriam, played by Sue Bowser) before he settles down and marries Gina. Unlike George Raft in the 1932 *Scarface*, Bauer doesn't have to flip a half dollar, he just needs to stand there and women presumably line up for him, except they don't.[22] This contrasts him with Tony who, as promiscuous as he is with a gun, is sexually monogamous in the course of the story, and that's with Elvira. (This may mean that he is saving himself for his sister, and the subtext supports it by inference rather than explicitly, but that's something for psychiatrists to debate.)

It's an easy dig to say that the men in *Scarface* (as well as American firearm culture in general) use guns instead of their penises. What DePalma achieves more than Hawks, thanks to five decades between the two films and the creation of film ratings, is the freedom to be honest about sexual politics as well as the politics of violence. As in his other works, by creating richer portraits of women, he increases their fascination and, if called for, the audience's concern when they are in jeopardy. In this way *Scarface* becomes a catalogue of contemporary morality that stands as contradiction to the charges of sexism that DePalma has endured for decades.

CHAPTER 6

Becoming Tony

avid O. Selznick, the producer of *Gone with the Wind*, frequently lamented, in his later years, that, no matter what else he would have achieved in his life, all of his obituaries were going to start, "David O. Selznick, producer of *Gone with the Wind*." And they did.

Likewise, Al Pacino—no matter how many indelible individual characters he will have created when his career winds down—is very likely going to be remembered for Tony Montana. Not Michael Corleone in the *Godfather* trilogy, not Sonny in *Dog Day Afternoon*, not Lt. Col. Frank Slade in *Scent of a Woman*, not Lt. Vincent Hannah in *Heat*, not Frank Keller in *Sea of Love*, not Carlito Brigante in *Carlito's Way*, certainly not Steve Burns in *Cruising*, and maybe not even Frank Serpico in that eponymous film (although IMDb's search engine continues to identify him that way). No, Al Pacino will be remembered as the mesmerizing, bombastic, uninhibited, but ultimately tragic Tony Montana, who went down in a cloud of cocaine—just him and his little friend.

From the days when only Francis Ford Coppola wanted him to today when everybody does, Pacino has been a dynamo. At eighty-two as this is being written, he is still going strong with a TV series (*Hunters*) and movie (*Sniff*) in production, and several films in pre-production. [1]

But why *Scarface*? Why has this character (who is arguably more extreme than any others in Pacino's repertoire), the one with which he has become so strongly identified?

By contrast, he played Michael Corleone three times, yet the only phrase anybody ever cites from that role is "Just when I thought I was out, they pull me back in." His Oscar-winning performance in *Scent of a Woman* is remembered only for "Hoo-ha" (and maybe "John Daniels"). Tony Montana, however, has enough quotable catchphrases to fill a quote-of-the-day calendar.

Is it because Tony Montana resonates beyond the story of a drug kingpin, such as being a metaphor for American capitalism? Or is it because he achieved that greatest of all actor's achievements, a person with whom people can identify?

"Well, I don't know what to say about that," Pacino told *Independent* interviewer Kaleem Aftab. "I look at *Scarface* and I don't see that as the metaphor. I see what Brian DePalma was talking about when we made it. It was the crazy eighties, the decade of avarice, greed and introducing that into the world . . . I thought it was a very socio-political statement . . . it's about a kind of ingenuity, suddenly coming from the bottom and rising, which is why the original was so inspiring for me."[2]

Once *Scarface* went from being a dream to becoming a production on Universal Pictures' release schedule, Pacino began his process. Coming from the South Bronx, he already knew street attitude; all he needed was the accent. But that was for the outside, and Actors Studio performers are trained to fill the inside. For that, he would assemble the pieces to make Tony real. First he collected a brain trust of advisors, the first time he ever went to such an extreme. They included costume designer Patricia Norris, a knife expert, and a trainer to get him in shape to play the wiry Tony. He discovered that, when he spoke Oliver Stone's dialogue, it came out best from a downturned mouth, almost a sneer that he could use to spit his words, a mannerism that makes his infrequent smile all the more powerful. He is both playful and deadly. Pacino's Tony is what he is, take him or leave him.

In addition to famed dialogue coach Robert Easton, Pacino's closer advisor and collaborator was his costar, Steven Bauer. Bauer, whose birth name is Esteban Ernesto Echevarría Samson, had a Cuban father and a German mother (the Bauer comes from his maternal grandparents).

"It was Steven that really helped me a lot with the Cuban," Pacino said in praise at the film's thirty-fifth anniversary panel at Tribeca. "We had a couple of months to be together, all summer, actually."[3] Getting to that place, however, was an adventure for the then-twenty-five-year-old Bauer, who was making his feature film debut opposite one of the screen's most electric performers.[4]

His gauntlet is instructive. Giving up school sports for acting (his rowing coach told him to make a choice, and he did, inspiring a teammate to do the same thing: Andy Garcia). He then acted in theater for a while. His adventures led him to a marriage in 1981 to Melanie Griffith when both were struggling newcomers. Her career was taking off and his was just about to. Then he met someone who changed his life.

"I'd met Stella Adler in a summer class in LA," he says. "I did a monologue for Stella: Marc Antony from *Julius Caesar*. I hadn't seen the Brando film version, I was just going off of the script. She stopped me about a third of the way, in front of all my friends, the whole class, and she said, 'That's very nice, you look nice to watch, your voice is great, but you need to study with me. You need technique. You can be like Marlon.' I said, 'Yes!' And she said, 'You have to come to New York and take my class.' And that was it. Melanie and I went to New York and signed with Stella Adler."[5]

When Melanie got work and he didn't, Bauer took a job moving furniture, "which was better than getting a hack license and driving a cab," he says. He also turned down modeling and soap operas, telling his agent and manager, "I'm gonna wait," which is not what they wanted to hear. Soon Melanie returned to LA to work and Bauer, still in New York, started preparing to fly out to join her when he got a call from his manager.

"'I know you have to get a plane,'" he recalls she told him, "'but they're casting a film called *Scarface* and it's starring Al Pacino and the second role in the film is you.' I said, 'Oh, really?' She said, 'Al Pacino's playing a Cuban immigrant and his best friend comes with him to Miami and they get into the drug trade.' She said, 'People are talking about you and the casting director is an old-timer named Alixe Gordin. They haven't opened the casting office yet, so she's at her apartment. She's waiting for you. She wants to see you before she sees anybody else.'

"So I ran up ten blocks and I rang her doorbell. She was vacuuming for a party. As she opened the door and saw me, I think I had my hair long and had facial hair, she said, 'Are you Steven Bauer?' I said, 'Yes.' She said, 'Oh my gosh, come in, come in, tell me all about yourself.' It was the movie I was waiting for."[6]

Gordin called Brian DePalma and said, "Brian, I found your guy." Bauer took the subway from Midtown to the Village (he lacked money for a taxi) and knocked on the director's door.

"Brian opens the door and, in his inimitable style, he said, 'Ah, so, you're Steven Bauer?' [Bauer does a spot-on DePalma impression.]

"'Yes.'

"'Are you really Cuban?'

"'Yes, yes.'

"'Then why is your name Baaaaauer?'

"'Because my grandparents came from Germany to Havana. I'm half-Jewish.'"[7]

Bauer was flown out to Los Angeles to meet Bregman, who confirmed that he spoke Spanish, and cautioned him that he was going to hear a lot of other names mentioned for the role of Manny, but to hang tight because, as Bregman said, "Al will go with my choice, but Al's not ready to meet anybody because he has something he has to do first before he considers anybody. So you're gonna have to bide your time."

Waiting was hell, and Bauer made the tough decision to turn down the lead in a Canadian film, *Running Brave* (eventually played by Robby Benson) when Bregman advised him, "How many people do you think will ever see that little Canadian film? How many people around the world do you think will see *Scarface*?"

When it came time for the two lead actors to meet, says Bauer, "Al arranged a meeting at Bregman's office in New York City. It was love at first sight, except we're two men. The first thing he said [Bauer does a flawless impression of Al Pacino as Tony Montana], 'I just have one question. You're really Cuban?' I said I was. He said, 'Okay. Why is your name "Steve Bauer"?' I said, 'It's not Steve, it's Steven.' And he goes, 'Bauer? What kind of Cuban name is that?' I said, 'I took my grandfather's name because nobody could pronounce my dad's name, which is Echevarría.' From that point on, we started working. I taught him everything I knew about the Cuban perspective of our place in the world. He liked this. You see, as Tony and Manny, we lost our country and found ourselves with the opportunity to get shipped to the United States of America and have a green card. We had been in jail and were released to come to America. And we built that whole background, him and I. We were exposed to a doctor who had worked in the jails in Cuba and worked in LA. He told us a lot."[8]

Bauer took a shack on the Pacific Coast Highway in Malibu and drove ten minutes up the beach to join Pacino in the expansive beach house that the star had rented. "We spent every day for just about a month," Bauer added, "not reading the script, just talking about our lives in Cuba, previous to the first shot. And what he taught me was 'That will imbue your performance.' Then Brian gave us the luxury of doing rehearsals."[9]

Tony's Cuban accent is an exaggeration, but so is Tony. It came out of the confluence of two tutors: Easton and Bauer. "Sometimes I had to correct Robert Easton," Bauer said. "His Spanish was okay and he gave Al the hard-and-fast rules of the language, like you say 'mang,' you don't say 'man.' That was good for Al, that was constructive for him. I wasn't reaching him that way, I was just talking like my father talked and he would imitate me. He would get the sound, 'thees' and not 'this.' Robert Easton was a great guy and he came every couple of days, and I thought it was humorous when he'd go, 'When you say, "Fuck you," you say, "Fok you."'"[10]

It's an acting adage that all characters have a secret that only the actor knows. Bauer struggled to find Manny's secret, and had to do so for the scene where he shoots Frank Lopez on Tony's command. It was not an easy stretch.

"There was a week when they [the studio people] saw me doing a reading with Al, and they said to my agents, 'He's perfect but we haven't seen that killer in him.' They wanted me to work with this great acting coach, Sandra Seacat, and she gave me some acute insight into what I needed to allow. What she said was 'You're a prince, and Manny's a prince to some degree, so that comes easy to you, but you will not allow the frog in you to be seen. You've got to open up and allow the frog, if called upon, to come out.' My dad also gave me pointers on that scene: 'You can't just walk up and shoot him. Your facial expression has got to be believable that you're going to pull the trigger and end a man's life that you're not mad at, you're not angry at him. If I had to do that,' he said, 'I would find something to be angry about so you can pull the trigger. If he hasn't wronged you it's very hard to end somebody's life.'"[11]

Watching the scene, one can see that Bauer has found something to be angry about, and that's his character's secret. And what was Manny angry about? Bauer won't reveal what it was, but he will go as far as saying, "If you see me in that scene, I'm muttering something in Spanish, something my dad said, like 'Fuck you, you motherfucker.' It's almost like I was angry to be called upon to do it, so I'm angry at Frank, and so now he doesn't mean anything to me and I'll do it so I won't be in trouble with my guys."[12]

The Pacino-Bauer tag team carried onto the set. "Al did not want to hear that much from Brian," Bauer says. "I was his conduit on the set to Al. Al does certain things by choice. Brian was very careful and when he got to take five he'd say, 'Okay, guys, what do you think? What do you think, Al?' And Al wouldn't deal with Brian, he would turn to me and say, 'I think we should do one more,' and I would turn to Brian and say, 'Could we do one more?' Al didn't want to talk about results, which was smart. But I could go in and out of Manny. It was easy for me, but Al had to 'be' Tony Montana."[13]

CHAPTER 7

Shooting the Movie

Hollywood has long taken pride in its chameleonic ability to pass for any other location in the world, at least as far as what the camera sees. The Golden State has mountains, valleys, surf, desert, forests, and plains, many of them within a few hours' commute of one another. This accommodating environment has caused more than one producer to reject a director's wish to shoot on a distant location, saying, "A tree is a tree and a rock is a rock. Shoot it in Griffith Park."

Scarface wasn't shot in Griffith Park (a mountainous stretch of scrub and trees in the Hollywood Hills), but it did make use of California's varied landscape as an alternative to actual Florida locations. A few days were also shot in New York. It fell to art director Ed Richardson, visual consultant Ferdinando Scarfiotti, and director of photography John Alonzo, among others, to find locations in the Los Angeles area (that is, within union driving distance of central LA) that could double for Miami. They were helped by the presence of sun, urban public works projects, eclectic architecture, and a wealth of Spanish-speaking extras to draw upon for crowd scenes. Among the first locations to use almost all of those was "Freedom Town," the refugee camp under the freeway where Tony, Manny, Angel, Chi Chi, and other Cuban Marielitos are warehoused while their immigration status is being determined. The camp was built, not in Miami, but underneath the nexus of the Santa Monica and Harbor freeways in downtown LA. It was then trashed in a scene where National Guardsmen and state police try to contain the rebellion during which Tony kills Castro partisan Rabenga as a favor to Frank Lopez, in revenge for torturing Lopez's brother to death. Forty stunt performers and translators were involved, the latter because many of the six hundred extras spoke no English.

Likewise, LA's Little Tokyo was redressed and fitted to look like Little Havana as the setting for the greasy spoon lunch counter where Tony and Manny slave while waiting for Frank Lopez to make good on his promise of jobs. The interior of the Babylon Club was built in a soundstage at Universal and designed to be torn apart by bullets in the assassination attempt on Tony that Lopez engineers. Special effects experts Ken Pepiot, Stan Parks, Ted Koerner, and George Zamora constructed fifty-two mirrored panels mounted on airtight SOLITEX boards of the kind used for home insulation. The fragile panels were then covered with tough, clear plastic so that, when they were hit with plastic rounds (the movie's safer version of live bullets) they would shatter but not explode into shards that would jeopardize the three hundred extras who dived for cover. The ambush took two weeks to shoot. At one point Pacino emerged from hiding behind the table with his face covered in blood. Every beating heart within earshot stopped until he said, "This tastes like chocolate!" One of the explosive squibs with which he was wired had splattered sugary prop blood into his mouth.[1] This is in contrast to an actual injury that Pacino suffered during the film's climax at Tony's mansion (more about that later).

Following that, the company moved to picturesque Montecito in Santa Barbara County, with its ornate Spanish-style villas, one of which served as the Bolivian estate of drug manufacturer Alejandro Sosa, and another of which was Tony's sumptuous (albeit garish) mansion complete with private zoo.[2] Alas, the weather didn't care that so much money was being spent, and rare California rainstorms caused delays. These only compounded the budget that had risen following the uncertainty of shooting in Miami.

Returning to Universal's studio facility, the production was slowed down again by the gunplay for which the small blood "squibs" would have to be taped and wired into the actors' and stunt performers' clothes every time a retake was needed, not to mention replacing the stained and tattered costumes. It got tense. Oliver Stone, visiting the set and no doubt itching to direct, noted that DePalma "was overweight, slow physically . . . [and] also, from what I gather, in the middle of a divorce from his wife, actress Nancy Allen, which must not have helped his mood."[3] Additional delays were caused by Pacino's need for several takes before coming up to performance level, draining the energy of the actors who appeared with him in the shot and got there earlier.

The production itself, as designed by Scarfiotti, was both impressive and stylized, a blend of legitimate opulence and tacky nouveau riche. The inside of Tony's villa was constructed on Universal soundstages. These sets included Tony's plush office and his gold-and-cream bedroom with its huge, round, sunken tub. But the standout feature was the increasingly paranoid Tony's home security system with video monitors covering every possible attack point. These monitors had to appear to be functional, so John Alonzo first had to shoot the images that would appear on the screens and then, using Panavision's playback system (which synchronized thirty-frames-per-second video to film's twenty-four-frames-per-second), later shot the dramatic footage of Tony looking at the screens. Unlike today, there was no CGI to superimpose images on TV screens in a moving camera shot.

It was during this complex sequence—when Sosa's gue-rillas invade Tony's fortress bent on revenge—that Al Pacino was seriously injured. Unfortunate as that was, the movie gods must have smiled, because his absence led to the Grand Guignol ending for which the film is so highly celebrated.

"In the finale," Pacino recalled, "and this is an opera, I remember firing off rounds, about thirty rounds. And somebody then shot me and I got hit and I flew in the air. I landed and I was still sort of alive but ready—that cocaine keeps you going—and I grabbed the barrel of the gun I'd just fired. My hand stuck to it. It just stuck to it. We had to go to the burn hospital." The injury kept Pacino off the film for two weeks during which, says DePalma, "we shot every-thing that Al was shooting. You see those eight thousand guys who come in and try to shoot him, we shot everything away from Al. That's why there's so much shooting because we just kept shooting."[4] Steven Spielberg, paying DePalma a visit, even directed a few second unit shots.

Other production delays physically affected Michelle Pfeiffer. Playing Elvira, a cocaine addict, the actress decided, as the story progressed, to actually starve herself to reflect her deepening addictive condition. "The movie was supposed to be a three- or four-month shoot," she said, "and of course I tried to time it so that, as the movie went on, I became thin-ner and thinner and more emaciated. The problem was, the movie went six months. I was starving by the end of it because the one scene, which was near end of the film, which is where I needed to be my thinnest, it was like next week, and then it was next week, and the next week. I literally had members of the crew bringing me bagels because they were all worried about me and how thin I was getting."[5]

On April 27, 1983, the *Scarface* company returned on the sly to Miami for pickups. Over the course of ten to twelve days they shot exteriors that could not be doubled in LA. To ensure privacy (and not trigger a resurgence of anti-*Scarface* protests), no local reporters were invited to the set, only national and international press whose stories would not break until after the crew had left town.

The official last day for principle photography was May 6, 1983. DePalma did not attend the traditional wrap party, telling Oliver Stone, "Do you think I want to be around these people another day? I'm outta here."[6] *Scarface* had begun shooting twenty-six weeks earlier. Its budget had risen from $10 million to $15 million to $21 million (per Martin Bregman)[7] to $23.5[8] to $37 million "according to some reports (which were false)."[9] And that was just the beginning of the film's ordeal

SIDEBAR

Synopsis of the 1983 Film

The Mariel boatlift (April 15 to October 31, 1980) from Cuba to Florida brings some 125,000 refugees to freedom in the United States. But Cuban president Fidel Castro has used the exodus as a cover to export violent criminals onto America's doorstep. One of them is Tony Montana (Al Pacino). Questioned by immigration officials who believe he is one such miscreant, he deflects their inquiries until they find a gang tattoo on his hand and send him to a refugee camp called Freedom Town. After some time in the stultifying surroundings, Tony's friend Manolo "Manny" Ribera (Steven Bauer) tells him they can get their release if they assassinate Emilio Rebenga (Roberto Contreras), a former Batista politician who has fled Castro and is arriving at the camp. Under cover of a riot, Tony knifes Rebenga to death. This deed wins him and Manny their release and work credentials through the connections of Frank Lopez (Robert Loggia), the cocaine trafficker who ordered the hit and has infiltrated the authorities.

Like Johnny Lovo in the first film, Lopez is more bravado than brains. Although he cautions Tony not to get high on his own supply, he himself is high on his perceived power and this, plus bad judgment of how to wield it, dooms him. Loggia's Lopez is a combination of Latin flash and Jewish homeyness; among the gold chains that hang around his neck is a chai pendant (a Hebrew symbol for life), and he occasionally spouts Yiddish, such as *chazzer*, meaning pig, which Tony spits back at him later before having him killed.

Tony and Manny slave at a greasy spoon in Miami waiting for Lopez to fulfill his promise of good jobs. Finally they meet Omar Suarez (F. Murray Abraham), Lopez's underboss, who offers them a shit job unloading a boatload of marijuana. When Tony arrogantly throws the job back in his face, Omar sets them up on a cocaine buy. Tony and Manny, accompanied by their detention friends Angel Fernandez (Pepe Serna) and Chi Chi (Angel Salazar), go to the Beacon Hotel (aka the Sun Ray) on Ocean Drive to meet Hector the Toad (Al Israel) for the transaction. Tony and Angel enter the room. Correctly suspecting Hector of wanting to steal the "buy money" that Tony has kept safely in the car with Manny and Chi Chi, Tony stalls the deal. Suddenly two of Hector's men ambush them, holding Tony at gunpoint while Toad uses a chainsaw to hack Angel apart. Manny and Chi Chi arrive from the car and together with Tony they kill Hector's bunch. The three of them escape with both the buy money and the cocaine. Manny is shot, but it's clean. Tony takes pleasure in shooting Toad in the head in the middle of Ocean Drive and in front of astonished onlookers.

Omar introduces the heroic Tony to Frank, who appreciates Tony's bravery and offers him a job. He also introduces him to his mistress Elvira Hancock (Michelle Pfeiffer), whose condescension toward Tony only makes him want her more.

Three months pass. Now flush with cash from working with Frank, Tony visits his mother (Miriam Colon) and sister Gina (Mary Elizabeth Mastrantonio), neither of whom he has seen in five years. His sister, who is studying to be a hairdresser, is happy to see him, but his mother disowns him and the corrupt way of life he has continued living in America. Tony tells his mother that if she had showed love to their father he would not have left her. Later he gives Gina the $1,000 cash their mother rejected, telling Gina to give some of it now and then to her. On leaving, when Manny admires Gina's look, Tony overreacts like a jealous brother, warning him to stay away from his sister.

Tony rises in Frank's organization. He travels to Bolivia with Omar to meet Alejandro Sosa (Paul Shenar), a powerful cocaine manufacturer. Sosa's hit man, "Shadow" (Mark Margolis), recognizes Omar as a police informer and Sosa has him executed by hanging him from a helicopter as Tony watches. Tony makes a deal with Sosa that is too rich for Frank to meet, and Tony lectures his mentor to expand his operation. Frank is wary of doing so lest he run up against rival dealers like the Diaz brothers. Tony is ready to kill them or anybody else who gets in their way. The two men agree to disagree and Tony goes off on his own, but not to compete with Frank (as a point of honor).

One day Tony visits Elvira while Frank is away. She warns him that Frank might return, but Tony doesn't care. He tells her that Frank is finished and asks her to marry him. She is charmed but refuses.

Entering the Babylon Club, where the swells mingle

with the hoods, Manny tells Tony, "All your enemies are gone." Here Tony meets Mel Bernstein (Harris Yulin), a corrupt Miami police detective. Bernstein knows about Tony killing Rebenga and the Colombian coke dealers, obviously having been told by Frank. The two men work out a bribery arrangement. Tony sees Gina at the club dancing with a man. Before he can act, Frank and Elvira arrive and Tony horns in on Elvira. Frank orders Tony to leave, but Tony, knowing Frank informed on him to Bernstein, refuses. Instead, Frank and Elvira leave. Now Tony sees Gina's dance partner leading her into the men's room. Tony follows them and scares the man away, berating Gina for dating someone who he knows is a member of a rival gang. She tells him that she's twenty and can do as she pleases. Tony remains at the club while Manny drives Gina home. On the way, she hints to Manny that she's attracted to him, but Manny shows his loyalty to Tony by refusing her advances.

Still at the club, and sinking into a drunken stupor, Tony survives an assassination attempt that he quickly deduces was called by Frank. Later that night he and Manny confront Frank at the Cadillac dealership that serves as front for his drug operation. Frank is there with Bernstein and the bodyguard Eddie. Frank breaks down and begs Tony not to kill him, so Tony has Manny do it. Then Tony kills Bernstein himself and asks a shocked Eddie if he wants to come work for him. After that, he visits Elvira and asks her to move in with him, and she does.

Tony is now at the top of the world—his world—and stands on the balcony of Frank's condo as a blimp flies over with "The World is Yours" in lights across its side.

Awash in cash from cocaine sales, Tony marries Elvira[10] and buys a mansion for the two of them. He buys a hairdressing salon for Gina, keeps a chained tiger on his grounds, and installs a statue for his swimming pool lounge, the top of which reads "The World is Yours."

The cocaine business in Miami is over the top, and corrupt banks are having trouble laundering the huge amounts of cash that dealers want to deposit, so the manager (Dennis Holahan) of Tony's bank insists on taking a larger service fee. When Tony balks, Manny recommends another business-man, Seidelbaum (Ted Benaides), who can handle it. Unbeknownst to Manny, Seidelbaum is a federal agent and busts Tony for drugs and nonpayment of taxes.[11]

Pressure mounts against Tony from all sides. The final straw occurs over dinner with Elvira, Manny, and him at a fancy restaurant, when Elvira's cocaine habit and his drinking make him snap. By now all love between them has gone, and she leaves him. Tony then stumbles out of the restaurant chastising all the well-heeled diners that they need a bad guy like him so they can feel superior.

Despite the mixed news that Tony's lawyer, George Shef-field (Michael Alldredge), gives him about his legal problems, Sosa surfaces to offer complete exoneration through his political connections if Tony will help Shadow, his assassin, kill a Bolivian journalist who is about to speak at the United Nations about the drug trade. Tony agrees.

In New York, Shadow[12] plants a bomb beneath the journalist's car, planning to explode it in front of the UN as a symbolic hit. Ready to follow the man's car the next morning, Tony sees his victim's wife and children getting in to join him at the UN. Tony refuses to carry out the hit and shoots Shadow in the head. This enrages Sosa, but Tony blows him off and snorts enough cocaine off a mound on his desk so that he doesn't care.

Tony tries to find both Manny and Gina, but his people cannot locate either of them. Giving in and visiting his equally worried mother, Tony learns from her an address where she followed Gina. Tony heads there to find his sister and Manny wearing bedclothes. Tony becomes incensed at the apparent shack-up and kills Manny, only to learn from a hysterical Gina that the two of them were married the day before and wanted to surprise Tony with the news.

Tony's bodyguards bring Gina back with a shocked Tony to his mansion fortress just as Sosa's squad of gunmen arrives to exact revenge. Tony barricades himself in his office, fortifies himself with cocaine, and prepares for a standoff. Gina enters and first offers herself to him sexually, then shoots him in the leg. When she moves closer to finish the job, one of Sosa's killers shoots her dead. Tony, hopped up beyond measure by the cocaine he has consumed, seems immune to bullets until he is blown away from behind and finished from the front. He falls bleeding into his swimming pool where the "The World is Yours" statue watches in silent judgment.

End credit: "This film is dedicated to Howard Hawks and Ben Hecht."

On-screen disclaimer: "*Scarface* is a fictional account of the activities of a small group of ruthless criminals. The characters do not represent the Cuban/American community and it would be erroneous and unfair to suggest that they do. The vast majority of Cuban/Americans have demonstrated a dedication, vitality, and enterprise that has enriched the American scene."

John A. Alonzo, ASC

John A. Alonzo was an inspired choice to photograph *Scarface*. A seasoned director of photography who had been shooting features since 1970 and, before that, documentaries, he had the advantage of being bilingual (English and Spanish), having been born in Dallas, Texas (on June 12, 1934) and growing up there and in Guadalajara, Mexico.

His collaboration with DePalma on *Scarface*—only the second time they worked together—yields a film that is visually interesting and inventive. As precise as DePalma always is in his framing and staging, Alonzo adds a sense of spontaneity that increases the energy and tension of the scenes. Yet they also know when to leave the camera alone to just watch the actors. In an age when directors distrust their audiences' attention spans to the point of destroying performances with fast cutting, DePalma and Alonzo let the actors do their job.

Like many people who rose to prominence in film, Alonzo started at the bottom, quite literally, cleaning up and building sets for Dallas TV station WFAA. Job definitions were vague at WFAA, and before long he was directing public service shows and then "acting" with performing partner Hank Williamson in a comedy duo when he wasn't carrying out other station duties. In 1956, his and Williamson's show *Señor Turtle* went to Hollywood, only to get canceled.[13] Alonzo found work in LA as a still photographer and began acting, landing roles in such episodics as *The Twilight Zone*, *Combat!*, and *The Alfred Hitchcock Hour*.

It was when he played one of the besieged Mexican peasants in John Sturges's *The Magnificent Seven* (1960) that he met its director of photography Charles Lang and became intrigued with cinematography. Becoming a journeyman cameraman, in 1965 he joined the David L. Wolper Organization and began photographing documentaries. After that, he worked as camera operator for James Wong Howe on John Frankenheimer's *Seconds* (1966), a film that drew notice for its inventive, subjective cinematography. Between the Wolper documentaries and *Seconds*, Alonzo polished his uncanny ability to shoot a handheld camera, a skill that involves both physical strength (a fully loaded 35mm Panavision rig weighs sixty pounds) and the instinct to know where the action is going to go before it heads there. By the time he made the leap to credited director of photography in 1970 with *Bloody Mama* for producer-director Roger Corman, he was becoming known as a fast shooter who had a knack for getting it right the first time.

His extensive credits since then include a number of extraordinary films that show his feel for just the right tone no matter what the genre: *Harold and Maude*, *Vanishing Point*, *Lady Sings the Blues*, *Wattstax*, *Chinatown*, *Farewell, My Lovely*, *Tom Horn*, and *Black Sunday*. His films for Martin Ritt make each moment come alive on its own honest terms: *Sounder*, *Norma Rae*, *Pete 'n' Tillie*, *Back Roads*, *Cross Creek*, *Conrack*, and *Casey's Shadow*, several of which, like Ritt and Alonzo themselves, were politically charged.

He first worked with Brian DePalma on *Get to Know Your Rabbit* (1972), whose tangled history kept him apart from the director for eleven years, until *Scarface*. He also directed several films himself including *FM* (1978), about rebellion against military recruitment ads at a progressive rock radio station, and a number of TV movies.

It has been said that the emotional temperature of a movie set can be taken by watching its director of photography, for it is he or she whose efficiency (or not) sets the speed and mood of everybody else. On each film, Alonzo had the boldness to shoot night-for-night under low light levels, in bright sunlight with flashy colors, and anywhere his directors chose to set their scenes. His ability to match his commanding yet sensitive personality with the stylistic requirements of a scene, whether with flowing dolly shots or in-your-face encounters in cramped quarters, results in *Scarface* becoming a visual textbook of how to make each scene its own yet also fit within a unified whole. Whether carrying out DePalma's complex, balletic set-piece crane shots or capturing nighttime walk-and-talk scenes with flawless handheld photography, Alonzo serves the film with astonishing verve.

John A. Alonzo died on March 13, 2001.

SIDEBAR

1932 vs. 1983

Although Scarface *is dedicated to Howard Hawks and Ben Hecht, the credits that usually appear on remakes acknowledge the writers of the original version. Hecht, Armitage Trail, Seton I. Miller, John Lee Mahin, and Fred Pasley, however, appear nowhere in the 1983* Scarface's *titles. Although Oliver Stone felt no particular obligation to the Hecht et al. original, he remained faithful to the theme and key story elements of the 1932* Scarface, *making the 1983* Scarface *one of the most satisfying and effective remakes in history. The key changes and resonances include:*

- The name Montana is phonically close to Camonte even though Spanish is not that close to Sicilian. Stone chose Montana to honor San Francisco 49ers quarterback Joe Montana.

- Both Tonys have scars, the origins of which vary [See Sidebar: "How Did Tony Get His Scar?"].

- Both Tonys kill someone at the beginning of their story to trigger their rise to the top. Camonte secretly kills "Big Louis" Costillo and Montana openly kills the politician Rebenga. Camonte's murder of Costillo is ostensibly his own idea (he was Costillo's ambitious bodyguard), where Montana's stabbing of Rebenga was ordered by Frank Lopez as a payback for Rebenga's torturing Lopez's brother to death in Cuba, not for drug trafficking dominance.

- Both Tonys' stories begin with the authorities already on to him: Camonte for unspecified earlier run-ins, and Montana because of his manner and hand tattoo.

- Tony is overly protective of his sister to the point where, at the end, she comes to him intending to kill him, but relents. Mastrantonio makes this work better than Dvorak. The 1932 version keeps the incest theme relatively hidden, where the 1983 version has her offer herself to him in so many words. Whether Gina means it literally or out of spite makes for lively discussion.

- Camonte's best friend is Guino and Montana's best friend is Manny. Both fall in love with his sister (Cesca and Gina, respectively) and Tony kills each of them, not knowing that he and Tony's sister have been married.

- Guino is far more astute than Manny. He keeps

his romances discreet and is played cool by
George Raft, versus the braggadocious Bauer.

- There is no counterpart in the 1983 version to
the St. Valentine's Day Massacre of the 1932
movie, and nobody dies under the sign of an
X. The nightclub massacre is ordered by Frank
Lopez against Tony, and not by Tony against the
Diaz brothers, whom he cites as competitors.

- Al Pacino's Tony Montana is brash and bright
despite a lack of formal education, whereas Paul
Muni's Tony Camonte is primitive and childish.
In short, Camonte is a sociopath where Montana
is a businessman.

- Camonte is never seen drinking any of the
hooch he bootlegs, whereas Montana becomes
the emblem for "Don't get high on your own
supply." His first on-screen snort occurs after he
has bought a $43,000 car and he borrows a hit
from Elvira's inhaler.

- Similarly, Guino is also never seen drinking, nor
is Manny seen doing lines, although he can be
heard snorting cocaine off-camera in the scene
where Jerry the banker demands a higher fee to
launder Tony's cash. DePalma chose not to show
a cutaway of Bauer hoovering.

- Both Camonte and Montana entrap their
mentor (Johnny Lovo, Frank Lopez) when their
assassination attempts fail, then have their
friend (Guino, Manny) do the revenge killing.
Where Tony Camonte does not kill a policeman
(per the Production Code), Tony has no problem

killing Bernstein (Harris Yulin). (N.B.: As Pacino said in *The Godfather*, "Where does it say you can't kill a cop?")

- Johnny Lovo's girlfriend Poppy (Karen Morley) and Frank Lopez's girlfriend Elvira (Michelle Pfeiffer) both reject Tony's first advances but happily join him once their first sugar daddy is killed. Neither apparently holds Tony accountable for the deaths, or cares.

- Michelle Pfeiffer's Elvira has much more to do and is a far more complex character than Poppy. In the end, she leaves Tony, and there's a suggestion that she can begin to straighten out her life. Significantly, Tony doesn't send Manny or his bodyguard Eddie after her, and she does not return to their mansion once she leaves the restaurant.

- Camonte's mother is uneasy with Tony's way of life but not insistent. Montana's mother disowns him. Yet both mothers show concern for their daughter, Mrs. Camonte by coming to Tony and Mrs. Montana by receiving him in her home even though she banished him earlier.

- Both Tonys become enamored of the promise "The World is Yours"—Camonte from a neon sign for Cook's Tours and Montana from an overflying blimp. The neon sign is for an actual travel agency established by Thomas Cook and his son in 1872. The company folded in bankruptcy September 2019 when consumers perfected booking their own travel accommodations online. "The World is Yours" was not their slogan. The blimp in the 1983 *Scarface* is an aerial display for Pan American Travel (not connected with the current PanAmerican Travel in Utah). It inspires Tony to commission a statue with that slogan for his atrium, and he names his sham money laundering corporation the Montana Travel Company (in an early script draft).[14] Perhaps like the people behind the 1986 remake of *The Fly* who included the catchphrase "Help me, please help me" from the 1958 original, the remakers of *Scarface* felt honor-bound to refer to their 1932 progenitor. In truth, Scene 124 has Tony looking out the window of Lopez's condo at a neon sign that reads "The World Is Yours: Pan American To Europe, Africa, South America." This is not apparent at 1:43:20 in the existing film.

- The 1983 film is thankfully devoid of the moralistic posturing jammed into the 1932 original by the Hays Office. Tony Montana is what he is and even the cops are happy to benefit from his way of life. Only both men's mothers hold their sons accountable.

- Instead of a showdown with the law as in the 1932 version, Tony's climactic end in the 1983 edition is with an army dispatched by a rival drug lord. Unlike Paul Muni's Camonte, who feigns cowardice in an attempt to break free of the police, Al Pacino's Tony Montana and his "little friend" stand their ground against Sosa's minions.

- In a rare display of decency, Tony Montana balks at blowing up the Bolivian journalist's family along with the journalist. Tony Camonte, however, is never seen showing any kind of compassion; in fact, it is even mentioned that children have been killed in crossfire he initiated against a foe. This disregard for "civilians" is what finally turned public sentiment against Al Capone.

- Tony Camonte has no hesitation going after O'Hara when Lovo backs off in fear, but Tony Montana eagerly forms an alliance with Alejandro Sosa to expand Lopez's (and soon his) empire. O'Hara and Sosa are not true counterparts; they serve to reveal to Tony the weakness of Lovo/Lopez.

- Elvira leaves Tony Montana after a public spat at a restaurant, disappearing from the film. Poppy's exit is stranger: Once Tony Camonte has Johnny Lovo killed, he tells Poppy to move in with him, but the last time she is seen is when she phones Tony after he has killed Guino and just before his sister arrives and the police storm his fortress.

- In the climax of both versions, while Tony is holed up in his fortress, his sister shows up to kill him over murdering Guino. In the 1932 version, Cesca makes an emotional turn and professes her love for Tony, apparently overriding her hatred of him for the murder. By 1983, Gina has done the math, and after pulling a gun on her brother, she asks him he if he wants to fuck her.

Then she shoots him, only to be killed, in turn,
by one of Sosa's hitters. Both sisters die in Tony's
arms, pushing him even further over his already
crumbling, paranoid edge.

Some people have disputed that *Scarface* 1983 is a remake per se of *Scarface* 1932, but rather, they say, it is a "reimagining." Words like *reimagining* and another one, *reboot*, are simply semantic justifications, as if any is needed, for bringing a story up-to-date for a new audience.

SIDEBAR

Deleted Scenes and Factoids

The 35th Anniversary DVD and Blu-ray of *Scarface* contain approximately twenty-two minutes of deleted scenes that enrich the character of Tony Montana and add tantalizing detail to the story without substantially altering it. The early screenplay cited here was called "second draft" and was presumably written in 1982 or earlier. A "shooting script" containing scene numbers for budgeting and scheduling purposes was also consulted for the book. It carries revisions dated from December 2, 1982, through January 18, 1983. Some scenes in the earlier screenplay were likely cut for budget purposes and their information was rolled into scenes in the final script, or that information was deemed extraneous to the plot. Deleted scenes from, or extensions of existing scenes that appear in, the shooting script also generally appear in the deleted scenes special DVD/Blu-ray feature.

Imagining how the deleted scenes would have changed the film is an exercise in examining how filmmakers apply their creative process. As written, acted, and directed, each deleted scene is compelling in itself, particularly once one knows its context. And yet, when gauging the overall rhythm of the film, it becomes clear why they were removed.

- Oliver Stone's second draft begins with a harrowing sequence in which Tony and Manny evacuate Cuba aboard a rickety vessel, the *Jolly Roger*, during the Mariel boatlift, with its captain ordered to take five "scum" for every family member unless he bribes the Cuban officials. Tony and Manny's boat hits rough seas and they launch a lifeboat. En route, Tony heroically rescues a small child from drowning. In the shooting script, as in the final film, this is replaced by a title card explaining the Mariel boatlift and then cuts to the Customs interrogation scene. "It was [cut from the script] pretty early," Oliver Stone says. "I remember that that went out pretty fast because of the cost factor, working in the ocean, the budget was too high."[15]

- Tony Montana's stated reason to immigration investigators for coming to America is to escape Communism (which neither they nor the audience are meant to believe). Later in the film, when the IRS is on his case, Tony complains about capitalism. No contrast in political messages, and the inherent hypocrisy, could be more powerful: It's all about the money.

- Sent to Freedom Town, Tony and Manny meet Chi Chi (Angel Salazar) and Angel (Paul Sema).

They also meet a "transvestite" [*sic*]; the script says she is a female wearing male clothing. They watch Humphrey Bogart in *The Treasure of the Sierra Madre*. The scene was apparently shot but later removed, partly for reasons of pacing, and perhaps because Universal Pictures didn't want to deal with Warner Bros. to license the footage.

- In Freedom Town, Tony declares his fraternal love for Manny. This is misinterpreted by a character whom the script calls a "transvestite" [*sic*] detainee, who offers Tony her services, which Tony playfully but respectfully rejects. Watching the raw footage of this encounter, one can see Pacino staying in character while other performers appear relaxed.

- A crane shot in Freedom Town shows Tony in a phone booth dialing his mother and sister (in his hand he holds Gina's school photo and reads her phone number off the back) but hanging up before there is an answer. This explains why, in the movie, he references five years until he is flush before contacting them, by which time fifteen-year-old Gina has become a woman (Scene 10).

- At Freedom Town, Manny and Angel hear of a riot in another detainment camp and fear that if there is one where they are, everyone will be shipped back to Cuba. Tony tells them not to worry because "the beard and cigar" (Castro) won't take them back, and thus they have the U.S. government by the balls. "And when you got 'em by the balls, their hearts and minds will follow." (The quote has been attributed to many people, including Theodore Roosevelt, General Douglas MacArthur, and John Wayne.) This shows how Tony is already gaming the system (Scene 10).

- Extended sequence of Omar, Tony, and others off-loading marijuana from boats in Miami and paying off cops. (So Tony and Manny took the low-paying pot job after all.)

- Tony, Manny, and Angel rob a bank but find very little cash. They hit a supermarket, with Tony posing as an undercover cop, and do much better by intimidating people.

- Buying Gina a designer dress, Tony is complimented by the saleswoman that his wife is good-looking. Tony corrects her that Gina is his sister. (In the film, this is a silent moment in a montage, but the saleswoman's lips are visible saying "your wife.")

- There is a brief scene in an early script where Tony, leaving a court appearance for drug and tax evasion charges, is celebrated by the press because he's good copy. So was Al Capone.

- Driving to their cocaine deal to meet Hector the Toad, Tony admonishes Angel not to indulge in spiritualism because there is no God. The beginning of one of the takes is unusable because a man is seen standing in a window in the background looking at the camera (Scene 32).

- Tony and Manny visit a drug dealer, Nick the Pig (Michael Moran), whose apartment is strewn with white bags. The man, who is overweight, offers them a quantity of quaaludes for a dollar apiece and then knocks the price down to 97 cents. They agree to take the pills off his hands. The scene has no place in the existing film but occurs in an early script between the supermarket robbery and before Tony surprises his mother with a visit.

- Nick the Pig joins Tony's gang and helps smuggle cocaine through Miami Airport in bottles of baby formula and a child's stuffed animal, fooling the Customs inspectors, who stop Tony but allow the "mules" to pass through.

- Tony waits for Frank to leave his apartment building before slipping in to see Elvira. This would alert the audience that Tony knows Frank is not returning soon, as Elvira warns he may (Scene 103).

- Tony and Sosa walk through Sosa's estate. Sosa tells Tony that he likes him because he doesn't lie. (In an early script Sosa is named Suarez, and Omar's last name is Sosa) (Scene 95).

- Tony and Manny pay the lawyer George Sheffield a $100,000 retainer well ahead of any actual need for him (Scene 102).

- Omar is seen in a close shot about to be pushed from the helicopter, then he falls off camera. Unlike the footage used in the final film, Omar does not appear to have been beaten first.

- On the way to being seated at his table in the posh restaurant, Tony speaks to a TV reporter sitting at another table. The reporter has editorialized against the cocaine cartels. Tony informs him that the 200-kilo bust he reported was actually 220 kilos and that he should think about investigating who skimmed the missing twenty kilos.

- After Manny kills Lopez and Tony kills Bernstein, Tony orders Lopez's Cadillac dealership torched. In the film it isn't even clear that Lopez's cover business is a Cadillac showroom.

- Early script drafts have two assassins. The man who is tasked with killing the Bolivian journalist is called Needles in an early script. He is not the servant, Alberto (Mark Margolis), who alerts Sosa that Omar is an informer. An early script has a Black "aide" identify Omar to Sosa (who was then named Suarez). The man who kills Omar is Shadow, and it is he who turns up at the end to shotgun Tony in the back.

- In New York to assassinate the Bolivian journalist, Tony is tipped off by his bodyguard that he is being trailed by the police. Tony takes the initiative to stop the squad car and ask if they have seen a little white poodle he is missing. This satisfies the officers and they depart, allowing Tony to let Sosa's assassin Alberto finish wiring the journalist's car with a bomb.

- In an earlier script there is an elaborate montage watching Needles construct the car bomb, which malfunctions at the crucial moment. Needles fixes it and is about to detonate the bomb when Tony shoots him with his Beretta, as in the final film.

- Angel's chainsaw amputation is described coldly in the screenplay: "A brief glimpse of ANGEL slumped by one arm like a cow on a strap, streaming blood, eyes conscious and horrified, a terrifying sight. The chainsaw whirrs once more."

- The Bolivian journalist and his family live at 5 Tudor City Place, New York, NY 10017. Google Maps shows this as a cul-de-sac (which, at this writing, is under renovation), where it was easy to block off streets for location filming.[16] (Aside: If only all journalists could afford to live in such a place.) Elvira walks out on Tony just before Sosa's army shows up to massacre him. She praises Tony for being kind enough not to kill the journalist, but leaves him anyway. Later the ghosts of Rebenga, Lopez, Bernstein, and Manny haunt Tony, who is incredibly strung out on coke. Although Shadow, Sosa's assassin, throws a grenade at Tony, Tony dies in a hail of unspecified bullets. Not until the shooting script does the assassin, by then called The Skull, personally blow Tony away from behind. Nevertheless, Tony is by then so strung out that it takes a volley of rounds to finish him. Most memorably, not until the December 21, 1982 script revision, Scene 226, do we see in writing:

Tony loading his rocket, intends to beat them to the punch, talking to himself.

TONY: "So you wanna play hunh, say hello to my
little friend here."

One of the unused takes has Pacino ending with "here." The
take that made it into the final film ends on "friend." Of
course, no one could have known at the time that it would
become one of the most quoted lines in film history. Even the
man who wrote it is modest. "It's not like a big deal," Oliver
Stone insists. "I mean, I know it's my line, but—I thought it
was in the first draft, but it wasn't. I was on the set for the
whole shoot and there was a lot of revising going on, so it's
probably one of those lines I added somewhere in there."[17]

CHAPTER 8

The Movie Novelization

Novelizations are the bastard child of Hollywood. They're not the movie, they're not a book, they're a second writer's idea of what the screenwriter and director were planning. And they seldom reflect the final film because, owing to publishing deadlines, they usually have to be started, if not finished, before the movie is complete. Yet they are designed to coast on the movie's success and expand on its content for readers eager for more. They are the sales department's way to profit from the publicity surrounding a new film, the production end's way of establishing prestige by bringing out a literary counterpart, and the studio conglomerate's way of keeping their publishing subsidiary busy. All three were at play with *Scarface*.

Novelizations are a cockamamie genre. As Alan Dean Foster (who has written some fine novelizations, among them *Star Wars*, without credit, and *Alien*) told *Vanity Fair* in 2014, "It's always amusing to me. You take a book, say, *To Kill a Mockingbird*, throw away three-quarters of it and win an Academy Award for best adapted screenplay. But if you take a screenplay and add three-quarters of original material to it— which is a much, much more difficult piece of writing—well, that's by definition hackwork."[1]

And yet, in the hands of a gifted writer, a novelization can add immeasurably to the enjoyment of a film, particularly because of the offset between book and film deadlines. As a result, many novelizations contain scenes that were cut or were never shot, adding to the novel's richness of character and story in ways that the film no longer contains.[2] Such is the case with Paul Monette's adaptation of *Scarface*.

What made a *Scarface* novelization attractive was its stealth nature, implied Universal marketing expert Stan Newman.[3] He pointed out that a bad book review for a novelization can be taken by the public to be a bad review for the movie, but since mass market paperbacks are rarely reviewed, movie novelizations, which are published in mass market only, are insulated.[4] If it was Newman's idea to hire Monette, he should be praised. Monette used the script as inspiration for his prose. Stone spent the first nine and a half pages of his screenplay describing the ordeal of the Cuban refugees on the Mariel boatlift. Tony Montana and Manny Ribera's crossing from Cuba to Miami in a rickety shrimp boat is fraught with danger. Never shot, the sequence ends and the script picks up with Tony's immigration interrogation, beginning with "Okay, so what did you say your name was?"

Monette not only expands those first nine-and-a-half pages into forty-seven pages (roughly twenty thousand words). He goes into vivid detail recounting Tony's past, starting when he was a kid picking pockets with his cousin Manny, ripping off people's homes by pretending to be sick and needing help, and ultimately becoming a Cuban marijuana mogul by organizing what had hitherto been a slapdash local gambit. He buys gifts for his sister Gina, including a gold necklace, and saves $16,000 to get to America, but has a run-in with the police first and loses everything. He earns his scar from being slashed with a razor wielded by the cuckolded general whose wife he has been screwing twice a week, blows the officer's head away in revenge with a sawed-off shotgun, is jailed, is forced into the Cuban army to fight a losing war in Angola, and returns only to get busted for stealing a few pesos' worth of marzipan candy. Because of his criminal record, he is rousted from his cell and shipped to Miami by the Castro government as they seize on America's naïve humanitarianism to slip criminals in among the Mariel refugees. En route, he pulls a struggling man onto a departing lifeboat, saves a boy from drowning, and is airlifted to shore by a copter, intending to use the boy as his immigration ticket, only to have the boy taken by the lad's uncle, Waldo Colon, who promises to do Tony a favor for his heroism.

Monette has drawn on individual dialogue and descriptive lines from Stone's script to construct this backstory from lines like "I was a kid" (the scar), "Oh, that was for my sweetheart" (referring to his hand tattoo), and others that suggest that he was in the army, and that his parents are dead (which his mother is not, as is revealed later). At times even single lines can inspire whole paragraphs.

Throughout the book, Monette expands on actions described in the script and adds other touches, some of them contradictory; unlike in the film, Tony does not reject Omar's offer to load and unload boats laden with pot—he and Manny do it. They also impersonate lawmen to shake down other crooks.

Because Monette had an early draft of the script that doesn't contain the line "Say hello to my little friend," it is not in the book. Instead, the last thing Tony says in the book as he is riddled with bullets is a self-aggrandizing, psychotic third-person line, "Tony Montana, he died doin' it." That line appears in the shooting script in a scene in which Tony tells Chi Chi how he'd like to be remembered.

Issued in paperback in August 1983 by Berkley Books, "by arrangement with MCA Publishing, a Division of CA Communications, Inc.," the book's copyright is held by MCA, not

Monette, who wrote it as what the copyright office calls "a work made for hire."

When the *Scarface* phenomenon became a juggernaut, Universal commissioned fantasy writer L.A. (Leslie Esdaile) Banks to write *Scarface: The Beginning* (New York: Dark Horse, 2006), which invented a version of Tony's backstory that built on Monette's earlier extrapolation.

Paul Monette is best known for writing *On Borrowed Time: An AIDS Memoir*, his 1988 book on the life and death of his partner, lawyer Roger Horwitz. His own memoir, *Becoming a Man: Half a Life Story* (1992), was his chronicle of coming out. He died in 1995 at the age of forty-nine. Before he died, he set up the Monette-Horwitz Trust with his second partner, producer Stephen Kolzak, to support LGBT activism and scholarship.

SIDEBAR

How Did Tony Get His Scar?

- Book by Armitage Trail: Facial injury in the Great War.

- 1932 film: Tony says he got it in the war, but Johnny Lovo says he got it "with a blonde in a Brooklyn speakeasy."

- 1983 film: "I was in a knife fight. When I was a kid. You should see the other guy."

- Novelization of 1983 film: Tony was slashed with a razor by a general whose wife he was screwing.

- Al Pacino's scar came from makeup artists Stephen Abrums and Barbara Guedel. Paul Muni's makeup artist is uncredited.

- Al Capone's scar came from Johnny Galluccio after Capone insulted Galluccio's sister at the Harvard Inn at Coney Island.

SIDEBAR

A Tale of Two Tonys

When Al Pacino said, at the thirty-fifth anniversary panel of *Scarface* at Tribeca in 2018, that he wanted to be Paul Muni after seeing the 1932 *Scarface*, what did he mean?[5] The two men couldn't be more different in their training, acting styles, careers, or personae. Other than thespic talent, what explains Pacino's fascination?

Muni's Tony Camonte is pure id. He acts entirely on his impulses, feels neither hesitation nor regret, and carries a sense of entitlement that overrides any adherence to society's mores. Although he kills to get what he wants, he also kills in angry revenge, not even caring that there's a chance he might not get away with it. A psychiatrist might call him a narcissistic sociopath, and he has counterparts strewn throughout history. For Muni it must have been liberating to portray someone who does what he wants with unrestrained glee, happy to make his tommy gun spit. Why wouldn't Al Pacino crave playing such a character?

That said, Muni and Pacino's differences emerge not only in how their performances turned out but in how they got there, and the journeys begin with the men themselves.

Frederich Meshilem Meier Weisenfreund was born in 1895 in Lemberg, in what was then the Austro-Hungarian Empire but which is now Ukraine. His parents, Salli and Phillip, were actors and spoke Yiddish, and young Muni (from his nickname

"Moony") assumed it as a first language. When he was seven, his family, which included two sisters, moved to Chicago. He was twelve when he entered the Yiddish theater in that city, impressing audiences in his first stage role, in which he played an eighty-year-old man. Makeup would become his specialty as his career progressed. At age twenty-three, he was scouted by Maurice Schwartz, the great Yiddish actor-producer, to join Schwartz's newly formed Yiddish Art Theatre (with an "re" to distinguish it from the Yiddish Art Theater with an "er") in New York's Union Square. It was there that he met and married Bella Frankel in 1921. He would become increasingly dependent upon her over the years, to the point where she would accompany him to guide his every move on and off the stage and screen.

The 1920s were still the days when movie studios sent talent scouts to see the shows in New York, including the Yiddish shows (where Edward G. Robinson, formerly Emmanuel Goldenberg, was discovered). Noticed there and signed to a Fox Film contract in 1929 in Hollywood's mad scramble to recruit talking actors with the arrival of sound, Muni made an artistic, if not commercial, success with his first film, *The Valiant*, and less of one with his second, *Seven Faces*, which also flopped financially. Discouraged, Muni returned to New York and restored his career with the hit play *Counselor at Law*. By chance, Howard Hawks caught the production and sought Muni to play Tony Camonte, whom he was then casting in Los Angeles.

Muni was methodical, if not Method. He was celebrated for compiling what people today would call a dossier on each of his roles. Exhaustive research was key to his absorbing a character. Although he was not a formal adherent of "the Method," which Konstantin Stanislavski had begun exploring in the 1890s at his Moscow Art Theatre, Muni's developing a character from the inside out was similar to their process,[6] although he was also aided by the use of makeup to alter his physical appearance.

Muni was challenged by the technical limitations of movies at the beginning of the sound era. Microphones were far from sensitive, and the actors in those first talkies were required to project several feet to the mikes, much as they had projected to the back rows from the stage. While Muni was renowned for being able to reach the highest balcony with a whisper, it gave him, in those first film performances, the appearance of overacting. This is particularly evident in *Scarface*, whose Western Electric sound system challenged spoken dialogue with a poor signal-to-noise ratio (digitally corrected for home video and new theatrical prints) and limited frequency range. All the performances suffer, but especially Muni's. Yet his facial expressions and the sheer flamboyance of his acting, for whatever reason, so perfectly fit Tony Camonte that it's no wonder Pacino became fascinated by him fifty years later.

Muni was thirty-seven when he made *Scarface*. Pacino was forty-two. Born in Manhattan on April 25, 1940, Alfredo (sometimes cited as Alphonse) James Pacino, is the son of Sal and Rose Pacino, who split up when he was two. His mother won custody and they moved to the South Bronx to live with grandparents. He attended public school so he could take advantage of working in school plays, and picked up habits such as smoking and drinking, which would vex him in later life. Pacino was admitted in 1966 to the Actors Studio under Lee Strasberg (whose character Hyman Roth he ordered to be murdered in *The Godfather Part II*) and won important roles in such off-Broadway landmarks as *The Indian Wants the Bronx*, *Does the Tiger Wear a Necktie?*, and *The Resistible Rise of Arturo Ui*. Although he'd had small roles in one feature film (*Me, Natalie,* 1969) and an episode of television's *N.Y.P.D.* in 1967, it was as the heroin addict in *The Panic in Needle Park* (1971) that drew his first broad acclaim. (His gambit with *The Gang That Couldn't Shoot Straight* is covered elsewhere.) Then, of course, came *The Godfather* (1972).

By the time Pacino hit the screen, the screen was ready for him. The 1970s was the era of average-looking leading men, Method-trained actors, and a vastly improved cinematography and sound recording technology that could capture actors' subtle, internalized performances.

In those days Pacino tended toward two extremes on the screen. One was wired, pressured, complicated people like the street denizen Lion in *Scarecrow* (1973), the endangered cop in *Serpico* (1973), the nervous Sonny in *Dog Day Afternoon* (1975), and the conflicted attorney in . . . *And Justice for All* (1979). The others were calculating and reserved: Michael in *The Godfather,* the dispassionate race car driver in *Bobby Deerfield* (1977), and the cautious, troubled undercover cop in *Cruising* (1980). The family man/playwright Ivan Travalian pointed Pacino in new directions leading to the breathtakingly complex journey that Tony Montana makes in *Scarface.* Pacino's Tony is at once playful, hard, challenging, sensitive, impatient, calculating, vengeful, paranoid, and exuberant. And it all makes sense. By the time of Tony, Pacino has not only expanded his range, he has solidified it.

The most profound difference between the Muni and Pacino Tonys can be found in the homecoming scene in which his mother rebukes him for activities that she clearly knows to be illegal. Mama Camonte (Inez Palange) suffers from the brevity of her role as a stereotyped Italian widow who can do little more than say tsk-tsk to her son and caution her daughter about ill-gotten gains. Mama Montana (Miriam Colon), by contrast, not only doesn't swallow Tony's excuse that he is a union organizer, she rebukes him with such resolve that one can see in Pacino's eyes that he has been eviscerated, then tries to cover it by an act of largesse to his sister that disguises his residual love for their mother. This pays off an unused plot point (noted elsewhere) in which Tony kept away from his mother and sister for five years. Tony Camonte, on the other hand, is seen as living with his mother and sister all along, though he probably spent little time under their roof. In both cases, Papa Camonte is gone, in 1932 by death and in 1983 by abandonment.

None of this is to say that Muni's was a one-note performance. A 93-minute film can't do as much as a 170-minute film. But Muni's Tony comes out swinging. In his early scenes when he is surveying Johnny Lovo's domain and thirsting after his moll, Poppy, Tony is both impressed and cocksure, flirtatious and contemptuous, clearly marking time like a lion waiting to take over another lion's pride. Muni almost strains to be charming (in a juvenile kind of way) as a device to gain others' confidence. He plays against Hecht's bravado dialogue and becomes ingratiating, much to the danger of those who are seduced by his contrived innocence.

Pacino's Tony is smarter and more devious, but as he is fond of saying, he only fucks those who fuck him. He remains coldly in control until cocaine clouds his brain; the transition from recreational user to human Hoover is admittedly sudden, coming after he kills Manolo. What's interesting in comparing each man's last moments is that Pacino's Tony goes out with an exuberant bang (killed from behind by Sosa's assassin, the swine, and then finished from the front by everyone else) where Muni's Tony feigns cowardice in an escape attempt only to be shot down by the cops. Both deaths are ignominious, but Pacino's Tony gets points for holding his ground where Muni's Tony had to buckle under the Production Code and come off even worse in the alternate ending.

Tony Montana benefited in other ways from the relaxed Production Code. He could have sex, drink, do drugs, swear, and kill on-screen. Tony Camonte could only be accused of these things and even then by the barest suggestion. Even though the Code wasn't being fully enforced in 1932, it still hovered enough over the Hawks-Hughes production to require Hecht and Hawks's expert footwork to let the audience know what was going on without actually showing it. This was most profound in Tony's suggested incestuous attraction to Cesca (there's no indication it was mutual) versus the more explicit showdown between Tony Montana and Gina Ribera (née Montana) when she returns to kill him.

Pacino's performance is daring. In *Scarface Nation*, Ken Tucker charts the star's explanation for what he calls a "garishly exaggerated" acting style. Pacino told Bernard Weinraub of the *New York Times* that it was an operatic movie and said that DePalma wanted him to go that way. To Lawrence Grobel he explained that he purposely made Tony two-dimensional (rather than three, although it raises questions of whether an actor of Pacino's skill can de-act). And to Britain's *Guardian* newspaper he defended Tony as a hero, despite his crimes, because he told the man with the chainsaw to "shove it."[7] What nobody seems to have noticed is that, in playing Tony over the top, Pacino was doing exactly what Paul Muni had done fifty years earlier. In other words, Pacino achieved his stated goal of being Paul Muni on his own terms.

"Al's always had a great affection for Bertolt Brecht's *Arturo Ui*," explains Oliver Stone, remarking on Pacino's stated "two-dimensional" choice. "Remember, he was playing on it, he went back to it and played it a couple of times, so he wanted to develop a character along those lines, I think, and

Arturo Ui is very broad and expressionistic. I think he saw a lot of Arturo Ui in the character. As I remember, he wasn't scared of the accent. He was bold in his choices. And I think that's good. He could easily have pulled it back and tried to sanitize it, but, on the contrary, he was pushing the language all the time." Significantly, Pacino delivers a brave performance. Most actors want to be liked. Pacino went all-in. "That's right," says Stone. "Most people misunderstand that. I love the fact that he committed completely to playing a guy like this. He was very straightforward; he was an honest man in his way."[8]

Ultimately, of course, comparisons become forced; Pacino and Muni are different people with different training. Yet even the differences between their interpretations show the richness and breadth of the possibilities in Tony's character and what he represents. Both Tonys enjoy their work. Viewers of both films can live vicariously through them, doing unto others as they would love to do themselves if they had the guts. Both Tonys want the world and, in the end, both of them get the world—or at least a six-foot hole in it.

SIDEBAR

Tony's Morality

No movie criminal, even a Bond villain, sees himself as evil. Not only would introspection muddle the plot, it would compromise the catharsis of the big finish when the bad guy gets his due. While self-justification monologues are useful for explaining antisocial behavior, they are seldom necessary for the plot, and these confessional "I once had a puppy" speeches are usually inserted to help the actor, not the character. With rare exceptions, evildoers must simply die by the end of the movie, preferably as outrageously as possible and, even better, by their own killing device backfiring.

Few filmmakers have managed to dispatch villains as gloriously as DePalma, who was, arguably, the first to do it so grandly: self-detonating John Cassavetes in *The Fury*; crucifying Piper Laurie in *Carrie*; drowning Gregg Henry in *Body Double*; blowing up Jon Voight in *Mission: Impossible*; and, of course, perforating Tony Montana in *Scarface*.

Yet Tony Montana doesn't start out evil in the film. One might say that he is simply a skilled businessman, except his business is criminal. How does his morality differ from, say, the United Fruit Company that engaged in atrocious activities in Central and South America;[9] collusion and other corporate miscreancy by Gulf + Western Industries;[10] Coca-Cola's worldwide effect on people, governments, and the environment?[11] The difference, of course, is that conglomerates like these enjoy the protection, if not the complicity, of the U.S. government. A look at the savings and loan crisis of 1987 and the recession of 2008, neither of which resulted in the imprisonment of any of the people who caused them, is a reminder that justice is indeed blind, only not in the right way.

Besides, Tony does have a good side, except it's buried within a more complex character than the one whom audiences meet on first viewing. Fortunately, Pacino embodies these textures and ambiguities in his performance even if the specifics remain locked in un-shot portions of various scripts.

Tony's introduction in the film is the interrogation scene in which he shows self-confidence, if not arrogance, under INS questioning. It is the first display of the textures in his character, and Pacino doesn't miss a beat in his performance, which is heightened by DePalma's shifting camera.[12] The movie is jockeying for a foothold in this new environment, same as Tony. In the course of the verbal do-si-do, we learn:

- Tony hates Castro and says that the U.S. can't do anything to him that Castro hasn't already done.

- He has no family (which is a lie; he has a mother and sister).

- He had to live by eating octopus every meal.

- His father was an American sailor who is now dead—so is his mother (which is also a lie).

- He got his facial scar as a kid in a knife fight.

- He learned to speak English by watching Humphrey Bogart, James Cagney, and Edward G. Robinson movies.

- Stone's description: "One of Tony's consistent mannerisms is rapid eye movement (over shoulders, sides, doors), and he does a lot of touching—objects—but lightly with the tips of his fingers."

- The tattoo on Tony's hand is revelatory. "It's some kinda code these guys use in the can," says INS Man #3. "I seen pitchforks on some of 'em. They're the hit men. This one I never seen before."

- Tony mentions quickly that he was in the army.

- He admits he was in jail in Cuba for possession of American dollars that he got from a Canadian tourist. The INS man says, "What'd you do, mug him first?"

None of Tony's background can be proven, and from Pacino's performance we gather that neither he nor the INS people believe it anyway. What we don't learn, because it is in script material from the second draft that was not put on the screen, is the ordeal Tony and Manny suffered getting from Mariel to Miami. Although this was discussed earlier, it bears closer examination here because, combined with other elements, it expands and enriches Tony's character.

In Oliver Stone's undated second draft script, which begins in the "grimy, industrial port" of Mariel Harbor, Cuba, Castro's officials are forcing shrimp boat owners and others to take an overload of passengers to Miami, specifically five deportees for every family member the boat owner wants to bring to America. Pro-Castro demonstrators are there to jeer the evacuees' departure. A sergeant takes the manacles off of a prisoners' wrists and tells "*Caracortada*" ("Scarface") to go to hell. Tony is described as being "in the young angry prime of his life" as he spits in the sergeant's face, saying, "Fuck you, fuck Castro," to his former captor, who is too surprised to respond. Tony is joined by Manolo Ray (later Ribera) as they board the boat. People and their belongings fill every inch of the rickety vessel.

Fifteen-foot waves rock the *Jolly Roger* as it crosses the Florida straits. Tony and Manolo hang on; Tony can't swim but tells Manolo, "I trust the gods." (This will be in contrast to what he tells Angel later that there is no God.) Then the mast begins to crack and the passengers panic. Refugees head for two small rowboats. A "strong man" slugs a "weaker man" for a seat and Tony throws the strong man overboard to save the weaker man. When the boat hits the water, Tony saves the life of a "retard" [*sic*] by pulling him aboard. He then sees a boy of three thrashing in the water. He dives in, even though he can't swim, and saves the boy. The "retarded" man throws them an inflated inner tube, and as they approach Miami, Tony and the boy are rescued by a helicopter. When he gets to the INS office, Tony is pulled aside for an interview, and the film as it now exists begins.

Paul Monette's novelization adds that Tony uses the boy, whom the author names Paco, to vault past the lines of arriving immigrants and avoid INS officials by claiming he is the boy's uncle. When little Paco sees his real uncle, Waldo Colon, he breaks away from Tony. A grateful Colon calls Tony a saint and says he will do anything for him. Called into interrogation by INS officials, Tony lies to them that his wife and children are waiting for him in Miami. The fact that Tony uses little Paco for his own ends is minor venality compared to his heroism risking his life to save him from drowning. This elaborate sequence was in the shooting schedule but was cut by the studio for budgetary reasons. It saved money, but it also eliminated important exposition and backstory for Tony and Manny's characters. Does screenwriter Oliver Stone feel its loss removes complexity from Tony's character? "I really can't answer that question because maybe it would have been seen as too leading, too sentimental," he says. "You know: Man saves baby in the first reel so we know he's a good guy. I don't know if you need to know that he's a good guy; I think it might be more interesting to some people to keep him dark. It might have been too much to go the other way."[13]

Later, confined to the ironically named Freedom Town, Tony engages in badinage with a "transvestite" [sic] (this scene partially appears in deleted footage on the film's DVD and Blu-ray). While hardly a sympathetic encounter, Tony displays casual acceptance. This is noteworthy, if not world-beating, for a character as macho as Tony is portrayed.

In another Freedom Town scene that appears in the deleted footage, Angel and Manny have heard that nine out of ten Marielitas at another detention facility are being shipped back to Cuba. Tony calms their fears of a similar fate by telling them, "This is America, they got lawyers here. Castro don't want us back, hey nobody wants us, so what are they gonna do with us. Put us in a gas chamber? They're stuck with us." And of course, he's right.[14]

Lastly, there is Tony's refusal to help assassinate the Bolivian journalist in New York when he sees that the man is traveling with his wife and children. Tony's shooting of Shadow, Sosa's hit man assigned to carry out the murder, brings about the film's climax and results in Tony's death.

Not that Tony's hands are clean; in addition to Shadow, he kills the chainsaw man Toad and others in the Colombians' hotel room; Bernstein the cop; countless gunmen sent by Sosa; his best friend Manny; and who knows how much collateral civilian damage? But to the extent that he justifies some killings and not others, his sense of honor (however fluid) prevails. The irony is inescapable that "no good deed goes unpunished," although no doubt the connection is lost on Tony in the orgy of recrimination and vengeance that surrounds him.

Then there are the drugs themselves. Although Tony sells cocaine, he at first is against using it himself. Explains Steven Bauer, who worked closely with Pacino to "Cubanize" him, he was fighting to create a character arc for Tony. "When Frank says, 'Don't get high on your own supply,' if you watch Al in that scene, he has no idea what they're talking about because, accurately, he's coming from Cuba. He and I talked about this. The [Cubans] were like, 'No, I don't do drugs. We do marijuana.' What was the idea of cocaine to real Cubans in that period? It did exist in the upper classes in Cuba in the 1930s. But for Al, to come from the working class, and after having been in prison, he never had contact with that until he came to the United States. His Tony thought that you can move this thing and get money and get power, but to use it is unthinkable. And yet he himself is the one who falls for it big time. Just when you think that you're above something, that's when you're headed for a fall."[15]

One final note on Tony's scruples: It's tempting to see him as a perversion of Horatio Alger, a man who rose to the top by means of opportunism, savvy, and his own brand of morality. Is Tony a villain or simply a bad guy? Like Al Capone and Tony Camonte, he wants it all, but—and this is important—he only wants it from his own kind. Like all levels of organized crime, real or fictitious, he does his best to leave the general public out of it.[16] A look at the victims of Tony's violence reveals that civilian casualties are the fault of Tony's enemies, not him or his men. Small comfort.

Early in the film, Tony says, "All I have in this world is my balls and my word, and I don't break them for no one." The fact that honor leads to his death is the kind of fatal flaw that makes for drama that reaches the level of Greek tragedy.

SIDEBAR

The Song of *Scarface*

Although it is merely one of his nearly a hundred screen credits, Giorgio Moroder's sensual, pulsating musical score for *Scarface* has become so closely identified with the film that when Universal Pictures asked Brian DePalma for permission to replace it with rap songs for a planned hip-hop rerelease, the director flatly refused. He respected Moroder's contribution to his film so much that he gave up the income that a new version would have generated.

Universal had good reason to want to add icing on DePalma's cake. For starters, there are currently five separate versions of Moroder's soundtrack album:

1983 original vinyl with ten cuts

1983 CD remastered with ten cuts

2003 CD remix with ten cuts

2016 vinyl and CD with ten cuts

2022 CD expanded limited edition with
    fifty-one cuts

Not only that, there are untold numbers of illegal uploads on YouTube and file-sharing sites, and the studio understandably wanted their share. Each iteration of the tracks has its fans and detractors, and this is not the place to attempt an album review. But it's a good spot to note that movie soundtracks are usually considered a promotional ancillary to a film's original release and rarely become a profit center. Exceptions include musicals, songs by successful recording artists, and albums from box office successes.

By any of these measures, Moroder's score scored. His and Pete Bellotte's featured single, "Push It to the Limit," has been covered by Ten Masked Men, Battle Beast, PelleK, Savación, Tumourboy, JCRZ, and sampled by Mobb Deep, Fonky Family, GOOD Music, Rick Ross, N-Wise Allah and Lou Fresco, Music Legends, Lowlight, and others. His original soundtrack featured Paul Engemann, Debbie Harry, Amy Holland, Elizabeth Daily, Maria Conchita Alonso, and Beth Anderson. The person formerly known as Kanye West also sampled "Tony's Theme" in his music. Five of the soundtrack's songs were even featured in the video game *Grand Theft Auto III* in 2001, a compendium that included Deborah Harry's "Rush Rush" and Amy Holland's "She's On Fire."

"The theme for Tony had to reflect the character and the person of Al Pacino," Moroder explained, "and, of course, the character of the movie. And it has to be a little dangerous, a little suspenseful, and a little deep, too. And I think it reflects quite well that atmosphere which was at that time in Miami with all the crime and all that stuff."[17]

DePalma came to Moroder after hearing the composer's evocative score for Paul Schrader's *American Gigolo*. It reminded him of the incessant disco music that he had heard in the dance clubs he'd visited while researching his film.

Moroder is widely credited with inventing modern disco[18] with his tracks for *Midnight Express* (1978), which, although thematically antithetical to the film's genre and setting, blew it into a different world and gave it a life that no traditional score could have conveyed. Suddenly the stock story of a young man in a Turkish prison took on an urgency that made it relatable to young people in the audience, and the motion picture Academy recognized Moroder's achievement with its 1979 Oscar.

Moroder's instrumentation, while largely electronic, is not strictly what's now recalled as disco; it is better termed "post-disco," a musical shotgun marriage that lowered the electronic component and drive more toward singles (and was created in reaction to the anti-disco riots in several northern cities) and a combination of synthesizer and rock music called "synth-pop." After *Midnight Express*, he became a movie institution not only through Paul Schrader's *American Gigolo* and Schrader's remake of *Cat People* (1982), but as one of the artists on Adrian Lyne's 1983 *Flashdance*.

The year after *Scarface*, Moroder produced and scored a controversial re-edited version of Fritz Lang's 1927 science fantasy film *Metropolis*, a visually stunning science fiction epic in which an inventor creates a female robot who plays havoc with the balance between labor and management in an underground city of the future. Moroder not only wrote an original score for a highly edited 83-minute version of the 153-minute silent German masterpiece, he color-tinted the scenes and tried to turn Lang's austere classic into a pop sensation. Although he proclaimed his appreciation for Lang's original film, his redo drew wide criticism and was quickly relegated to being a cheeky curiosity.

His work for *Scarface*, however, is subtle and unexpected. He uses traditional character melodies—particularly "Tony's Theme," "Gina's and Elvira's Theme," and their interpolation—but they function more as background music than traditional movie underscoring. He will often use slow, methodical music against fast-paced screen action to create a contrast that forces viewers to consider what's being shown, rather than involving them. Much of the score sounds divorced and nonspecific, like someone has left a radio running in the background. He will also introduce an ominous, low rumbling that telegraphs danger. Unlike traditional movie music that underlines specific on-screen action or interacts with dialogue,[19] Moroder goes for mood, quite often doing nothing except filling the silence. It becomes a key contribution to *Scarface*'s sensory overload. Yet it also dates the movie in ways that the costumes and cars do not.

Moroder wrote specific themes for the main characters. "The theme for the two girls was a little tricky," he said, "because I wanted to have the same feel for both because Tony's in love with the sister and in love with Elvira and so the sounds are very similar. The melodies are slightly different, but that was done on purpose so to create a little bit of ambiguity and to show the people that Tony is in love with both."[20] It's a stretch to call them leitmotifs, but there is a similarity. Like most movie composers, Moroder wrote his themes after the film was cut and he had seen it.

At the time the film was being shot, Moroder and his close group of fellow musicians were in their North Hollywood office, called Oasis Studios. They had earlier knocked out eight songs to be used as diegetic (source) music in the Babylon Club and coming from car and home speakers. When the Babylon Club scenes were shot, however, as is the custom, no music was played and the background extras mimed dancing and talking to one another so the main characters' dialogue tracks would be clean. The songs were kept for use in the final mix and were added when the film's soundtrack was built. Unusual for a studio film, editors Jerry Greenberg and David Ray—who were putting the footage together while it was being shot so that DePalma could have a look at it the day after he finished shooting—didn't use temp music. They just handed it over to Moroder, who started composing the underscoring that would enhance the dramatic scenes. Music editor Jim Henrickson was liaison between composer and editors in rushing to meet the December release date.

It was the songs that sold the film. Tracks such as "Push It to the Limit" and "Rush Rush" (referring to a cocaine high) are used to underscore montages. The music drives the film more than it adds to emotion for the viewer. It is disconnected and very much anchored in the era in which it was written, a period that includes Moroder's electronic contemporary Vangelis (*Chariots of Fire*, 1981), Wang Chung (*To Live and Die in L.A.*, 1985), Tangerine Dream (*Thief*, 1981), and other synth-pop groups. His key changes, tonal progressions, and repetitions are also reminiscent of Philip Glass.

Moroder acknowledged, in an interview with Robert Kraft on the *Spitfire Audio/The Score* podcast, that he went with mood and key changes rather than following dramatic beats. He also revealed that he had little contact with DePalma when the director was editing *Scarface* in New York. "I think he was very little involved," Moroder said. "Even the dance songs, I don't think he was very interested in. The first notes,

I just sang them to him and he liked it. That happened in New York. Then I came out [to Los Angeles] and I started to work on it. And those bass lines, I loved them. They are never on the dominant, they are always on the third or the fifth."[21]

By all these means, Moroder's score, however much it may be disconnected from time to time, provides a constant level of menace and tension that matches the threats that define the world where Tony Montana lives, and the rules under which he increasingly forces others to live as he rises to the top of a mountain built on white powder and red blood.

CHAPTER 9

The Critics Are Raving (and Ranting)

John Frankenheimer used to say, whenever people praised his remarkable 1966 film *Seconds*, which died at the box office, that it went from being a flop to being a classic without ever being a hit. *Scarface* flirts with the same fate, what with an unreliable (but widely circulated) negative cost of between $23.5 and $37 million and a domestic gross on its first release of $44,668,798 which, at last reporting, had grown to $65,884,703 worldwide.[1] Given the additional cost of prints and advertising and the generally accepted formula that a film returns to its distributor half of what it grosses in theaters—plus payments off the top to Pacino, DePalma, and Bregman if they had what are known as gross points—*Scarface* is still anywhere from $5 to $10 million from breaking even without taking into account Hollywood's infamous bookkeeping.

But if its current popularity and cultural impact are any gauge, *Scarface* is one of the most beloved and influential movies of all time. People who love it watch it repeatedly, with some having memorized whole stretches of dialogue, dressed themselves to emulate Tony Montana, festooned their walls with artwork from the film, and, in one case, assumed the name "Scarface" as a performing pseudonym. The one thing they seem to have in common is that none of them read the reviews.

This author seldom quotes critics, but in this case it's necessary in order to illustrate the hostility that greeted *Scarface* on its initial release.

First there were the reviewers themselves. In 1983—before *Ain't It Cool News*, *Rotten Tomatoes*, and the blogosphere made credentials superfluous—critics still meant something to a film's success. Not always, but diligent reviewers could often attract attention to a film that had fallen into a distributor's black hole.[2] It helped to have a powerful press advocate. This was especially true for Brian DePalma when his early champion, Pauline Kael, was reviewing for the *New Yorker*. The revered if mercurial critic had her favorites and her bête noirs and made no bones about vaunting or condemning each as appropriate. She also had a cadre of acolytes who called themselves "Kaelites" (but were dubbed "Paulettes" by those not enfolded) who followed both her lead and her lede. Kael didn't like *Scarface*, and she didn't like it in such a way that was both condescending and nasty, taking it personally that her protégé DePalma had betrayed her. In her December 26, 1983, review she pouted, saying, "Maybe in giving up his artistry DePalma was trying to identify with Pacino's performance, and trying to persuade himself that the methods he was using here were more honest, more truthful than the way he'd worked on his other pictures. *Scarface* is a long, druggy spectacle—manic yet exhausted, with DePalma entering into the derangement and trying to make something heroic out of Tony's emptiness and debauchery. The director is doggedly persistent—compellingly so—but the whole feeling of the movie is limp."[3] Her review wasn't so much an artistic appraisal as a gut reaction that read like a personal rebuke to a naughty child who had dared stray from his mother.

She was not alone in her lack of affection. Others were more harsh.

"*Scarface* . . . suffers from grotesque over-inflation," began Sheila Benson of the *Los Angeles Times*. "Brian DePalma and screenwriter Oliver Stone have started with Howard Hawks' great 1932 lean juggernaut of a film and have turned it into one of the largest empty vessels to float on an ocean of celluloid." It gets worse: "Tony Montana is unchanged from first to last dreadfulness [making] almost three hours in his company seem never ending," she spewed, and finished by calling it "the *Grand Bouffe* of filmmaking."[4]

Even the usually astute *LA Weekly*'s Michael Wilmington missed the boat when he wrote, "For about half an hour, I thought *Scarface* was going to be a great movie, or at least great trash, then suddenly it went haywire. The violence loses its edge." He ended by saying that the film should have scrapped more of the plot of the 1932 original and concentrated on the psychosis of its main character.[5]

The *New York Times*'s Vincent Canby seemed to have taken Pauline Kael's review to heart by admitting that he had been uneasy with DePalma's *Carrie* and *The Fury* while praising *Blow Out* and *Dressed to Kill*. His evenhanded notice praised the performers, especially Michelle Pfeiffer, but warned readers that "there are dismemberments, hangings, knifings, and comparatively conventional shootings by small arms and large." The review is almost cautious, as if Canby senses there is greatness on the screen but doesn't feel confident calling it such. Instead, he criticizes Hollywood for perhaps not thinking that cocaine is as big a problem as everybody outside of Hollywood knows it is, but admits that the bloody climax "is as arresting as it is terrifying."[6]

David Ansen, however, reviewing for *Newsweek*, quickly dismissed the predictable plot of the film so he could write with sophistication about the freedom filmmakers were able to enjoy in a more adult atmosphere. "What makes *Scarface* so satisfying is the obvious relish with which DePalma tells his first epic-sized tale. . . . This is a nouveau riche *Godfather*, not only a study in the brutality of first-generation criminal thugs but a panorama of arriviste bad taste." As for the gore, "Any recent horror film is more graphically grisly. If *Scarface* makes you shudder, it's from what you *think* you see and from the accumulated tension of this feral landscape. It's a grand, shallow, decadent entertainment which, like all good Hollywood gangster movies, delivers the punch and counterpunch of glamor and disgust."[7]

David Denby, in *New York* magazine, wrote with perceptive detail but ultimately dismissed *Scarface* as "a sadly overblown B movie. . . . DePalma doesn't share Scorsese's ability to make lowlife characters complex and tragically screwed-up. After the sixtieth or seventieth 'F-you!' the word loses its savor, and you long to see someone on the screen who can speak a complete sentence in English. Tony, it seems, isn't very smart or interesting. Yet the movie treats him as a classic tragic hero—we get a pattern, not the working out of an individual destiny."[8] Denby noted, in particular, the chainsaw scene in which DePalma plays off Tony rather than doomed Angel, lamenting why we couldn't see Angel's eyes pleading with Tony for help. It's a valid observation but raises a core question about the very essence of film criticism: As DePalma has said, should the critic review the film he saw or the film he wanted to see?

Andrew Sarris ventured into similar speculation but chose to trash not only the film but anybody who went in not expecting what they got. Asking quite legitimately how anybody could be shocked by finding violence in a gangster movie, he opined that the gunplay is the film's only redeeming aspect. "The trouble with the movie," he wrote, "is that there are about 20 minutes of action and two and a half hours of middle-brow attitudizing [*sic*]. It is a pity because there was a very original and very colorful movie to be made about the Cuban drug scene in Miami." Backhanding Pacino, he summarized, "Despite all the undeniable force and intensity of his talent, he just gets sillier and sillier until that awesomely awful moment when he snorts cocaine from a mountain of the white stuff on his desk and emerges like Bambi with a white nose. Perhaps the movie can be marketed as camp for the coke crowd."[9]

In dismissing *Scarface* as "another remake," Stanley Kaufman also took belated shots at the 1932 original, calling it, "overrated as are most good American films by rhapsodists eager to create pantheons." His *New Republic* pan suggests that DePalma was inspired by *The Texas Chainsaw Massacre*, that Oliver Stone's screenplay is "the very boring and predictable arc of a criminal's rise and fall," and lays into Pacino as an actor. It's unclear whether Kaufman is referring to the character or the actor when he writes that Pacino (Tony?) "has no range; he just sells violence wherever anyone will hire him to do it, like a mercenary soldier who doesn't care whom he shoots so long as he's paid. It's disgusting to see Pacino pouring the gifts he has used well elsewhere into this sewer. (He does assume a good Cuban accent.)"[10]

These major critics were not alone. Others joined the voices of discord: Ken Turan, "It's lonely at the top when you don't know any words with more than four letters" (*California* magazine, January 1984); Merrill Shindler, "The *Reefer Madness* of the 80s" (*Los Angeles* magazine, January 1984); *Time*'s Richard Corliss called DePalma "another artist of atrocity" who "applies his film school expertise" (*Time*, December 5, 1983); *Playboy* (unsigned), "nearly twice as long but not half as good" [as the 1932 version], March 1984); and the *UCLA Daily Bruin*'s headline was "DePalma's *Scarface*: Misogynistic Sleaze" (January 18, 1984). Only Guy Flatley of *Cosmopolitan* dared, in the February 1984 issue, to praise: "hypnotically operatic, impudently adventurous."

What was it that ticked off so many critics, especially given how the film's aggressive survival has repudiated all the naysayers? "It's a hugely influential movie," *Newsweek*'s David Ansen elaborates with a perspective of forty years, praising *Scarface* as "a gorgeous film, very stylish. That was the first thing I responded to. It was embraced by younger audiences, embraced by people of color, none of whom were the critics. Hollywood is filled with so many examples of movies that audiences take in a different way than the filmmakers intended. In a way, they weren't wrong; the movie was embraced by a lot of younger people who want to emulate its lifestyle. It's like when Hollywood made *The Wild One*, Brando's movie. [The filmmakers] thought they were making a movie against juvenile delinquency. But that's not how people reacted; they thought Marlon Brando was the coolest thing they'd ever seen. And I think a lot of people thought that *Scarface* was really cool even though there's no question that Tony Montana is, as I said in my review, a tragic-comic figure. DePalma doesn't think he's a great guy, but he (DePalma) sure revels in his destruction. Movies send off all sorts of different messages and it isn't always the ones that they think they're making. People watch this movie over and over again; for many young people, it's their favorite movie. They didn't care what the critics said about it." As for the violence, Ansen recalls, "People got up on their moral high horse, which happens frequently throughout history, that the sky is falling, but I think it's a combination of the very stylishness of it, which is what makes it so good, which may have made people uncomfortable. It might have been a class element involved because it's both a celebration and a satire of bad taste. That might have set them off."[11]

Having the benefit of decades of hindsight and several hits since 1983, DePalma could opine, in 1998, "The critics didn't like *Scarface* because the film was too cynical, brutal, violent, exaggerated."[12] He also recalled, "Believe me, you didn't want to be around for the preview of *Scarface*. I remember the opening night party, I thought they were going to skin me alive."[13]

"Scarface wasn't understood," Pacino told Lawrence Grobel for their memoir-interview. "It was about excess and avarice and everything being out of proportion. The character didn't try to explain himself. It was originally conceived so brilliantly by Paul Muni in the thirties, and that's who I emulated. Oliver Stone did a tremendous job bringing the character to life. It was a real piece of writing—when you hear lines quoted to you in the streets everywhere you go, and not the same lines, either. I'm walking, and somebody says, 'Hey, Tony, can I go now?' These are the kinds of lines they quote. The picture had a fire to it. That was part of Brian's concept, to do everything in an extraordinary way—to have the violence blown up, the language blown up. The spirit of it was Brechtian, operatic. It didn't opt for sentiment but had an almost fable-like quality to it. It was probably the most popular picture I ever made, but the reaction to it was stranger than to any of my other films. The picture was perceived by some as a failure, but it wasn't. It was a lot of movie. You go to a movie, you get a *lot* of movie with *Scarface*. That picture did something to me."[14]

One surprising critic of the film was Oliver Stone, who complained that the politics were buried in "a lot of superficial trivia. To some, it's a movie about cars, palaces, money and coke . . . it's about what those things do to you. That theme got lost."[15]

Was DePalma ahead of his time? Were his critics wrong? Did they fail to see the same movie that audiences saw, or were they turned off by something that subsequent audiences no longer care about? Perspective might be gained by referring to the reception that Howard Hawks's 1932 *Scarface* received from the critics whose positive but qualified reaction at a private screening was used by Howard Hughes to pry the film away from the censors' hands. The comments from 1932 hauntingly presage those of 1983. "After giving this Howard Hughes production all the credit it deserves for gripping characterizations, fine direction, and other unusual production values," guardedly wrote the trade magazine *Film Daily* in 1932, "it still remains a most unpleasant affair, not to be recommended for family trade or for anyone with anything but a stout heart and hard-boiled aspect toward human life."[16] Mourdant Hall in the *New York Times* wrote, somewhat condescendingly, "It is a stirring picture, efficiently directed and capably acted, but as was once said of *The Covered Wagon*, that it was all very well if you liked wagons, so this is an excellent diversion for those who like to take an afternoon or an evening off to study the activities of cowardly thugs."[17] Only James Agee, who was frequently ahead of his time, called it "the masterpiece of gangster films [without] a trace of sentimentality."[18]

And yet, allowing for public reaction to their plaudits, one senses that the major critics in 1932 were more in tune than their 1983 brethren. How could this happen? Were the reviewers inveighing against the Production Code that was, even with its lax enforcement, eviscerating the movies? When and how did 1983's *Scarface* cease to be merely a movie and become a cultural phenomenon? And when would Brian DePalma be able to utter one of the biggest *I told you so*s in Hollywood history?

Code Blues

The first Motion Picture Production Code included a list of *Don't*s and *Be Careful*s compiled in 1930 by motion picture industry advisors at the behest of Will H. Hays, president of the Motion Picture Producers and Distributors of America. It was no secret that it was created to forestall a nationwide movement to establish censorship boards all over the country that could decide, on a local basis, which films and what part of those films could or could not be shown in their area theaters. If only to avoid death by a thousand cuts, Hollywood took the bull by the scissors and insisted they could do it better.

For its first four years the Code was de facto voluntary; there was too much money to be made with salacious, suggestive, and even vulgar content. Soon, however, public outcry from moralists elevated, and the studios, hit financially by the Depression, found themselves vulnerable when ticket sales dropped off, and they were ready to listen. In 1934, Hays promoted Joseph I. (for Ignatius) Breen, who had been doing public relations for Hays, to enforce the Code.

Breen, a staunch churchgoer and skillful diplomat, ran the Production Code office with an unwavering hand until his retirement in 1954. He was succeeded by Geoffrey Shurlock, who was more urbane but just as tough. Not until 1968, under Jack Valenti, would the Code awaken to the massive changes in the social fabric of America and revise itself almost out of existence with the introduction of the first version of what is now the movie rating system.

Cleverly, the Code office studiously refused to call itself a censorship bureau. Rather, they simply withheld the essential

Production Code Seal until the filmmakers censored themselves. It was de facto censorship then, and still is. In the pre-Code seal days of 1932, when *Scarface* was in production and nearing release, Will Hays and his staff still exerted pressure to make cuts, to add moralizing scenes, and to change the ending in order to bring the film into compliance with Code ideals. Despite this, an unusual number of probable Code violations managed to get through for reasons that do not always appear in MPPDA correspondence, among them:

- The waiter cleaning up after Louis Costillo's stag party at the beginning of the film finds a brassiere and falsies. (Violation: showing personal undergarments. Stag parties are also to be avoided)

- When Tony is first seen in the barbershop, he tells the detective that he is getting a massage. In Chicago in those days, some massage parlors were being used as fronts for whorehouses, and getting a massage came to mean—well, the Code prohibited showing that, too. (Violation: prostitution)

- Tony strikes a match on the detective's shield. (Violation: disrespect for the law)

- A police detective asks, "Should I slap it out of him, chief?" meaning should he beat Tony Camonte. (Violation: third degree and aggressive forms of interrogation)

- Poppy calls Tony's jewelry "effeminate." (Violation: mention of "sexual perversion" [*sic*])

- When Tony chases away Cesca's suitor and tells

her, "I'm your brother!," she responds with the leading "You don't act it! You act more like . . . I don't know, sometimes I think you're . . ." before he cuts her off. (Violation: incest)

- There's innuendo about O'Hara "hanging out in a flower shop." (Violation: "sexual perversion")

- When a dead body is thrown from a car as a warning to Lovo, one of Lovo's men says, "Jesus!" (Violation: use of the Lord's name in vain)

- Poppy is portrayed as a kept woman. (Violation: A mistress who doesn't suffer a sad fate, unless you count getting written out of the picture)

- Tony and his boys attend the play *Rain* and refer to Sadie Thompson as a hustler. (Violation: prostitution)

- The half-salute that Tony gives police could be construed as flipping someone off. (Violation: obscene hand gestures)

- Trying to locate Guino at various women's homes, Tony refers to him as a tomcat. (Violation: referring to a man as being randy and use of the term *tomcat*)

- The portrayal of Italian-Americans could be considered offensive to foreign or ethnic groups. (Violation: as stated)

- Tony's display of affection to the dying Cesca in the final shoot-out could easily be interpreted as incestuous. (Violation: incest).

But the 1932 *Scarface* had nothing compared with the pageant of profanity that writer Oliver Stone, producer Martin Bregman, director Brian DePalma, and ad-libbing actors put into their 1983 remake. Even though the Code had been relaxed in 1968, the shock of violence, swearing, and attitude that exploded from the screen was something the Classification and Rating Administration (CARA) hadn't encountered since, well, since DePalma's provocative 1980 film *Dressed to Kill*.

The boundaries of screen violence had been shifting since 1966, when Arthur Penn included the brutal beating of Marlon Brando in *The Chase* (not that Brando had shunned violence in his own 1961 film, *One-Eyed Jacks*). Penn continued with the then-shocking "face shot" in 1967's *Bonnie and Clyde*, in which Clyde Barrow (Warren Beatty) fires a gun through his getaway car window into the face of a pursuing bank teller (Russ Saunders). Showing a gun fired in the same frame as its victim was banned by the Code, which was weakening as American audiences matured. The next year, Peter Yates staged an anatomically correct shotgun murder in *Bullitt* (1968), blowing away half a man's face and shoulder. Finally in 1969, Sam Peckinpah did it all at once in slow motion in *The Wild Bunch*. The revised Code found a way to deal with each of them by marking *Bullitt* as "Mature/PG" and *The Wild Bunch* "R."

Brian DePalma outdid everything to that date in *Scarface*. His film was so powerful that CARA couldn't handle it. It was not DePalma's first tangle with them, but this time he vowed to win on his terms. Mindful that studios don't like X-rated (now NC-17) films because they restrict audiences and limit advertising outlets, they almost always demand an R rating or better, and it is usually the filmmaker's contractual duty to deliver it.

The criteria of ratings constantly shift, and this add to both the confusion and the controversy. What earns an X? What needs to be cut to earn an R? What is the context—i.e., how is the violence justified and what does it do to the people involved?

DePalma's attitude was surprising and encouraging. At a thirty-fifth anniversary reunion in 2018 at Tribeca in New York, he recalled that he submitted his film four times to the ratings board and each time it received an X. Finally he said, "I've had it with these people. I'm not taking anything more out. And I told Marty [Bregman], and Marty said, 'We'll go to war with these people.'"[19] They filed for an appeal and Bregman wanted to take in the third cut. DePalma held firm and insisted that they put the movie back the way he originally edited it, figuring that, if he was going to get an X anyway, he might as well get it with his preferred cut. The studio objected, but DePalma said, "Why not? They didn't have an answer for that. And we won! It was one of the great moments that we had to beat the censor board."[20]

The details of the skirmishes were excruciating and filled the newspapers. During the ordeal, DePalma and Bregman complained that ratings board chief Richard Heffner was "overly demanding" and "had an axe to grind" because of the public opposition the filmmaker had given him over the X forced at first on *Dressed to Kill*.[21]

"Heffner told me it was the skill with which I rendered the scenes that made them seem excessively violent," DePalma told Aljean Harmetz of the *New York Times*. "I was being censored because of my skill. Now Heffner wants to make me sweat." Responded Heffner, "That's nonsense, and how do you respond to nonsense? We aren't waging a vendetta against Mr. DePalma. I never considered anything he said as a personal attack. The cult of personality looms large in

Hollywood and it is difficult for some people to understand that we rate films, not their makers."[22]

Predictably, when the ratings board upheld their X, Bregman and DePalma appealed to the full board of the MPAA and submitted letters of support from critic Jay Cocks (an old friend of DePalma's), Roger Ebert, producer Bob Rehme, and Nick Navarro, a narcotics officer who urged young people to see the film because of its accurate portrayal of the "ugliness behind the drug trade."[23] (This reasoning will become noteworthy in discussing the film's resurgence within the hip-hop community.)

When two psychiatrists—Dr. H. Feinberg and Dr. Richard Atkins—were engaged by the producers, they testified that children above the age of thirteen would not be harmed by the film because, by that age, they are able to distinguish screen life from real life, the board agreed to give the film an R, and it premiered in New York on December 1, 1983, with a national break on December 9, 1983.[24] Producers also made the argument that Tony's violent ending would serve as a lesson to anyone who might have been tempted to enter the drug trade. Even Pacino has been quoted as saying, "I don't think you feel like you want to have coke when you leave that movie. It doesn't seem to be pro-drug at all."[25]

Oliver Stone has a more cynical view of the way the film was rated, and one can infer that it's a "nudge-nudge, wink-wink" alliance between the studios and the censors, with the filmmakers caught in the middle. "The divorce between reality and political correctness is enormous," he says, "and the movie industry has never been able to solve it. We know, everyone knows, what's going on in the sense that, in a war, the GIs know before the generals, and in the front lines of the movie business the people on the set know what's going on, they know the score; they're very sophisticated people. They always pull you back, the censorship boards. This film was messed with so much, and turned up so much publicity about how many times DePalma had to go back to the MPAA, it became silly. And I think DePalma—at that time we were not talking anymore—but I had nothing to do with the postproduction process, and I drifted away from it, but I heard these stories, and I know he was frustrated about that. I had these same problems later with *Natural Born Killers* [1994], bringing me back and making cuts. It's a demeaning process. It wears you out."[26]

In other countries, not surprisingly, the film was heavily censored. Amazingly, there is a television and airline version that uses alternate shots, cutaways, and looped (substituted) dialogue to create a presentation suitable for general viewing. Because the loss of violence and profanity noticeably shortened the TV version, some deleted scenes were restored to bring the television and airline editions up to normal length. The results are a triumph of the editorial and censorial arts. Samples can be seen and heard—or, rather, not seen and not heard—on the 35th Anniversary DVD and Blu-ray.

Scarface may contain an overwhelming amount of violence, but it has no sex. There is only one moment that comes close, and that's seeing Manny in bed with a woman when Tony calls to meet him at Frank's office after the nightclub assassination attempt. The film does, however, contain liberal use of a well-known word for sex, a word that begins with the letter "F."

The F-Word

Scarface contains a blistering number of *fuck*s. Not the act, the word. Its use of rough language was second only to its use of even rougher violence. Yet the overkill of the F-word seems entirely appropriate to the over-the-top story being told. At the same time, it's a reflection of the decline of American speech, so much so that the well-born Elvira is driven to ask Tony in one scene, "Can't you stop saying *fuck*?" As social observer/comedian Lewis Black says, "In New York, *fuck* isn't a word, it's a comma." And its use in the screen has a complicated history.

For starters, there is no agreement on the number of F-bombs. The Family Media Guide says 207, IMDb trivia says 226, someone on the social media site Mastodon says 132, a posting on Funtrivia says 170, a *Scarface* tribute blog says both 206 and 218, and YouTube has two frenetically edited compilations of the word's use in the movie itself, one of which says 196 and the other of which goes uncounted. This author counted an even 200 *fuck*s, plus or minus 10 percent because some of them were mumbled, and that will be the number used herein. At times they zoomed by so fast that it was like counting taxicabs in Midtown Manhattan at rush hour. The real heroes in the enterprise were the people who wrote the DVD/Blu-ray subtitles and the studio clerks tasked with typing an exact cutting continuity for copyright and foreign language purposes. Even Oliver Stone, who wrote them into his script, says that Pacino "added a lot of the *fuck*s that I didn't write."[27] In fact, the film's shooting script contains, by the author's count, 122 *fuck*s in its 182 pages (including their use in scenes that do not appear in the finished film).

However many times *Scarface* gives a *fuck*, it is no longer the movies' most prolific wielder of the fabled swear word. Jeremy Urquhart, who braved the fusillade of F-bombs for *Collider*, lists ten films with more F-words (as of June 1, 2022) than even *Goodfellas* (1990) with its 315. By this ranking, *Scarface*'s 200 Fs is practically virginal:[28]

The Outpost (2020): 355

Alpha Dog (2006): 367

Straight Outta Compton (2015): 392

Nil by Mouth (1997): 428

Summer of Sam (1999): 435

Casino (1995): 452

Uncut Gems (2019): 560

The Wolf of Wall Street (2013): 569

F*ck (2005): 857

Swearnet: The Movie (2014): 935

Mainstream movies have always been uncomfortable with the F-word. While the Production Code, when it was revised by Jack Valenti in 1968, acknowledged that profanity was sometimes necessary, its ratings board nevertheless came down hard on its use. If a child character swears, for example, the film suffers. There is also alleged bargaining between the board and producers over the number of each cuss word that can appear (e.g., "I'll trade you one *fuck* for three *shits*."). From the days when *Gone with the Wind* (1939) gave the censors nosebleeds with its use of the word *damn*, by 1970 Robert Altman was able to include John Schuck's ad-lib "all right, bub, your fuckin' head is comin' right off" in the football game that concludes *M*A*S*H* (1970), making it the first American studio film to go there and still get an R rating rather than an X.

Use of the F-word used to earn a film an automatic R rating, but the MPAA has flirted with duality over the years, most famously with two important films in the 1970s: *All the President's Men* (1976) and Woody Allen's *Manhattan* (1979). In *All the President's Men*, Jason Robards warns Robert Redford and Dustin Hoffman not to "fuck up" their Watergate investigation, yet the film earned a PG. Three years later, *Manhattan* was given an R because Diane Keaton used the F-word in the phrase, "I'm honest; I say what's on my mind and if you can't take it, then fuck off," and it was determined that this use meant sex. The difference is arcane but clear: If you say it, you get a PG, if you mean it, you get an R, but if you do it, you get an X.

Western civilization has had a long and uncomfortable relationship with the F-word. Part of this comes from an overriding Christian ethic that sex is dirty (or, as Woody Allen says, "It is if you're doing it right"). Of its many alleged derivations, the one that seems the most constant is that its origin, according to the *Oxford English Dictionary*, is Germanic (*ficken*), Dutch (*fokken*), Afrikaans (*fuk*), and Icelandic (*fokka*), meaning variously "to strike" or "to breed" and, yes, even Old French ("to have sex"), thereby indirectly legitimizing the exculpatory phrase, "Pardon my French."

It did not, however, arise as an acronym for "For Unlawful Carnal Knowledge," "Fornication Under Consent of the King," "Forbidden Use of Carnal Knowledge," or similar wordplay. In point of fact, nobody really knows where it came from, but there is little question that it's here to stay and continues to shock.

Shock, of course, is the purpose of profanity in general. *Scarface*'s use of the F-word exists on several levels.

First, of course, is to shock filmgoers of 1983. After a while, however, its abundance becomes almost comical, so much so that Elvira even mentions it to Tony. And yet, thirdly, it becomes symbolic of Tony's ultimate powerlessness, and not just Tony's but the powerlessness of disenfranchised people in general. Tony may have guns, a snazzy car, a mansion, a pet tiger, and nifty clothes, but he is still street. In America, money may buy status but it cannot buy class. The insult hurled at Hollywood's founding moguls reflected this when it was said of them, "from Poland to polo in one generation." Just as Eliza Doolittle's Cockney vulgarity returns when she is surprised by her absent father's reappearance in *Pygmalion*, so is language a dead giveaway for one's origins. The promiscuous utterance of *fuck* in *Scarface*, as in other films, where it ceases to be shocking and does, in essence, become a comma, is a demonstration of its users' impotence. Viewers who identify too closely with Tony Montana are saying as much about society as they are admitting it of themselves.

CHAPTER 10

Renaissance

If Luke 4:24 is correct that "No prophet is accepted in his own country," then *Scarface* has enjoyed not just a renaissance but a resurrection. It has become a film that people watch, rewatch, and quote—a picture whose lifestyle some seek to emulate; a work in which others find a metaphor for America; and a viewing experience that is both inspiring and cathartic.

It's a safe bet that none of this was imagined by the people who made the film.

More to the point, where were all those fans when the picture was new?

In their November-December 1974 issue, the journal *Film Comment*[1] published a list of reasons—"Why a Film Flops"—that reflected the way the industry thinks, or how its executives deflect blame. Excuses included "It was ahead of its time"; "It was over the heads of its audience"; "the weather"; "sports competing on TV"; and other flimsy pretexts. In truth, as William Goldman said, "nobody knows anything," a sentiment that is misunderstood to mean ignorance when, in fact, he meant that the elements for movie success are unknowable and unpredictable.

What makes a film popular? If anyone knew, they'd bottle it. As Sam Goldwyn once said, "If people don't want to see a film, nothing can stop them." For over 120 years the film industry has honed its advertising and publicity machinery to the point where they still don't know for sure what will work. Sure, they can spend a fortune to "buy a gross" on opening weekend, but come Monday morning the film itself must stand on its own, after which word-of-mouth will do the rest. The trick, as in any matchmaking enterprise, is finding the audience who can best appreciate the product and then pray that there are enough of them to put it into profits.

Universal Pictures had no way of knowing that the audience for *Scarface* was different than the audience they thought it would be. Even Martin Bregman, Brian DePalma, Oliver Stone, and Al Pacino had no idea. But they were smart enough to ride the crest of the popularity wave once it appeared.

It had happened before. Some films became popular for reasons opposite those that their makers intended. *Reefer Madness* (1936), for example, was meant to warn people about the dangers of marijuana until it was discovered and ridiculed by potheads in the 1960s, who got stoned and laughed at it. *The Rocky Horror Picture Show* (1975) flopped first run but became a celebration when it was discovered by an alienated fan base at midnight shows. Did the people who made *The Wizard of Oz* (1939) predict that an album like Pink Floyd's *The Dark Side of the Moon* (1973) would prove more profound than the film's own soundtrack?[2] Did Ed Wood know that *Plan 9 from Outer Space* (1959) would become beloved for all the wrong reasons? Did Walt Disney want kids to catch a buzz before seeing *Fantasia* (1940)?[3] The same for *2001: A Space Odyssey* (1968) that was drifting at the box office until it was advertised as "the ultimate trip," a phrase conferred upon it by, of all places, the *Christian Science Monitor*, the newspaper of a church that eschews drugs. *The Shawshank Redemption* is the most well-known modern film that became a hit on cable TV and home video rather than on its 1994 theatrical release.

But *Scarface* goes beyond all of those. It is a phenomenon. Not only was it discovered by a generation that wasn't old enough to see it when it was new, it has acquired a place in cultural history by being celebrated as an endorsement of a way of life that its own makers reject.

"It was ahead of its time," says Christine La Monte, who was Universal's director of publicity in New York at the time it came out. Her appraisal, which hasn't changed since then, was "There were so many great performances in it: Michelle Pfeiffer, Mary Elizabeth Mastrantonio. And especially the art direction. The choreography was like a dance of war of drug lords. It was opera on the scale of Coppola, in a way; the same kind of vision."[4]

That regard was shared by the whole studio, who put major effort behind promoting it. Universal prepared for the December 1, 1983, New York premiere with a VIP screening followed by a party at Sardi's landmark theatrical restaurant. The guest list included such luminaries as Kurt Vonnegut, Jr., Cher, Raquel Welch, Lucille Ball, and Eddie Murphy. "Martin Scorsese sat behind me," Steven Bauer recalls, "and Cher was with us. The movie's about to start. I had not seen it. The moment I come on the screen with my hair slicked back, Cher goes, 'Rocky!' [Rocky is Bauer's nickname]. I was just trying to concentrate, what do I come off as? I was really comfortable because I saw that my performance, I was part of the story, I was believable. And then afterwards the praise from all our peers, at Sardi's, they all lined up, all these people, all these New York actors and they lined up and came to our table to tell us how they loved our movie. I'm so proud of it. But then I remember Al telling me, "Don't read the reviews tomorrow." And the next day 94 percent of the critics were horrible."[5]

The first hint that something was wrong was when Vonnegut walked out of the screening during the chainsaw scene. The audience's discomfort continued to the end, when the film's thoughtful dedication to Howard Hawks and Ben

Hecht drew boos.[6] Then the critics, who were aware of the filmmaker's tussle with the MPAA ratings board, piled on.

Although it earned fair theatrical receipts, in summer 1984 *Scarface* went where all soft grossers went at the time: home video and laserdisc. Priced at $79.95 in the days before affordable sell-through, the two-cassette, two-disc sets nevertheless set records with sales of 100,000 units (approximately $5 million) as of June 22, 1984, primarily to Blockbuster and other rental stores who seemed to sense something that theater owners did not.

Meanwhile, to say the least, Universal was disappointed. "It makes me think of painters who were not accepted in the time they did their work," La Monte says. "People couldn't understand it, and then, decades later, they were appreciated, and sometimes even more than that."[7]

There's no way of knowing for sure, but it was probably the film's repeated showings on HBO starting in 1985 that exposed it to its more appreciative audience: rappers.

"*Scarface* was dead and buried until hip-hop rediscovered it," Steven Bauer told an audience at Tribeca in April 2018, as reported by Hardeep Phull. "In the early 90s I would start getting recognized on the street by rappers. They would say, 'Oh, I gotta give you respect—that's *the* movie.' I didn't know all of them, so I would have to ask someone, 'Who was that?'"[8]

Even Brian DePalma confessed that he was unaware of its popularity with the hip-hop generation until Universal approached him in the 1990s for permission to rerelease it with a hip-hop soundtrack replacing the Giorgio Moroder score. He instantly turned them down.

"*Scarface* is loved by rappers with an unwavering devotion that can safely be called an obsession," wrote Miakkanatisse in the *Grio*. "Jay-Z has dedicated countless rap lyrics and interludes to the film, from the intro to his debut album all the way up to the lyric, '*Scarface* the movie did more than Scarface the rapper for me.' It definitely wasn't for the masses. But the film found an unlikely home in the black community, slowly becoming a requirement in hip-hop references 101."[9]

Historian Lucas Garrison cites rappers Kool G Rap and Nas [Escobar]'s "Fast Life" as the first song to sample *Scarface*. It was released in New York on November 14, 1995.[10] Also in the mix was Raekwon from the Wu-Tang Clan with "Criminology," from his album *Only Built 4 Cuban Linx*, also 1995. Pop culture observer Ken Tucker in *Scarface Nation* links the earlier 1992 song "Bush Killa" by the rapper Paris as the start of the wave.[11] Jay-Z—who has declared *Scarface* his favorite film— referenced it with "Can't Knock the Hustle" (*Reasonable Doubt*, 1996).[12] A partial list of additional samplings and inspirations includes "Me" (Chief Keef), "Scarface" (Soulja Boy), "Get TF Out My Face" (Rich Homie Quan featuring Young Thug), "I'm Still" (DJ Khaled featuring Ace Hood, Chris Brown, Wally and Wiz Khalifa), "Rhyme Room" (Yelawolf featuring Killer Mike and Raekwon), "Live Freestyle" (The Notorious B.I.G. and Tupac Shakur), "Tony Montana" (Future featuring Drake), "Ghetto Dreams" (Common featuring Nas), "Trap Boom" (Three 6 Mafia featuring Project Pat), "Hogg in the Game" (Pimp C), "Hood Fame" (Big K.R.I.T.), "Money Machine" (Chainz), "Fine China (Remix)" (Chris Brown featuring Common), "Thief's Theme" (Nas), and the list goes on. There's even a rock band, Blink-182, named for how many times the F-word is used in the film.[13] Some of the songs play tribute in lyrics, some sample dialogue, and some use a combination to celebrate Tony Montana's rise to power. But rarely, it needs to be said, his fall.

Therein lies the film's fascination, and with good reason. "After *Scarface* comes out, the effect on my crew of those who went to see it immediately was overwhelming," recalls Bill Stephney, who created the rap group Public Enemy with his friend Chuck D and is further credited with bringing politics into the hip-hop mix. "Everybody's speaking in a Tony Montana patois accent and quoting him. It's a phenomenon. Around '80 and '84 hip-hop is developing in the New York area, and then the movie comes out that celebrates a guy on the streets with nothing [who turns] the drug trade into a fortune. I think that resonated with young black men who were largely now being raised by the culture of hip-hop, of aggression, of an in-your-face aspect to the culture. It's also the time of the boom box where you're walking around cities in neighborhoods and basically putting your culture in people's ears. You're saying, 'If my grandfather and great-grandfather were the invisible men, marginalized—*I'm not.*' Those elements seemed, to me, around '83 or '84, to coalesce, and that's where you get Tony Montana and *Scarface* being a foundational influence for hip-hop."[14]

Why did it take a new generation to discover the film? Prevailing wisdom says that young people born into the seventies and eighties saw their own values and aspirations reflected on the screen, and they were cynical aspirations in conflict with those of their parents. "I started to hear *Scarface* mentioned on the MTV *Cribs* shows," says Charles Coletta, PhD, professor of popular culture at Bowling Green State University. *Cribs* began in 2000 visiting (as the promos said) "the domestic sanctuaries that some of today's most favorite stars call home." Some of them would make Tony Montana's mansion look like a Motel 6.

"Not that I was a frequent watcher," Coletta goes on, "but I did notice that a lot of the hip-hop and rappers did like it. I think a lot of it goes back to that gangster persona or archetype in American popular culture: someone who's independent, maybe a little shady, but they're a go-getter and they see what they want and they go get it. That archetype resonates, and it's such an over-the-top film that people just get immersed in it."[15]

As for the film's infamous disclaimer that was appended to mollify the Cuban community, Coletta—whose PhD thesis was on Hollywood's portrayal of Italian-Americans—says, "I'm half Italian and half Irish. No group is ever satisfied by how they're portrayed. Hollywood does deal in stereotypes. Every Italian isn't a gangster and every German isn't a Nazi, but that's part of popular culture. I don't need a disclaimer. I know what I'm getting into. I know it's a movie and that they're acting."[16]

What's interesting is that African American audiences see *Scarface* as their story even though Black actors have no significant presence in the film. Bill Stephney knows why the story transcends race. "For that generation—for those who are nineteen, twenty, or twenty-one in 1983 to 1984—you're a product of the Civil Rights generation and integration. You're relating to people beyond race. We thought, from our generation, that white people were segregated on the basis of race, not black people. Tony Montana, for teenagers, at that point, is just a cool guy that teenagers are into.

"It developed this cult status," he continues. "Then, later on, as the crack trade developed in New York City in the eighties, where's the area that it's going to be most prominent in terms of the trade? I always say that you probably can put the impact of *Scarface* culturally in the area of young black males who decide that the drug game, even if they had a mom who was a teacher and a dad who was a corrections officer, fell in love with the romanticism they found in *Scarface*, and that's where the energy for gangsters and hip-hop derive from."[17]

For whom was the movie originally intended? Given the

track record and appeal of the filmmakers, in 1983 it would have been a general audience, "general" meaning (for an action film) males eighteen to forty-nine with no racial distinction. And since males under eighteen follow males over eighteen, this is why the R rating was so important. But how closely did Universal break it down?

Although he didn't handle the film, Kevin Goetz offers insight into the process. Goetz, author of the book *Audience-ology: How Moviegoers Shape the Films We Love*, is an entertainment research expert whose company, Screen Engine/ASI, has guided thousands of films to market. "In general," he explains, "all studios look at race and ethnicity both ways. It's important to look at the total audience, but still not ignore the cultural cues of any one community. The U.S. has turned very much toward 'minority/majority.' In fact, California, Hawaii, Arizona, Texas, and Washington, DC, have turned already, that is to say that there are more minority residents than Caucasian residents. By the 2040s, it will be the entire country—and that's driven mostly by the younger generations. When you look at moviegoing habits today, that number of Caucasians decreases more than the general population. African Americans make up twelve percent of the population but make up sixteen percent of moviegoers today. So that demographic segment is indeed an important part of box office success."[18]

"It was probably the right movie at the right time," says Charles Coletta. "Cocaine was in all the media in the late seventies and early eighties, but I think it was sort of a perfect storm. It hit all the cultural buttons at the right time. It is a well-made film. Is it the greatest gangster movie of all time? Probably not. But it does carry you along, and Pacino is over the top, maybe more so later [in the film], but it's a well-made film and that's why people like it."[19]

It also carried the cache of being "discovered" by people who, arguably, were not targeted in the original advertising campaign and therefore were unaware of it. "It got a number of Razzies and was pooh-poohed by the mainstream press and characterized as, sort of, weird and operatic and certainly not the same movie that Howard Hawks made fifty years earlier," explains Kevin Goetz. "But the thing about *Scarface* is that the depth of affection and breadth of impact across the world was completely unexpected and no one at the studio anticipated just how hot it would perform, and it was driven almost entirely by DVD.

"It was not just a U.S. thing," he continues. "I have only seen that cult status occur with a small number of movies through their DVD life after their initial theatrical runs. That model really doesn't exist anymore. We have a different model now. But, yes, the urban audience took a shine to it and really could relate to it in some deep way. And the younger generation discovered it as a sort of 'retro-cool' movie. I believe people are enamored by Tony and his story. I think, at the heart of it, there is this unabashedly, unapologetic character in Tony that was, in some way, the ultimate underdog. There have certainly been a number of underdog stories, but this is a true immigrant experience and, in its own perverse way, it's the American Dream. The urban audience quite likely recognized that in a more visceral way. Here's this guy who manages to do whatever it is his way—how fucked anyone coming in from the outside is, how fucked the system is, how fucked the odds are, and this was the gritty, authentic representation of that. There's an archetypal reason for it resonating, particularly with disenfranchised groups."[20]

Accordingly, author L. A. Banks, who wrote *Scarface: The Beginning*, recognized early on this affinity in the audience that would soon make the movie their own. "I went and saw *Scarface* in the hood," she recalls. "I was in the Black neighborhood. It was West Philadelphia on the big screen and it was one of those movies where you could yell back at the screen. And people went, 'Oh! Yeah!' Everybody was engaged with the movie."[21]

These yearnings often manifest themselves in wretched excess. Actress-singer Maria Conchita Alonso, who performs "*Vamos a Bailar*" on the soundtrack (as Maria Conchita), says, "When people who come from nothing all of a sudden have a lot, you overdo things. You overdress, you buy everything because you never had anything. So that was the way I saw it. It was ridiculous, but they used to do that."[22]

Scarface is an unashamed 170-minute commercial for overindulgence. Audiences, particularly in communities of color, are attracted to it because of Tony's excess and the unfiltered joy he takes in getting even with his enemies. The irony is that this is the exact opposite of the argument its producers made to persuade the MPAA ratings board to change the film from an X to an R, namely that Tony gets his comeuppance at the end, so how could it inspire young people to enter the sordid drug trade? "But the movie is more about the journey, not the ending," notes Kevin Goetz.[23]

Agrees Bill Stephney, "There was a cognitive dissonance to this day. There were drug dealers from that era from New York City who began to name themselves after Tony Montana. There is a rapper who calls himself Scarface.[24] It's so interesting because a lot of our struggle today is 'How did we get to that point where the central influence on young black culture is drug dealing and gang-banging?' Point to the top ten rappers at any one time today and nine out of ten came out of a gang or drug dealing experience. How do you compare that to young black artists of forty years ago where everybody came out of playing in bands?"[25]

Music referencing aside, *Scarface* has lately also generated a grotesque amount of merch (merchandising)—*grotesque* in that collectors want to own a piece of the Tony Montana experience beyond the excitement of the movie itself.

Traditional movie merchandising includes T-shirts, action figures, baseball hats, lapel pins, and other novelties that may be specific to the theme of a particular film. *Scarface* knows no limits. Not only is there a vast assortment of T-shirts, but there's an entire fashion line, including sport shirts, shorts, athletic jackets, socks, hoodies, and sunglasses. There are blankets, wall clocks, neon signs flashing "The World is Yours," metal and canvas art posters, stickers, smartphone protective boxes,[26] commemorative plaques with a frame of film embedded, a coloring book, leatherette wallets, twelve-inch authentic faux brass "The World is Yours" statues, perfume (presumably Elvira's fragrance, not Tony's), party decorations, pop sockets (rubber grips), a wall decoration with Tony Montana replacing Jesus Christ, a "Scarface Street" road sign, and action figures for the kiddies. Some of the drawings of Tony Montana even manage to look like Al Pacino. There are also CDs of the original, remastered, and expanded musical score by Giorgio Moroder. Those wishing to possess deluxe copies of the DVD have a choice of several limited edition boxed sets starting at $30, including the film, stills, and fancy packaging. All that's missing is branded amber cocaine vials, crack pipes, scales, toot straws, and pill grinders.

Perhaps the most spiritually connected merch is sold on the Scarface Store website[27] belonging to Dennis Plaksin and his business partner Angel Salazar, the movie's Chi Chi. "The clothes sell, especially around Father's Day because it's a great gift," Plaksin reports. "We have beach slippers on the website, T-shirts, towels, bags—just kinda cool merchandise. Coasters are available. We try to do father/ guy gifts, but you'd be surprised how many females follow *Scarface*. There've been some music videos, commercials; whatever we can do to promote. And whenever Angel's here, we try to go out and promote. Starting this year, I'm going to source out some more artists to come up with more creative stuff. And these artists come from all over the world: One guy's from Brazil, one guy's in Argentina, I have a guy in Russia, I have a guy in Denmark doing stuff, and a couple of local guys. The fan base spreads worldwide. It's amazing."

Plaksin has avoided selling more scurrilous merchandise such as 1-gram amber bottles and pill crushers, but he does hold out hope for an offbeat tie-in. "We spoke to Gurkha, which is a cigar company. My idea was to make a cigar box—matter of fact, I'm still gonna follow up on that—so that, when you open the cigar box, there's a mirror. Then it becomes a table with a mirror, and need I say any more?"[28]

Naturally, there's a video game. *Scarface: The World Is Yours* was created by Radical Entertainment in 2006 for PlayStation 2, Xbox, and Microsoft Windows and was published by Vivendi Games. It was written by David McKenna with underscoring music by Marc Baril. A version with enhanced graphics was released the next year for Wii. A point-of-view driving and shooter game which hypothesizes that Tony Montana survived assassination to wreak revenge on those who opposed him, it dodges the film's moral that the world may be yours, but not for long. Tony is voiced by Andre Sogliuzzo (who was reportedly personally approved by Al Pacino) with Steven Bauer, Robert Loggia, and Al Israel recreating their roles of Manny, Frank, and Hector the Toad, respectively. A three-and-a-half-hour playthrough (in which the viewer is passive) was posted on YouTube by Mafia Game Videos in 2022.[29] Like all such games it is monumentally violent and searingly profane, no one ever has to reload (in the film, they do), and while lip movement leaves a lot to be desired with the current state of rendering, the animators and designers have perfectly captured Pacino's/Tony's swagger.

The plot is that four rival gangs have taken over Tony's empire (Little Havana, Downtown, South Beach, and North Beach) and Tony must recapture them in order to take on Sosa. Like many video games, it suffers from the uncanny valley in being unable to render human figures with believable eyelines, but the action is appropriately cathartic. Songs are provided by Giorgio Moroder, Debbie Harry, Beth Anderson, Arthur Barrow, Peter Bellotte, Rick James, Earth, Wind & Fire, the Dazz Band, Cameo, 20/20, Iggy Pop, Treacherous Three, Run DMC, Planet Patrol, Public Enemy, LL Cool J, Grandmaster Flash, Mongo Santamaría, Peter Tosh, Black Uhuru, Toots and the Maytals, Waylon Jennings, and a dozen equally eclectic recording artists. In other words, when Universal couldn't re-score the film, their music division had a field day with the video game.

Together with the continuing sale of anniversary DVDs and Blu-ray editions, including the 4K Ultra High Definition release, *Scarface* should be well into profits by now, on paper, at least. Not bad for a movie that pushed the limits, broke the rules, played to the wrong audience, and sidetracked the careers of the talented yet unknowingly prescient people who created it.

SIDEBAR

The World Is Still Yours (Remakes)

Albert Einstein said that the definition of insanity is doing the same thing over and over and expecting a different result.

While this certainly applies to the scientific method, it also has echoes in Hollywood, where the creative method is anything but scientific. Forty years after *Scarface* failed to meet initial commercial expectations, they're trying to remake it—specifically director Luca Guadagnino (*Suspiria*, 2018) and producer Dylan Clark (*The Rise of the Planet of the Apes*, 2011) from a screenplay by Joel and Ethan Coen (*Fargo*, 2014), according to a report by Gabriella Paiella in GQ.[30]

At this writing, Paiella's is the latest in a string of reports that began in 2011 with an item on the industry trade site Deadline.com announcing that Martin Bregman would produce a version which was neither a sequel nor a remake, to be written by David Ayer (*The Fast and the Furious*, 2001) and directed by David Yates (*Harry Potter and the Order of the Phoenix*, 2007).[31] A sequel titled *Son of Tony* with Cuban rapper Cuban Link (Felix Delgado) writing and starring was mentioned on Wikipedia, but the citations are incomplete. Bregman's death in 2018 presumably aborted the project.

Whether called a remake, a reboot, or a reimagining, *Scarface* has passed through more hands than a Kardashian. Pablo Larraín (*Tony Manero*, 2008) was announced to be directing a script by Paul Attanasio (*Quiz Show*, 1994) in 2014[32] that moved the setting from Miami to Los Angeles and changed Tony from Cuban to Mexican while keeping his ruthless pursuit of the American Dream intact.[33] In 2015, Jonathan Herman (*Straight Outta Compton*, 2015) was named to rewrite the Oscar-nominated Attanasio.[34] By 2016, Antoine Fuqua (*Training Day*, 2001) was set to direct a new script by Terence Winter (*Boardwalk Empire*, 2010)[35] but departed the project in 2017[36] only to return in 2018[37] to do the Coens' script, which was being rewritten by Gareth Dunnet-Alcocer (*Miss Bala*, 2019).[38] This brings the carousel back round to the 2020 announcement, yet to be realized, of Luca Guadagnino.

Guadagnino, speaking at the Venice Film Festival in 2020, told Adam Chitwood of the Italian online journal *BadTaste*, "[Tony Montana] is a symptom of the American Dream. I think the important thing about these movies is not the fact that they're lush and fundamental like Brian DePalma's one. The important thing is knowing that Tony Montana is an archetypal character. It's almost 100 years that Tony Montana affects the imagination of the audience, and this happens in part because we are attracted by what is capable of producing evil." He then cautioned, "It has to be well done."[39]

The remake flame continued to burn at Universal, reported Mike Floorwalker at the beginning of 2022. Noting that Guadagnino had lost actor Diego Luna, who had been attached for a considerable amount of time, Floorwalker offered replacement suggestions, imagined a summer shoot, and predicted a possible release early in 2023[40] as a 40th Anniversary event.

What could be the basis for a sequel? Dennis Plaksin of the Scarface Store spitballed that Tony might have impregnated Elvira and, years later, their son begins to take over neighborhoods in New York. This could work, except that Tony specifically criticizes Elvira for doing so many drugs that her body is polluted, revealing that he had been trying to conceive with her. But this would not be a problem given that it would come from the studio that found ways to resurrect Frankenstein's monster in at least two sequels.

One mitigating fact that might concern Universal Pictures is that the 1929 magazine serialization and the original Armitage Trail book *Scarface* fell into the public domain when their copyrights were not renewed. This was revealed by a chain-of-title copyright search conducted by Jane E. Currier of the firm Thompson & Thompson and reported to Mildred Basch of MGM/UA on October 25, 1989.[41] Why or how Trail's publisher assumed the book's copyright but not the serialized magazine story's copyright is not known. Current editions of the novel from Dean Street Press carry no copyright notice or credit. Technically this means that anyone may make their own version of *Scarface* as long as they stick to the book and do not take anything created expressly for any of the film adaptations.[42]

Scarface is the gift that keeps on giving. Its legacy as a cultural icon years after its release is a testament to the craft of its creators on all levels. Even though it might now be seen as cinematically dated in an age when frenetic editing has replaced its elegant, moving long shots, the fact that it retains its power the way it was originally filmed should be taken as a lesson that well-made movies are ageless. Young audiences raised by the manipulative construction of *Transformers* or the Marvel Universe can still appreciate *Scarface* because of its integrity and character.

Unlike what Peter Allen and Carol Bayer Sager wrote in their hit song, not everything that's old is new again, only the best.

SIDEBAR

Chi Chi, Get the Yeyo

Angel Salazar, who plays Chi Chi, Tony Montana's cohort, is partners with businessman Dennis Plaksin in the Scarface Store. The company began informally when Plaksin was introduced to a Miami man who licensed the rights from Universal to sell Scarface pajamas. "We did pretty good," Plaksin says. "I helped my buddy out, and at that point I said, 'Wait a minute, why stop with pajamas when we can do something else? Let's get creative and come up with a website.' I bought as many domain names as I could and launched the project and, not to infringe on any copyrights, we started to get creative." They reversed the r in *Scarface* and launched the program called Scarface Renaissance to keep the film's spirit alive.

"I hired a couple of local artists," Plaksin continues, "and said, 'Look, here's the movie. We're all huge fans, we all know exactly what it is, Chi Chi's involved, Angel Salazar from the movie, let's get something.' The artists came up with some really cool designs. That's how it all started. Then we started promoting. We did some promotions with local businesses, clubs; a couple of retail stores have ordered from us. It's a niche market. There's a huge *Scarface* fan base out there."

One of his and Salazar's most telling experiences happens when they're together in public. Says Plaksin, "We were in the Hard Rock Casino. He's a comedian, so he fills up a Ziploc bag full of white powder—nothing illegal, just powder—and he's walking through the casino. All of a sudden he drops this bag in front of a lot of people, and a guy sitting in the restaurant gets up—and this is not worked out, this is a hundred percent organic—and this guy yells out, 'Chi Chi, get the Yeyo.' We literally fell to the floor."[43]

SIDEBAR

Life After *Scarface*

Scarface may be the film for which many of its creators are best remembered, but it wasn't the only thing any of them ever did. At this writing forty years later, most of the people whose talents brought Tony Montana to life are still practicing their trade.

Director Brian DePalma's most recent film is *Domino* (2019), but he has more films in development. Funding has been challenging in a streaming industry.

Oliver Stone (writer) directed the alternative energy-themed documentary *Nuclear* (2022) and is preparing *White Lies*, a multigenerational story of love, lust, and family starring Benicio del Toro.

Martin Bregman (producer) died in 2018 at age ninety-two. He produced *Carlito's Way*, *Dog Day Afternoon*, *Sea of Love*, *The Shadow*, and *Betsy's Wedding*.

John A. Alonzo (director of photography) was known for his handheld camerawork and expertise in lighting in such films as *Sounder*, *Conrack*, *Chinatown*, *Steel Magnolias*, and *The Grass Harp*. He died in 2001.

Ferdinando Scarfiotti (visual consultant) was the highly acclaimed art director and/or production designer on numerous stylish films, including *Death in Venice*, *The Last Emperor*, *The Conformist*, and *Daisy Miller*. Scarfiotti died in 1994.

Al Pacino (Tony) was finally directed by Oliver Stone in 1999's *Any Given Sunday*. At age eighty-three he has six films and a TV series in various stages of production.

The prolific career since *Scarface* of Steven Bauer (Manny) includes TV episodics (*Ray Donovan*, *Better Call Saul*, *NCIS*), features (*Nothing Is Impossible*, *A Song to Kill For*), and the occasional short subject to keep himself even busier.

Michelle Pfeiffer (Elvira) effortlessly switches between superhero movies (*Avengers: Endgame, Ant-Man and the Wasp*) and prestige dramas (*People Like Us*) and TV series (*The First Lady*).

Robert Loggia (Frank), a beloved actor with a prolific career (*Big, Independence Day, The Sopranos*), died in 2015.

Mary Elizabeth Mastrantonio (Gina) became a major star in James Cameron's *The Abyss* and continued with *Robin Hood, Prince of Thieves*. Her work in the TV series *Limitless* and *Blindspot* kept her visible.

F. Murray Abraham (Omar) remains a popular character actor with *The White Lotus*, before which he appeared in such varied films as *The Ritz, Mighty Aphrodite*, and *The Grand Budapest Hotel*. His Academy Award for *Amadeus* is remarkable given that he was shooting *Scarface* at the same time and had to constantly commute between America and Europe.

The more than 130 roles of Harris Yulin (Bernstein) made him a familiar face, though not necessarily a familiar name, in *Night Moves, Doc, Candy Mountain*, and TV series such as *Ozark* and *Cagney and Lacey*.

Paul Shenar (Sosa) was a founding member of the American Conservatory Theatre in San Francisco and played mostly menacing villains in TV and movies. His more than fifty roles included *The Night That Panicked America* (as Orson Welles), *Big Blue*, and *Raw Deal*. He died in 1989.

Miriam Colon (Mama Montana) was only four years older than Al Pacino when she played his mother. She also appeared in the first two *Godfather* films and individual television series episodes. She died in 2017.

Angel Salazar (Chi Chi) continues to be a presence in numerous films and TV shows, including *Carlito's Way* (for Brian DePalma), *In Living Color*, *Night Rapper*, and *On Our Own*. He is also partners in the merchandising website scarfacestore.com.

Pepe Serna (Angel) survived the chainsaw to continually act in dozens of movies and TV shows, such as *The Black Dahlia* (for Brian DePalma), *Criminal Minds*, *Downsizing*, and *Flamin' Hot*.

Mark Margolis (Shadow) is a familiar face in TV series such as *Waterfront*, *Santa Barbara*, and *Breaking Bad*. More recently, his character from the latter, Hector Salamanca, was given a multi-season backstory in its sister series *Better Call Saul*.

A Very American Film

"To a certain extent, *Scarface* is about the film industry," confirms Julie Salamon, the *Wall Street Journal* reporter who covers the movies. "I think in his depiction of the gangsters surrounding Tony Montana, I think that's how [Oliver Stone] wrote the studio executives."[1] The comparison is facile but not incorrect. Whether one looks at the alleged Mob ties with MCA/Universal[2] or a shared taste for diamond pinky rings between Mafia dons and Hollywood's founding moguls, it might better be said that any business with money, power, and glamor is bound to be compared with organized crime.

As discussed in Chapter 2, the colorful men who codified the Hollywood system by the late 1920s shared a fascination with gangsters. Nowadays, however, the multinational corporations who own Hollywood don't need the likes of Al Capone or Frank Nitti, they call upon Congress and the U.S. State Department to assure their dominance in world markets. Agents and studio heads don't kill actors, they kill careers.

Tony Montana's stated philosophy in the script is "This country, first you gotta get the money, then you get the power, and when you got the power, then you get the women—then, Chico, you got the world by the balls. *Por los cojones!*" The ethic is not unique to *Scarface*. One remembers the remarks of Hyman Roth (Lee Strasberg) to Michael Corleone in *The Godfather Part II*: "We're bigger than U.S. Steel," also attributed to the real-life Mob mogul Meyer Lansky, upon

215

whom Roth was based. It's only a short jump to say that, while such thinking applies to any big business, it seems especially apt to Hollywood. This becomes especially true in light of the industry's ongoing consolidation into international, integrated conglomerates.

Is *Scarface* a satire of Hollywood? Or America? Knowing Stone's progressive politics and DePalma's less flamboyantly stated but equally radical beliefs, it's likely both. From the very start of his career, DePalma called out abuses of national power. *Hi, Mom!* is a kick in the face of token liberalism with its excruciatingly pointed and painfully prolonged "Be Black Baby" sequence in which white middle-class playgoers are abused by actors who force them to "be Black," after which they remark how exciting the experience was as they head home—no doubt to their Upper East Side high-rises. *Greetings* is founded in the desperation to escape the draft in opposition to an illegal war (into which, no doubt, the Black actors in the play-within-the-film "Be Black Baby" will be drafted in their stead). More pointedly, DePalma's *Casualties of War* (1989) is an unflinching indictment of a system that protects the guilt of war criminals with a bureaucracy that is designed not to recognize guilt. When America itself raped Vietnam, DePalma and screenwriter David Rabe are saying, to whom do you go to turn in a squad of soldiers who did the same thing to a Vietnamese girl? In his other films—*The Bonfire of the Vanities* (1990), *Blow Out* (1981), and *Redacted* (2007), among others—he likewise calls out a system that protects itself by ignoring infractions of its own rules when it suits the rule makers.

Oliver Stone, like his films, is more overtly political and draws fire for stating what people in power don't want to hear: Greed is *not* good (*Wall Street*, 1987), Lee Harvey Oswald did *not* act alone (*JFK*, 1991), freedom of speech has a price from opposite sides of the law (*Talk Radio*, 1988, and *Snowden*, 2016), and the media are accessories (*Natural Born Killers*, 1994). Even when written by and with others, Stone's films speak his heart and soul, and his critics bristle at his (often irrefutable) claims.

The combination of DePalma and Stone, even though Stone hadn't yet become a media target when *Scarface* was released, made for a heady blend of text and subtext. The text was blatant: Tony Montana is American Exceptionalism to the Nth degree, with all the arrogance, duplicity, and hypocrisy inherent in that philosophy. Stone calls it out and, in Tony's decline and fall, plays it out. DePalma, stressing the subtext, shows the seductiveness of Tony's choices and his willingness to co-opt the system, how easily it comes to someone who has reconciled his morals with his desires, and how all-fire terrific the rewards can be, at least at first. For Tony, nothing exceeds like excess. With America in the early 1980s rampant with hostile corporate takeovers, greenmail, junk bonds, Iran-Contra, housing bubbles, and an approaching savings and loan crisis, the simplicity of the toot trade was the perfect symbol of an imminent crash. The fact that people of color—that is, the community traditionally excluded from mainstream rewards—took the film to their heart was not only predictable, it had the tinge of bread and circus. To many, it still does. The film serves as a lesson, not a prediction. Everybody loves the first two acts and insists they will not make the third act their own.

Tony Montana believes in the American Dream—cynically, at first, as he jives his way out of immigration detention, and then for real as he celebrates his financial success. He bribes police, co-opts the banks, acts as he pleases in public, helps his sister, and buys his way with guns or money, one being a substitute for the other. He says the U.S. can't do anything to him that Castro didn't already do and that he is a proud capitalist, and as if to prove it, an hour later he is griping about having to pay taxes—which, being a drug lord, he doesn't do anyway, leading to his downfall. How much more American is that?

"It's a satiric comment on capitalism and success and what it means to succeed and what happens to you when you succeed," says actor Keith Gordon, who appeared for DePalma in *Home Movies* and *Dressed to Kill*. "He happens to be doing it as a killer and drug dealer, but is he really that different from the banker in the movie who's laundering his money or the shadowy government guy who's in that last meeting that they all have? It's really talking about American society a lot."[3]

"Hollywood didn't want to acknowledge it as 'this was representative of our filmmaking, of what our great filmmakers are doing,'" Steven Bauer said in retrospect. "It's not a human story that everybody can relate to, it's fucking *Dante's Inferno*."[4]

Scarface's morality is situational. Is it immoral because it wallows in sin, or is it an over-the-top cautionary tale? As reported earlier, the producers won an R rating instead of the dreaded X by claiming that Tony's fall teaches a lesson to wannabe teenage drug lords who would, given the R rating, presumably attend with their parent or adult guardian, who would reinforce its message (yeah, sure). In this naïve way, *Scarface* reflects the ethic of Hollywood's founding hypocrite, Cecil B. DeMille, whose biblical epics and social dramas preached morality, but only after giving the audience an eyeful of the immorality that he was condemning.[5]

No such duplicity exists in *Scarface*. The film is plainly the rise and fall of a man who wants it all and pays the price. If there is any hypocrisy, it is perhaps better called denial, and not from the filmmakers, but from the audience who enjoys the joyride and then ignores the toll at the end of the highway. Perhaps this is the unspoken explanation of the film's resurgence in the hip-hop community. When you are a person of color in America, where African American youths are four times more likely to be placed in the penal system than white youths or to be shot by the police, you learn early on to live for today because you may not be allowed to have a tomorrow.[6] Perhaps white critics and early audiences didn't realize this. Audiences of color did, and they were on board from the beginning, later spreading word to a new generation of fans.

No wonder the knives were out when *Scarface* was released. "*Scarface* was hated right from the beginning," DePalma recalled. "Hated by the industry. I remember a screening where people were walking out and cursing our names up and down the aisles. People loved it, people hated it, but the only way you can judge the real significance of a movie is whether people are still looking at it and talking about it ten, twenty years later."[7]

By that measure, *Scarface* took it to the limit. And has stayed there.

Bibliography

Battcock, Gregory, ed. *The New American Cinema, A Critical Anthology.* New York: E. P. Dutton & Co., 1967.

Bergan, Ronald. *The United Artists Story.* New York: Crown Publishers, 1986.

Ceplair, Larry, and Steven Englund. *The Inquisition in Hollywood: Politics in the Film Community 1930–1960.* Chicago, Illinois: University of Illinois Press, 1979.

Denby, David. "The Great Hollywood Screenwriter Who Hated Hollywood." *New Yorker.* February 11, 2019.

Goetz, Kevin, with Darlene Heyman. *Audience-ology: How Movie-goers Shape the Films We Love.* New York: Simon & Schuster/Simon Element, 2021.

Grobel, Lawrence. *Al Pacino in Conversation with Lawrence Grobel.* Foreword by Al Pacino. New York: Simon Spotlight Entertainment, 2006.

Harmetz, Aljean. *Rolling Breaks and Other Movie Business.* New York: Alfred A. Knopf, 1985.

Hecht, Ben. *A Child of the Century.* New York: Simon & Schuster, 1954.

Keesey, Douglas. *Brian De Palma's Split-Screen: A Life in Film.* Jackson, Mississippi: University Press of Mississippi, 2015.

KRS-ONE. "The Science of Rap." New York: L. Parker, 1995.

Mast, Gerald. *Howard Hawks Storyteller.* New York: Oxford University Press, 1982.

McBride, Joseph. *Hawks on Hawks.* California: University of California Press, 1982.

Monette, Paul. *Scarface* novelization. California: Berkley Books, 1983.

Pye, Michael, and Lynda Myles. *The Movie Brats: How the Film Generation Took Over Hollywood.* New York: Holt, Rinehart, and Winston, 1979.

Rode, Alan K. "The Chicago Way." *Noir City* 26. filmnoirfoundation.org/noircitymag/The-Chicago-Way.pdf.

Scarface (1932). Cutting continuity, prepared November 6, 1979 (Universal City Studios). 139 pages.

Seal, Mark. *Leave the Gun, Take the Cannoli.* New York: Gallery Books, 2021.

Stone, Oliver. *Scarface* screenplay. January 18, 1983. 183 pages.

Stone, Oliver. *Scarface* screenplay, second draft. Undated. 153 pages.

Taylor, David. *The Making of Scarface.* London, England: Unanimous, Ltd., 2005.

Trail, Armitage. *Scarface* novel. New York: Edward J. Clode, 1930. (Dean Street Press reprint, 1994).

Tucker, Ken. *Scarface Nation: The Ultimate Gangster Movie and How It Changed America.* New York: St. Martin's/Griffin, 2008.

Wiley, Mason, and Damien Bona. *Inside Oscar.* New York: Ballantine Books, 1993.

Zuckerman, Ira. *The Godfather Journal.* New York: Manor Books, Inc., 1972.

Extended Credits

AMPAS (Academy of Motion Picture Arts and Sciences) in a citation refers to the source of the material being quoted. Hawks, Howard. *Scarface* (United Artists, 1932). 1932. MS Hollywood, Censorship, and the Motion Picture Production Code, 1927–1968: History of Cinema, Series 1, Hollywood and Production Code Administration. Margaret Herrick Library. Archives Unbound, link.gale.com/apps/doc/SC5106192261/GDSC?u=gdscacc1&sid=bookmark-GDSC&xid=ee5a2d7d&pg=1. Accessed August 10, 2022. Used by permission of AMPAS.

LeRoy, Mervyn. *Little Caesar* (First National Pictures, 1931). 1931. MS Hollywood, Censorship, and the Motion Picture Production Code, 1927–1968: History of Cinema, Series 1, Hollywood and Production Code Administration. Margaret Herrick Library. Archives Unbound, link.gale.com/apps/doc/SC5106190494/GDSC?u=gdscacc1&sid=bookmark-GDSC&xid=e76385bd&pg=1.

Mayo, Archie. *The Petrified Forest* (Warner Bros., 1936). January 1935–November 3, 1936. MS Hollywood, Censorship, and the Motion Picture Production Code, 1927–1968: History of Cinema, Series 1, Hollywood and Production Code Administration. Margaret Herrick Library. Archives Unbound, link.gale.com/apps/doc/SC5106211189/GDSC?u=gdscacc1&sid=bookmark-GDSC&xid=e4de1181&pg=1.

Van Dyke, W. S. *Manhattan Melodrama* (Metro-Goldwyn-Mayer, 1934). November 21, 1933–May 20, 1940. MS Hollywood, Censorship, and the Motion Picture Production Code, 1927–1968: History of Cinema, Series 1, Hollywood and Production Code Administration. Margaret Herrick Library. Archives Unbound, link.gale.com/apps/doc/SC5106208194/GDSC?u=gdscacc1&sid=bookmark-GDSC&xid=4b8a2ad7&pg=1.

Wellman, William A. *The Public Enemy* (Warner Bros., 1931). 1931. MS Hollywood, Censorship, and the Motion Picture Production Code, 1927–1968: History of Cinema, Series 1, Hollywood and Production Code Administration. Margaret Herrick Library. Archives Unbound, link.gale.com/apps/doc/SC5106190776/GDSC?u=gdscacc1&sid=bookmark-GDSC&xid=5066723e&pg=1.

Additional credits and permissions:

Grobel, Lawrence. *Al Pacino in Conversation with Lawrence Grobel.* Foreword by Al Pacino. New York: Simon Spotlight Entertainment, 2006. Used by permission of Lawrence Grobel.

Excerpt from *A Child of the Century.* New York: Simon & Schuster, 1954. ©1954 by Ben Hecht, © renewed 1982 by Charles A. Mantione as executor of the estate of Ben Hecht. Copyright transferred to the Newberry Library in 1994. Originally published by Simon & Schuster in 1954. Published in paperback by Primus in 1985. This edition published by the Yale University Press. Used by permission of Yale University Press.

Konow, David. "Writing in a Very Dark Room—Oliver Stone Revisits Scarface." *Creative Screenwriting*, January 20, 2015. creativescreenwriting.com/writing-in-a-very-dark-room-oliver-stone-revisits-scarface/. Used by permission of the author.

Stone, Oliver. *Chasing the Light: Writing, Directing, and Surviving* Platoon, Midnight Express, Scarface, Salvador, *and the Movie Game.* Boston, Massachusetts: Houghton Mifflin Harcourt, 2020. Used by permission of the author.

The author attempted to source quotations from interviews posted without citation on YouTube. Here a claim of fair use is made for such quotes.

Some sources used as reference had neither notes nor bibliographies, so the limited quotations from them appearing in this book are used under a claim of fair use crediting the source in which they appeared.

Photo Captions and Credits

1-A   "The Musketeers of Pig Alley," D.W. Griffith, 1912. This seventeen-minute drama is considered the first American gangster film. Frame enlargement.

1-B   Ben Hecht publicity photo. He was twenty-five at the time. Culver Pictures. Wikimedia Commons. commons.wikimedia.org/wiki/File:Hecht_Earlyportrait.jpg.

1-C   Josef von Sternberg, director of *Underworld*. Studio publicity photo. Wikimedia Commons. commons.wikimedia.org/wiki/File:Josef_von_Sternberg,_Mary_Pickford._Pickfair_Estate,_Beverly_Hills,_California._1925.jpg.

1-D   *Underworld* lobby card. Wikimedia Commons. commons.wikimedia.org/wiki/File:Underworld_lobby_card.jpg.

2-A   George Bancroft in *Underworld*. Studio publicity photo.

2-B   Book cover, *Scarface* reprint. Author's library.

2-C   *Scarface* (1932) main title. Frame enlargement.

2-D   Howard Hawks, director of *Scarface* (1932). Studio publicity shot. Wikimedia Commons. commons.wikimedia.org/wiki/File:Howard_Hawks_head_shot.jpg.

3-A   Publicity shot of Paul Muni as Tony Camonte in *Scarface* (1932). Studio publicity photo. Wikimedia Commons. commons.wikimedia.org/wiki/File:Paul_Muni_in_Scarface_(1932).jpg.

3-B   Tony taunts the police to come for him. They do. Wikimedia Commons. commons.wikimedia.org/wiki/File:Comante_Taunt.jpg.

4-A   Al Capone summoned to Chicago's FBI office for questioning. Photo by Chicago FBI Bureau/Wide World Photos. Wikimedia Commons. commons.wikimedia.org/wiki/File:Al_Capone_in_1930.jpg.

4-B   Al Capone photographed around 1935. Photo by Chicago FBI Bureau. Wikimedia Commons. commons.wikimedia.org/wiki/File:Al_Capone-around_1935.jpg.

5-A   Willie Bioff, the Mob's designated hitter, who came to Hollywood in the 1930s to take over the unions and shake down the studios. Photofest.

5-B   The classic image from *Scarface*. Paul Muni (CENTER) with Vince Barnett (LEFT). Wikimedia Commons. commons.wikimedia.org/wiki/File:Scarface_1932.jpg.

6-A   St. Valentine's Day Massacre, 1929.

6-B   Caption for St. Valentine's Day Massacre photo.

7-A   Paul Muni and Ann Dvorak as the Camonte siblings in *Scarface*. Wikimedia Commons. commons.wikimedia.org/wiki/File:Scarface-Muni-Dvorak.jpg.

7-B   Paul Muni and his wife Bella at the 1937 Academy Awards. Photo by *Los Angeles Daily News*. Wikimedia Commons. commons.wikimedia.org/wiki/File:Paul_Muni_and_his_wife_Bella_at_the_1937_Academy_Awards.jpg.

8-A   *Scarface* (1932) 22x28 poster. Wikimedia Commons. commons.wikimedia.org/wiki/File:Scarface_(1932_film_poster).jpg.

8-B   *Scarface* (1932) insert poster. Wikimedia Commons. commons.wikimedia.org/wiki/File:Scarface_(1932_film_poster).jpg.

9-A   Oliver Stone, screenwriter of *Scarface* (1983), when he served in Vietnam. Photo by Press Service of the President of Russia. Wikimedia Commons. commons.wikimedia.org/wiki/File:Oliver_Stone_(2019-06-19).jpg.

9-B   Oliver Stone, screenwriter of *Scarface* (1983). Photo by Oliver Stone via Towpilot. Wikimedia Commons. commons.wikimedia.org/wiki/File:Oliver_Stone_01.jpg.

10-A   Director Brian DePalma at Venice Film Festival, 2007. Photo by John Rubin, Flickr. Wikimedia Commons. commons.wikimedia.org/wiki/File:Brian_De_Palma_(Venice_2007).jpg.

10-B   Director Brian DePalma at Guadalajara Film Festival, 2008. Photo by Festival Internacional de Cine en Guadalajara. Wikimedia Commons. commons.wikimedia.org/wiki/File:Brian_De_Palma_(Guadalajara_2008)_13.jpg.

10-C   Director Brian DePalma at Guadalajara Film Festival, 2008. Photo by Festival Internacional de Cine en Guadalajara. Wikimedia Commons. commons.wikimedia.org/wiki/File:Brian_De_Palma_(Guadalajara_2008)_20.jpg.

10-D   Giorgio Moroder, composer for *Scarface* (1983). Photofest.

11-A   Cuban refugees escape Castro on the Mariel boatlift. Photo by Robert L. Scheina, U.S. Department of Homeland Security. Wikimedia Commons. commons.wikimedia.org/wiki/File:Mariel_Refugees.jpg.

11-B   Steven Bauer, who played Manny in *Scarface* (1983), today. Photo by Romina Espinosa, rominaespinosa.com. Wikimedia Commons. commons.wikimedia.org/wiki/File:StevenBauer08.jpg.

11-C   Angel Salazar (Chi Chi in *Scarface*, 1983) and Dennis Plaksin, partners in the Scarface Store. Photo courtesy of Dennis Plaksin, The Scarface Store.

11-D   Angel Salazar (Chi Chi in *Scarface*, 1983) models the most popular shirt in the Scarface Store, "Chi Chi get the Yeyo." Photo courtesy of Dennis Plaksin, The Scarface Store.

12-A   LEFT TO RIGHT: Producers Martin Bregman and Louis Stroller confer with flak-jacketed director Brian DePalma on the sidelines of *Scarface*. Photofest.

12-B   Al Pacino, as Tony Montana, about to get even with Frank Lopez in *Scarface* (1983). Photo accredited to Al Pacino. Wikimedia Commons. commons.wikimedia.org/wiki/File:Ytdhhte.jpg.

13-A   Al Pacino and Steve Bauer check out the sights on Miami Beach and discuss their future. Photofest.

13-B   Steven Bauer plays Manolo (Manny) Ribera, "Scarface" Tony Montana's best friend. Photofest.

14-A   Mary Elizabeth Mastrantonio, as Gina Montana, dances with a fella, to the disdain of her overprotective brother, Tony. Photofest.

14-B   The duplicitous Omar (F. Murray Abraham, LEFT) and his menschy boss Frank Lopez (Robert Loggia, RIGHT). Photofest.

15-A   Brian DePalma directs Michelle Pfeiffer, who plays Elvira, Tony Montana's trophy wife. Photofest.

15-B   Tony Montana (Al Pacino) marries Elvira (Michelle Pfeiffer) as the romance of Manny (Steven Bauer) and Gina (Mary Elizabeth Mastrantonio) blooms under their cocaine-dusted noses. Photofest.

15-C   Michelle Pfeiffer as Elvira, the stylish woman who finally realizes enough is enough. Photofest.

16-A   Tony Montana (Al Pacino) introduces Sosa's invading army to his "little friend." Photofest.

16-B   Tony Montana's (Al Pacino) last stand against the invasion by his drug overlord enemy's army. Photofest.

Endnotes

Introduction: "I'm proud of that film and what we did."

1. "DVD & Games: Video," *Billboard*, July 8, 2021.

Chapter 1: "Get out of my way, Johnny, I'm gonna spit"

1. U.S. Bureau of Alcohol, Tobacco, and Firearms: https://www.atf.gov/our-history/timeline/18th-amendment-1919-national-prohibition-act.

2. James C. Howell and John P. Moore, "History of Street Gangs in the United States," *National Gang Center Bulletin*, May 2010.

3. Ibid. Al Capone would become associated with the Bowery Boys and Five Points.

4. In a "making-of" featurette designed to promote *The Godfather* (1972), Al Pacino says, "An island that was invaded as much as Sicily, the people formed families so that they could have this trust within the family compound. If you had this sense of loyalty, you could combat the invaders." When Paramount executives felt that this quote excused the Mafia, they pulled the featurette and ordered its publicity team to confiscate all copies. Only years later when the feature itself came out on DVD was the featurette restored. (The author was working for Paramount at the time and was ordered to implement the cancellation.)

5. YouTube: https://www.youtube.com/watch?v=AzyuKxrHGoM.

6. Tom Dirks, https://www.filmsite.org/crimefilms.html, undated.

7. *The Musketeers of Pig Alley* on YouTube: https://www.youtube.com/watch?v=Bnlf7YqYPNc&t=657s.

8. *Underworld* on YouTube: https://www.youtube.com/watch?v=P4SQecahEkk.

9. Ben Hecht, *A Child of the Century* (New York: Simon & Schuster, 1954). *Bawds* means bawdy, or indecent, and sometimes a prostitute.

10. The Motion Picture Production Code.

11. Mark A. Viera, *Sin in Soft Focus: Pre-Code Hollywood* (New York: Harry N. Abrams, Inc.), 1999.

12. Lee Grieveson, Esther Sonnet, and Peter Stanfield, *Mob Culture: Hidden Histories of the American Gangster Film* (New Brunswick, New Jersey: Rutgers University Press, 2005).

13. Not the current actor James Woods, who starred in *Salvador*, *Videodrome*, and *The Onion Field*.

14. It is not generally known that *The Public Enemy* was originally planned as a sequel to *The Doorway to Hell* (Archie Mayo, 1930), which starred Lew Ayres and James Cagney as mobsters trying to organize Chicago's gangs. Source: January 6, 1931, letter from Warner Bros. production vice president Darryl F. Zanuck to Colonel Jason Joy of the Production Code Administration, AMPAS. This raises the question of why Zanuck didn't recognize Cagney's charisma earlier.

15. Lee Server, *Encyclopedia of Pulp Fiction Writers* (New York: Checkmark Books, 2002).

16. Joseph McBride, *Hawks on Hawks* (Berkeley, California: University of California Press, 1982).

17. Max Wilk, *Schmucks with Underwoods: Conversations with Hollywood's Classic Screenwriters* (Milwaukee, Wisconsin: Hal Leonard Corporation, 2004).

18. McBride notes that screenwriter John Lee Mahin attributes the Borgia idea to Hecht, not Hawks.

19. A telegram from Leland Hayward to Sam Briskin concerning another film recalled that Hecht wrote *Scarface* in twelve days. AMPAS.

20. Hawks always collaborated with his writers but never took credit because, as he told McBride, "If I did, I couldn't get such good writers to work with me."

21. Ben Hecht, *A Child of the Century* (New Haven, Connecticut: Yale University Press, 1985), reprint.

22. Joseph McBride, *Hawks on Hawks* (Berkeley, California: University of California Press, 1982).

23. Technically he was not nominated, as only the winners for this early Oscar ceremony were announced in advance.

24. Joseph McBride, *Hawks on Hawks* (Berkeley, California: University of California Press, 1982).

25. He was also known for low-key performances that hid his limited acting ability. George Burns once joked, "I saw a scene where George Raft and Gary Cooper [another low-key actor] were talking in front of a cigar store and it looked like the wooden Indian was overacting."

26. For trivia buffs: Raft played a gangster in Billy Wilder's 1959 comedy, *Some Like It Hot*. In one scene he sees a young hood flipping a coin and snaps at him, "Where did you pick up that cheap trick?" The young hood is Edward G. Robinson, Jr.

27. Gerald Mast. *Howard Hawks, Storyteller.* New York: Oxford University Press, 1982.

28. Notation in Colonel Joy's diary. AMPAS.

29. Clipping (no source), AMPAS. Percy was a stage and screen actress.

30. Joy to Hughes, AMPAS.

31. E. B. Dorr to Joy, AMPAS. True to his word, the film did not actually say "Chicago," but they showed it on the masthead of a prop newspaper.

32. Dorr also wanted "pretty smart boy" in dialogue to be changed to "dirty thug," Detective Guarino made kindly, and the deletion of "cold shower" because it was salacious.

33. June 4, 1932, letter from Joy to Dorr, AMPAS.

34. David Taylor. *The Making of Scarface*. UK: Unanimous Limited, 2005.

35. September 31, 1931 memo from Colonel Joy that Hughes agreed to the new ending. There is evidence that screenwriter Lamar Trotti wrote the new material (memo from Trotti to Joy, September 22, 1931, AMPAS). Trotti's involvement predates any of his plentiful writing or producing credits. At the time he was transitioning from journalism to being a 20th Century-Fox executive.

36. YouTube: https://www.youtube.com/watch?v=6pBnk_vxLcI.

37. September 22, 1932, Joy memo. On September 21, they ran the film for Irving Thalberg at MGM, who loved the anti-gun message that had been inserted. AMPAS.

38. AMPAS files.

39. Telegram, Trotti to Julia Kelley, AMPAS.

40. Schenck to Hays, letter, AMPAS.

41. *Motion Picture Herald* review, March 12, 1932. The screen date can only be inferred as having taken place in the days prior.

42. Telegram, AMPAS.

43. Tippy to Colonel Joy, September 1, 1932, AMPAS.

44. Breen to D. Biederman, Atlantic Pictures Corporation, AMPAS.

45. How this happened is anybody's guess. As reference, the author knows a performer who, when his TV show ended after one season, simply backed his car up to the studio vault and loaded the master tapes into the trunk. Years later they were conveyed to the proper owner (which wasn't the studio).

46. The author unapologetically admits that this was how he first saw the film: by borrowing a "hot" print, screening it for friends, and returning it to its source immediately after rewinding it.

47. On April 21, 1986, reporter Geraldo Rivera went into Capone's former offices in Chicago's Lexington Hotel, 2136 South Michigan Avenue, hoping to find artifacts, even bodies, in the huge vault-sized safe. Instead, it was full of dust. Commendably, Rivera posted the entire show, *The Mystery of Al Capone's Vaults*, on his website: http://geraldo.com/folio/mystery-of-al-capone-s-vault.

48. Speculation is that he got a dose in a Chicago brothel but did not seek treatment. Perhaps he was an early anti-vaxxer.

49. A conundrum that remains controversial: In order to obey the law by paying taxes on illegal income, one has to admit to having illegal income, a violation of the Fifth Amendment against self-incrimination. Thus the government's power to enforce the Sixteenth Amendment (income tax) trumps the people's rights under the Fifth Amendment.

50. Attributed.

51. *Encyclopedia Britannica*, https://www.britannica.com/biography/Ben-Hecht.

52. https://www.jewishvirtuallibrary.org/ben-hecht.

53. July 19, 1929, memo to Colonel Jason S. Joy, AMPAS.

54. January 13, 1932, letter from R. E. Plummer to unnamed PCA recipient, AMPAS.

55. January 27, 1931, advisory letter to Jason S. Joy from Will H. Hays's executive assistant, identified only as "Maurice," AMPAS.

56. January 27, 1931, note from Jason S. Joy, AMPAS.

57. April 28, 1931, letter from R. E. Plummer, AMPAS. There is no character named Bess in the film. This may be a reference to the Mae Clark character, Kitty, who famously gets grapefruited. Tom is wearing pajamas, indicating a probable sleepover.

58. AMPAS, Undated memo, Breen to file.

59. August 13, 1953, letter to the files by "J.A.V." (J. August Vollmer), AMPAS.

60   W. S. Van Dyke was known as Woody "One Take" Van Dyke because he routinely went for the first try rather than working on getting a good one, causing the studio to have to reshoot much of his work. But damn, he kept on schedule.

61. March 6, 1934, Joseph I. Breen to Louis B. Mayer, AMPAS.

62. April 17, 1934, Joseph I. Breen to Louis B. Mayer, AMPAS.

63. May 15, 1934. Will H. Hays to Joseph I. Breen. AMPAS.

64. This is the date that John Dillinger was ambushed by, among others, Melvin Purvis of the FBI. Purvis was later driven out of the Bureau by FBI director J. Edgar Hoover, allegedly for stealing Hoover's public thunder. On February 29, 1960, Purvis took his own life, supposedly with the same gun that he had used in Dillinger's assassination twenty-six years earlier.

65. January 17, 1935 unsigned report of the stage play to unknown PCA recipient. AMPAS. There is some dispute whether John Dillinger ever killed anybody himself.

66. This is where the deleted yacht sequence would have gone.

67. Incidentally, there is a moment in *Underworld*, whose story Ben Hecht wrote, where the hero gangster, Bull Weed, points to a neon sign on a building that reads "The City is Yours."

68. On that same date, the Nobel Prizes were awarded in Sweden and D. W. Griffith's final film, *The Struggle*, was released.

Chapter 2: The Moguls and the Mob

1.   United States v. Motion Picture Patents Co., 225 F. 800 (E.D. Pa. 1915), was the most significant decision limiting the power of the motion picture industry until U.S. v. Paramount Pictures, Inc.

2. U.S. v. Paramount Pictures, Inc., et al., 334 U.S. 131 (1948), divorced film production companies from their theaters, ending vertical integration with a consent decree. Both the Patents Trust and Paramount actions were brought under the Sherman Antitrust Act, which seems to have been forgotten by the United States Department of Justice for the last forty years.

3. Sam Kashner, "The Color of Love," *Vanity Fair*, September 3, 2013. The threatened hit scared Davis into marrying someone else, but Kashner says the performer was never really in jeopardy because, as a Las Vegas star, he was worth more to the Mob alive than Cohn was.

4. Murray Ross, "Labor Relations in Hollywood," *The Annals of the American Academy of Political and Social Science*, November 1947.

5. Mason Wiley and Damien Bona, *Inside Oscar: The Unofficial History of the Academy Awards* (New York: Ballantine Books, 1993).

6. "Three Studio Unions Strike in Hollywood," *New York Times*, May 1, 1937.

7. Holding Hollywood hostage by threatening a projectionists' strike was also used by Roy Brewer, a notorious Red-baiter and head of the projectionists union during the Blacklist era, when he vowed to order his members not to run any film made by alleged Communists.

8. "George Browne Runs Against General President William Elliot," IATSE website, accessed July 25, 2022. Kudos to the IATSE for facing up to their own history.

9. "Film Extortion Plan Charge: Union Official Found Guilty," *Sydney Morning Herald*, December 24, 1943.

10. This story is told in vivid detail by Alan K. Rode in "The Chicago Way," *Noir City* (The Film Noir Foundation), no. 26.

11. "Willie Bioff's Last Shakedown," *Variety*, November 9, 1955.

12. Alan K. Rode, "The Chicago Way," *Noir City* (The Film Noir Foundation), no. 26.

13. *Las Vegas Desert Sun*, November 5, 1955.

14. Cecile Rasmussen, "L.A. Then and Now: Mobsters Muscled into Film Industry," *Los Angeles Times*, January 2, 2000.

15. Mark Seal, *Leave the Gun, Take the Cannoli* (New York: Gallery Books, 2021); Ira Zuckerman, *The Godfather Journal* (New York: Manor Books, 1972).

16. In 1976, the author heard about "guys" hanging around the set of the original *Godfather* and rumors of such investments from an accountant who had been involved with Paramount at the time.

17. Scott Burnstein, "The Cotton Club Movie Mob Affair," *The Gangster Report*, https://gangsterreport.com/cotton-club-movie-mob-affair/.

18. The anti-Semitic goals of HUAC have been cited by scholars, including Ceplair and Englund in *The Inquisition in Hollywood* (Illinois: University of Illinois Press, 1979); Gordon Kahn, *Hollywood on Trial* (New York: Boni & Gaer, 1948); Michael Freedland, *Witch Hunt in Hollywood* (Berkeley, California:

Autumn Press, Ltd., 2014); and in interviews with, and memoirs by, numerous blacklistees.

19. *Congressional Record*, November 24, 1947, 80th Congress, First Session. Referring to Jewish entertainers who changed their names: "There are others too numerous to mention. They are attacking the Committee for doing its duty in trying to protect this country and save the American people from the horrible fate the Communists have meted out to the unfortunate Christian people of Europe."

20. The author is cowriter, with Daniel M. Kimmel and Arnie Reisman, of the 1993 play *The Waldorf Conference*.

Chapter 3: A Few Lines About Cocaine

1.   Before he took on the coked-out lead in *Bright Lights, Big City* (1988), Michael J. Fox learned from Al Pacino that the substance they had tooted in *Scarface* was milk sugar. *Hit* magazine in *People* magazine, April 25, 1988.

2.   Dominic Streatfeild, *Meth: An Unauthorized Biography* (New York: Macmillan, 2003).

3.   "The Birth of a Refreshing Idea," *News & Articles* newsletter, the Coca-Cola Company, www.coca-colacompany.com. The Coca-Cola company insists that cocaine was never present in their product.

4.   "Traveling a Primeval Medical Landscape," *New York Times*, April 27, 2010.

5.   https://oig.justice.gov/sites/default/files/archive/special/9712/ch06p2.htm.

6.   https://www.npr.org/2007/05/15/10192766/cocaine-prices-have-fallen-steeply-since-1980s.

7.   Nicknames for cocaine include blow, toot, flake, snow, dust, line, nose candy, Peruvian Marching Powder, yeyo, and other colorful sobriquets. For crack there are dice, gravel, grit, rocks, cookies, and candy. Like all slang, these terms are transitory and by the time they appear in print may have become laughably archaic.

8.   https://www.businessinsider.com/us-cocaine-prices-change-2016-10; www.crackcocaineaddiction.com/Cocaine_Prices.htm.

9.   https://www.ussc.gov/topic/powder-cocaine.

10. https://action.aclu.org/send-message/congress-end-racist-sentencing-disparities-now, posting not dated, accessed September 4, 2022.

11. Sophia Cai. "Garland orders end to cocaine sentencing disparities." *Axios*. December 16, 2022. https://www.axios.com/2022/12/16/doj-garland-end-sentencing-disparities-crack-powder-cocaine.

12. Alfred McCoy, *The Politics of Heroin in Southeast Asia* (New York: Harper & Row, 1972).

13. Gary Webb, *Dark Alliance: The CIA, the Contras, and the Crack Cocaine Explosion* (book), Foreword by Rep. Maxine Waters (New York: Seven Stories Press, 1998).

14. Numerous books and news stories have documented this subject, including Laurence E. Walsh, *Firewall: The Iran-Contra Conspiracy and Cover-Up* (New York: W. W. Norton and Company, 1997).

15. Nick Schou, *Kill the Messenger: How the CIA's Crack Cocaine Controversy Destroyed Gary Webb* (New York: Nation Books, 2006).

16. Ken Tucker, *Scarface Nation: The Ultimate Gangster Movie and How It Changed America* (New York: St. Martin's/Griffin, 2008).

Chapter 4: "I Want to Be Paul Muni"

1. Author's conversation with Beatty for *Ishtar* (1987).

2. Brian Gallagher, "Scarface Invades Los Angeles," Movieweb.com, August 25, 2011.

3. Speaking at the film's thirty-fifth anniversary panel at Tribeca, *Scarface* 2018 DVD bonus features.

4. Lawrence Grobel, *Al Pacino* (New York: Simon Spotlight Entertainment, 2006).

5. Clive Barnes, *New York Times*, April 25, 1977.

6. The author was privileged to see Pacino in the memorable Boston engagement.

7. A more elaborate version of this story is told in Mark Seal's *Leave the Gun, Take the Cannoli* (New York: Gallery Books, 2021), in which Paramount's production VP Bob Evans called his friend mob lawyer Sidney Korshack, who threatened MGM to release Pacino. MGM then sued the actor for everything he had at the time. But he landed the *Godfather* role.

8. Jason Bailey. "Revisiting the Controversy Surrounding Scarface." *Vulture.com.* April 20, 2018. Bregman died June 16, 2018 with the conflict unresolved.

9. Ken Tucker, *Scarface Nation* (New York: St. Martin's Griffith, 2008).

10. Colin Dangaard, *Marquee*, November 1983.

11. AFI Catalogue.

12. *Los Angeles Herald Examiner*, August 17, 1981. DePalma later said that the studio, United Artists, fired him and Rabe. DePalma was conflating studio executives; the studio was Orion, whose officers had recently left United Artists.

13. *Hollywood Reporter*, June 11, 1981. On August 3, 1981, *Variety* reported that DePalma would direct "a contemporary action-adventure set in Chicago and South America" for United Artists, as confirmed by UA's Worldwide production VP Raphael Etkes. No additional information was given, nor was anything else ever said about it.

14. Comments to the Film Society of Lincoln Center, June 10, 2016. https://www.youtube.com/watch?v=guAwJZ5wbZs&list=RDLVgSo_Ds9_9O0&start_radio=1&rv=gSo_Ds9_9O0.

15. Ken Tucker, *Scarface Nation* (New York: St. Martin's Griffin, 2008).

16. Stone made his feature debut with the horror film *Seizure* in 1974 for Cinerama Releasing Corporation, which was in the process of going out of business and couldn't give it exposure or bookings.

17.   Columbia (which was bought by Coca-Cola in 1982) would change their mind about Vietnam movies in 1989 to make DePalma's and Rabe's *Casualties of War.*

18.   *Cruising* was based on Gerald Walker's novel about a series of murders of gay men in New York's leather culture. DePalma was interested in directing it and even wrote a script before dropping out, although elements of his script made it into *Dressed to Kill.* Before Friedkin picked up *Cruising* and wrote his own adaptation, Steven Spielberg was mentioned as a possible director. The mind reels.

19.   Author interview with Oliver Stone.

20.   Author interview with Oliver Stone. He is referring to the character of "Charles Goodson" (Gregg Henry) who appears at Sosa's compound when Tony agrees to kill the Bolivian journalist.

21.   Comment to Cinema Garmonbozia, https://www.youtube.com/watch?v=PuCqcvORq5Y, and to the Film Society of Lincoln Center, June 10, 2016, https://www.youtube.com/watch?v=guAwJZ5wbZs&list=RDLVgSo_Ds9_9O0&start_radio=1&rv=gSo_Ds9_9O0.

22.   Ken Tucker, *Scarface Nation* (New York: St. Martin's Griffin, 2008).

23.   *Hollywood Reporter*, February 18, 1981. Says Bregman, Pacino initially wanted Glenn Close. Ken Tucker, *Scarface Nation* (New York: St. Martin's Griffin, 2008).

24.   Studios generally borrowed money from banks, but Universal was so cash rich at the time that they could self-finance, immensely reducing interest rates by not having to borrow from a bank.

25.   *Firestarter* (1984) wound up being directed by Mark Lester, *Psycho 2* (1983) by Richard Franklin, and *Halloween III* (1982) by Tommy Lee Wallace.

26.   *Weekly Variety*, April 7, 1982.

27.   David Taylor, *The Making of Scarface* (United Kingdom: Unanimous, Ltd., 2005).

28.   *Variety*, May 24, 1982.

29.   *Variety*, August 23, 1982.

30.   Colin Dangaard, *Marquee*, November 1983.

31.   Francisco Alvarado, *Miami New Times*, December 13, 2012.

32.   *Daily Variety*, August 23, 1982.

33.   *Daily Variety*, August 23, 1982.

34.   Later reported in *Variety*, April 27, 1983.

35.   Tina Daniell. "'Scarface' Remake Scheduled to Film, Opposition Expected," *Hollywood Reporter*, August 26, 1982.

36.   *Daily Variety*, September 1, 1982.

37.   *Variety*. September 10, 1982.

38. *Hollywood Reporter*, November 22, 1982.

39. *Daily Variety*, November 1, 1982.

40. *Daily Variety*, November 17, 1982.

41. Author interview with Steven Bauer.

42. *Daily Variety*, December 2, 1982.

43. Posted May 12, 2017, https://www.youtube.com/watch?v=nmSnoGtVMkM. Clarified in comments to James Lipton, *Inside the Actors Studio*, August 6, 2007.

44. Gerri Hirshey, "The Bat's Meow," *Rolling Stone*, September 3, 1992.

45. Graham Fuller, "Michelle Pfeiffer: Woman Who Runs with the Wolves," *Interview*, July 1994. Retrieved from Douglas Keesey, *Brian DePalma's Split Screen* (Jackson, MS: University Press of Mississippi, 2015).

46. Ken Tucker, *Scarface Nation* (New York: St. Martin's Griffin, 2008).

47. *Weekly Variety*, November 17, 1982.

48. Milos Forman, "How I Came to America to Make a Film and Wound Up Owing Paramount $140,000," *Show*, February 1970.

49. Fabiola Santiago, "History of the Cuban Revolution Marked by Tens of Thousands Fleeing the Island for the U.S.," *Miami Herald*, November 26, 2016.

50. JFK Library, https://www.jfklibrary.org/learn/about-jfk/jfk-in-history/the-bay-of-pigs.

51. "Cuban-Americans: The Miami Mirror," *Economist*, March 24, 2012.

52. Jorge Duany, "Cuban Migration: A Postrevolution Exodus Ebbs and Flows," Migrationpolicy.org, July 3, 2017.

53. "Castro Would Free 3,000," *New York Times*, November 23, 1978. Castro disingenuously gave amnesty to these people so they could enter the US under its immigration policy that otherwise barred criminals. Castro also passed word to the anti-Castro Cubans in Miami to send boats.

54. Peter Baker, "U.S. to Restore Full Relations with Cuba, Erasing a Last Trace of Cold War Hostility," *New York Times*, December 17, 2014. Trump strategically excluded Cuba from his list of "shithole countries."

55. Unsourced, David Taylor, *The Making of Scarface* (London: Unanimous, Ltd., 2006).

56. Mark Harris, *Five Came Back: A Story of Hollywood and the Second World War* (New York: Penguin Press, 2014). Many Hollywood figures served, but the ones Harris covers are John Huston, William Wyler, George Stevens, John Ford, and Frank Capra.

57. When Columbia backed out of *Platoon*, they introduced Stone to the producers who were looking for a screenwriter for *Midnight Express*.

58. This is not to impugn these filmmakers, merely to note the changing times and their reaction to an illegal, immoral war. A notable exception is John Milius,

whose severe asthma prevented enlistment. Instead, he wrote *Apocalypse Now* for George Lucas, that Francis Ford Coppola later directed.

59. Quoted by Christopher Hooton, *Independent,* January 11, 2017, https://www. independent.co.uk/arts-entertainment/films/news/scarface-film-1983-cocaine-oliver-stone-screenplay-tony-montana-brian-de-palma-a7521051.html.

60. David Konow, "Writing in a Very Dark Room—Oliver Stone Revisits *Scarface,*" *Creative Screenwriting,* January 20, 2015, https://www.creativescreenwriting. com/writing-in-a-very-dark-room-oliver-stone-revisits-scarface/.

61. David Taylor, *The Making of Scarface* (London, England: Unanimous, Ltd., 2005).

62. Oliver Stone, *Chasing The Light: Writing, Directing, and Surviving* Platoon, Midnight Express, Scarface, Salvador, *and the Movie Game* (Boston: Houghton Mifflin Harcourt, 2020).

63. Ibid.

64. Stone also referred to the film on occasion as a "comedic Richard III," referencing Shakespeare's drama about a pretender who murders his way to the throne of England only to be undone on the battlefield for lack of a horse.

65. David Konow, "Writing in a Very Dark Room—Oliver Stone Revisits *Scarface,*" *Creative Screenwriting,* January 20, 2015, https://www.creativescreenwriting. com/writing-in-a-very-dark-room-oliver-stone-revisits-scarface/.

66. Noah Baumbach and Jake Paltrow, *DePalma,* documentary, 2015.

67. Oliver Stone, *Chasing The Light: Writing, Directing, and Surviving* Platoon, Midnight Express, Scarface, Salvador, *and the Movie Game* (Boston: Houghton Mifflin Harcourt, 2020).

68. Cowritten by Stone and Cimino from Robert Daley's novel.

69. Oliver Stone, *Chasing The Light: Writing, Directing, and Surviving* Platoon, Midnight Express, Scarface, Salvador, *and the Movie Game* (Boston: Houghton Mifflin Harcourt, 2020).

Chapter 5: The DePalma Dilemma

1. Interview comments to Mark Cousins, "Scene by Scene," in association with the Edinburgh International Film Festival, https://www.youtube.com/ watch?v=rh_nbTfvfYc&t=1483s.

2. Ashley Clark, "Brian DePalma: Film Lies All the Time—24 Times a Second," *Guardian,* June 7, 2016; Marc Cousins, "Scene by Scene," in association with the Edinburgh International Film Festival, https://www.youtube.com/ watch?v=rh_nbTfvfYc&t=1483s.

3. Jason Guerrasio, "Brian DePalma, Legendary Director Of 'Scarface' and 'Carrie,' Explains Why He 'Left Hollywood Completely,'" *Business Insider,* June 3, 2016. This is one of the few stories DePalma tells about his youth. Unlike other filmmakers, he does not claim his work is autobiographical.

4. Remarkably, some of these have been posted on YouTube, if not by DePalma himself, then with his passive consent.

5.   Recalled in the film *DePalma*.

6.   When the X was introduced, it just meant grown-up, not obscene, but since the MPAA purposely did not trademark the X rating, pornographers quickly self-applied and exploited it.

7.   Shawn Levy, "When Mike Nichols Fired Robert De Niro: Excerpt from 'De Niro: A Life,'" *IndieWire*, December 28, 2014. Simon retooled the script into *The Goodbye Girl*, replaced De Niro with Richard Dreyfuss, Nichols with Herbert Ross, and scored a hit in 1977, for which Dreyfuss won the Best Actor Oscar. Sharp-eyed viewers can see a poster of De Niro (or a close look-alike) on the wall of Marsha Mason's apartment when she throws a bottle of cologne at it in anger for being abandoned.

8.   As an aside, calling DePalma a Hitchcock imitator is as ill-informed as, say, calling Howard Hawks a D. W. Griffith imitator. Every director builds on those directors who came before, and Hitchcock—like Griffith—perfected a vocabulary for screen storytelling that all subsequent filmmakers adapt for use. Why not call Neil Simon a George S. Kaufman imitator because they both wrote comedies, or Maya Angelou a Robert Frost imitator because they both used English in their poems?

9.   For the record: *Phantom of the Paradise*, *Obsession*, *Carrie*, *The Fury*, *Home Movies*, *Dressed to Kill*, *Blow Out*. One is a horror satire, one a coming-of-age story, and four are suspense thrillers.

10. Wade Major, "Brian DePalma," *Mr. Showbiz*, August 1998, http://mrshowbiz. com.

11. Lawrence Grobel, *Al Pacino* (New York: Simon Spotlight Entertainment, 2006).

12. Interview comments to Mark Cousins, "Scene by Scene," in association with the Edinburgh International Film Festival, https://www.youtube.com/ watch?v=rh_nbTfvfYc&t=1483s.

13. https://www.youtube.com/watch?v=gSo_Ds9_9O0&t=3s.

14. Tony Sokol, "Filmmakers Thought Al Pacino's Scarface Should Never Be Made," *Den of Geek*, September 11, 2022.

15. Charlie Rose, 1992 interview, https://www.youtube.com/watch?v=gSo_ Ds9_9O0&t=3s. Also: Jim Hemphill, *Filmmaker*, June 2, 2016.

16. Michael Pye and Lynda Myles, *The Movie Brats: How the Film Generation Took Over Hollywood* (New York: Holt, Rinehart, and Winston, 1979).

17. Tom Smothers played a tap-dancing magician. The film was written by Jordan Crittenden and was partially reshot and re-edited by Peter Nelson when the studio and Smothers disliked DePalma's footage.

18. https://www.youtube.com/watch?v=-Var3kWOjHc.

19. David Taylor, *The Making of Scarface* (United Kingdom: Unanimous, Ltd., 2005).

20. Author interview with Oliver Stone.

21. In early scripts her last name is Snodgrass, to which Tony replies, "Is that a name or an attitude?"

22. The image of Raft and the half dollar hounded Bauer. "When I had the role," he recalls, "there were old-timers who knew I was the guy who had gotten this role, flip the coin. Old guys would say, 'You know, George Raft did that role. Have you seen it? Are you gonna flip the coin?' I said, 'No, I have no reason to. It's not 1932.'" Author interview with Steven Bauer.

Chapter 6: Becoming Tony

1. IMDbPro. Accessed December 5, 2022.

2. Kaleen Aftab, *Insider*, Friday, July 17, 2015.

3. *Scarface* 35th Anniversary Reunion at Tribeca, *Scarface* 2018 DVD Bonus Features.

4. Bauer had previously appeared in a handful of TV episodics and a tiny role in *Valley Girl* (1983).

5. Author interview with Steven Bauer.

6. Author interview with Steven Bauer.

7. Author interview with Steven Bauer.

8. Author interview with Steven Bauer.

9. *Scarface* 35th Anniversary Reunion at Tribeca, *Scarface* 2018 DVD Bonus Features.

10. Author interview with Steven Bauer.

11. Author interview with Steven Bauer.

12. Author interview with Steven Bauer.

13. Author interview with Steven Bauer.

Chapter 7: Shooting the Movie

1. Army Archerd, *Variety*, January 10, 1983.

2. Mizner's huge hacienda. The other—seen as Tony's Coral Gables, Florida, mansion—was designed by Bertram Grosvenor Goodhue for J. Waldron Gillespie, one of whose Cuban estates was appropriated by Fidel Castro as his headquarters.

3. Oliver Stone, *Chasing The Light: Writing, Directing, and Surviving* Platoon, Midnight Express, Scarface, Salvador, *and the Movie Game* (Boston: Houghton Mifflin Harcourt, 2020).

4. *Scarface* 35th Anniversary Reunion at Tribeca, *Scarface* 2018 DVD Bonus Features.

5. *Scarface* 35th Anniversary Reunion at Tribeca, *Scarface* 2018 DVD Bonus Features.

6. Oliver Stone, *Chasing The Light: Writing, Directing, and Surviving* Platoon, Midnight Express, Scarface, Salvador, *and the Movie Game* (Boston: Houghton Mifflin Harcourt, 2020).

7.   Tina Daniel. *The Hollywood Reporter*. August 30, 1983.

8.   *Los Angeles Times*. November 10, 1983.

9.   Tina Daniel, op. cit. In the winter 1983/1984 issue of *Movie* magazine, Eric Estrin writes that he was in Martin Bregman's office at Universal when DePalma arrived with a copy of *Variety* that reported the budget at $37 million. Bregman immediately phoned the paper's Todd McCarthy and said, "Why don't you get off your little bottom and get over here and I'll show you the cost runs which are currently at $22 million, and after having seen that, I would love you to retract that statement."

10.   The cross-cutting to Gina and Manny as they become attracted to each other surfaces on additional viewings, particularly at Tony's and Elvira's wedding, where Manny and Gina make eyes at each other, and then, later on, in a sequence that was cut, in which they have stand-up sex against a tree in the woods not far from Tony's tiger.

11.   An observation: It was Manny whose unnamed connection helped liberate him and Tony from Freedom Town, but it was also Manny's unnamed connection that entrapped Tony into the FBI sting. Tony had the prescience to keep Manny out of what became the DEA and FBI sting, although he holds it against him later.

12.   The film combines the characters of the screenplay's Sosa's bodyguard Shadow (Mark Margolis) with the Bolivian journalist's intended assassin Needles so that Tony is "ripped apart by machine gun fire, grenades, and gas," rather than by a lone killer with a shotgun as in the film.

13.   Turner Classic Movies biography, undated.

14.   In the film it is called Montana Management Co., at 9461 Brickell Avenue, Miami.

15.   Author interview with Oliver Stone.

16.   https://www.google.com/maps/place/5+Tudor+City+Pl,+New+York, +NY+10017/@40.7483494,-73.9709732,3a,75y,127.25h,82.51t/data=!3m6!1e1!3m 4!1ssA8lUx7rdPeyiir2cWscFA!2e0!7i16384!8i8192!4m5!3m4!1s0x89c2591b517fc 545:0xc2507f3f58750a5e!8m2!3d40.7479568!4d-73.9709044?hl=en.

17.   Author interview with Oliver Stone.

Chapter 8: The Movie Novelization

1.   In his 1979 film *Manhattan*, Woody Allen chides Diane Keaton for doing a novelization: "What, what do you waste your time with a novelization for? It's like another contemporary American phenomenon that's truly moronic. The novelizations of movies. You're much too brilliant for that. You should be doing other stuff." The key is what she says back to him: "Why? Because it's easy and it pays well."

2.   Perhaps the most celebrated instance of this phenomenon is Foster's novelization of *Star Wars* that contains the whole Biggs-Luke subplot on Tatooine that was famously cut from the movie.

3.   Tina Daniel, *Hollywood Reporter*, August 30, 1983.

4. *Esquire* magazine noted the existence of the book, but no more, in an article in their March 1984 issue written by Stan Berkowitz, Samuel Graham, and John Milward.

5. Speaking at the film's 35th Anniversary panel at Tribeca on *Scarface*, 2018 DVD bonus features.

6. This is a gross oversimplification of the Method, but it will suit this purpose.

7. Ken Tucker, *Scarface Nation* (New York: St. Martin's Griffin, 2008).

8. Author interview with Oliver Stone.

9. Report Prepared by the National Security Council Planning Board, June 1, 1953, https://history.state.gov/historicaldocuments/frus1952-54v04/d45.

10. Seymour M. Hersh, *New York Times*, July 24, 1977, https://www.nytimes.com/1977/07/24/archives/sec-presses-wide-investigation-of-gulf-and-western-conglomerate-sec.html.

11. Center for Ethical Organizational Cultures, Auburn University, "The Coca-Cola Company Struggles with Ethical Crises," https://harbert.auburn.edu/binaries/documents/center-for-ethical-organizational-cultures/cases/coca-cola.pdf.

12. DePalma decided that he didn't like the voices of two of the INS agents in the interrogation scene, so he had actors Charles Durning and Dennis Franz come in and revoice them during ADR (automated dialogue replacement, sometimes known as looping).

13. Author interview with Oliver Stone.

14. It may be noted that the same situation arose in 2022 when Florida governor Ron DeSantis and Texas governor Greg Abbott transported Hispanic migrants, many of whom had applied for status, across state lines to other states, the legality of which continues to be debated.

15. Author interview with Steven Bauer.

16. The drug consumers, of course, are the ultimate victims, but they are never shown on screen, a noteworthy and wise decision.

17. https://www.youtube.com/watch?v=gHnHrcDgRWY.

18. Tim Greiving, *Scarface* CD liner notes, 2022.

19. When done to extreme, this musical punctuation is called "Mickey Mousing" after the on-the-nose synchronization used in many cartoon shorts.

20. https://www.youtube.com/watch?v=gHnHrcDgRWY. Also used by Tim Greiving in his *Scarface* CD liner notes, 2022.

21. Excerpted from *Score: The Podcast*, Season 2, Episode 15: "Giorgio Moroder and Raney Shockne, Kings of the South," https://www.youtube.com/watch?v=Vz1icPXDJ4Y&t=1s.

Chapter 9: The Critics Are Raving (and Ranting)

1. Boxofficemojo.com.

2. Author's statement: Film criticism is not a plebiscite; that's for the *People's Choice Awards*. Bona fide film criticism from experienced reviewers—not navel-gazing, but perceptive analysis—can be helpful to the art of cinema, and its near-disappearance from American letters is to be lamented.

3. Pauline Kael, "A DePalma Movie for People Who Don't Like DePalma Movies," *New Yorker*, December 26, 1983.

4. Sheila Benson, "Scarface Ods on Drugs, Violence," *Los Angeles Times*, December 9, 1983. *La Grande Bouffe* was Marco Ferreri's 1983 comedy about two men gorging themselves to death.

5. MW (Michael Wilmington), *LA Weekly*, December 19, 1983.

6. Vincent Canby, "Al Pacino Stars in *Scarface*," *New York Times*, December 9, 1983.

7. David Ansen, "Gunning Their Way to Glory," *Newsweek*, December 12, 1983.

8. David Denby, "Snowed Under," *New York*, December 19, 1983.

9. Andrew Sarris, "Pacino's Cuban Capone Comes a Cropper," *Village Voice*, December 20, 1983. But Sarris does make a good point about Bambi.

10. Stanley Kaufman, "The World Is Theirs," *New Republic*, January 6, 1984.

11. Author interview with David Ansen,

12. Service Cinema, "*Un entretien avec Brian De Palma, cineaste voyeur*," *Les Inrockuptibles*, May 11, 2000. Retrieved from Douglas Keesey, *Brian De Palma's Split-Screen: A Life in Film* (Jackson, MS: University Press of Mississippi, 2015).

13. Ann Thompson, "The Filmmaker Series: Brian De Palma," *Premiere*, September 1998. Retrieved from Douglas Keesey, *Brian De Palma's Split-Screen: A Life in Film* (Jackson, MS: University Press of Mississippi, 2015).

14. Lawrence Grobel, *Al Pacino* (New York: Simon Spotlight Entertainment, 2006).

15. David Taylor, *The Making of Scarface* (United Kingdom: Unanimous, Ltd., 2005).

16. Unsigned, *Film Daily*, August 17, 1932.

17. *New York Times*, May 20, 1932.

18. Quoted by Jonathan Rosenbaum in his October 16, 2017, *Film Comment* review of *James Agee's Complete Film Criticism*, Vol. 5, edited by Charles Maland.

19. Jason Bailey, "Revisiting the Controversy Surrounding *Scarface*," Vulture.com, April 20, 2018.

20. Comments at panel, 35th Anniversary Reunion at Tribeca, *Scarface* 2018 DVD Bonus Features.

21. *Los Angeles Herald Examiner*, November 9, 1983.

22. Aljean Harmetz, "DePalma Disputes Rating for 'Scarface,'" *New York Times*, October 26, 1983.

23. Many in the industry wished there was some middle ground between R and X. A. Alan Friedberg, president of Sack Theaters in Boston, who had seen the film at a preview, told Aljean Harmetz of the *New York Times* on October 30, 1983, that *Scarface* showed the need for an "M for Mature" or "A for Adult" that would avoid the stigma of an X. Friedberg said it was a powerful movie "that should not be lumped with *Debbie Does Dallas.*"

24. Julie Salamon covered the appeal for the *Wall Street Journal* ("X-ploiting the Ratings System," September 21, 1983) and would later write the book *The Devil's Candy* (New York: Houghton Mifflin, 1991) chronicling DePalma's 1990 film *The Bonfire of the Vanities.*

25. Lawrence Grobel, *Al Pacino* (New York: Simon Spotlight Entertainment, 2006).

26. Author interview with Oliver Stone.

27. Author interview with Oliver Stone.

28. https://collider.com/the-10-most-profane-movies-of-all-time-ranked-by-the-number-of-f-words/. Jordan Hoffman places the count at 207, or 1.21 times per minute (*Guardian,* April 20, 2018).

Chapter 10: Renaissance

1. Nat Segaloff, "Why a Film Flops." *Film Comment*. New York: The Film Society of Lincoln Center, November-December 1974.

2. For those who want to try, here's how: https://www.goldminemag.com/features/how-to-view-the-wizard-of-oz-with-dark-side-of-the-moon.

3. Absolutely true author story: I was close to Herb Schaefer, the avuncular branch manager of Buena Vista Distribution Company, which handled the Disney films in Boston, where I had gone to school. One day in summer 1969, Herb asked me to come to his office. He closed the door and confided that the company was thinking of rereleasing *Fantasia* but was afraid it would attract young people on marijuana. Did I think that was a risk? Being no stranger to the demon weed myself, I assured Herb that Disney had nothing to worry about. I'm not saying that I had anything to do with it, but the film's December 17, 1969, rerelease finally put *Fantasia* into profits.

4. Author interview with Christine La Monte, September 23, 2022.

5. Author interview with Steven Bauer.

6. Tim Gray, "Looking Back at 'Scarface' and How It Became a Cinematic Classic," *Variety*, December 6, 2019.

7. Author interview with Christine La Monte.

8. Hardeep Phull, "People Hated 'Scarface' Until Hip-Hop Gave it Cred," *New York Post*, April 12, 2018.

9. Miakkanatisse, *Grio*, August 26, 2011.

10. Lucas Garrison, DJ Booth, May 18, 2015, www.djbooth.com.

11. Ken Tucker, *Scarface Nation* (New York: St. Martin's Press), 2008.

12. Unsigned, *Hiphop News Journal*, November 30, 2018, http://hiphopnewsjournal.com/scarface-legacy-with-hiphop/.

13. Their count is short. See Sidebar: "The F-Word."

14. Author interview with Bill Stephney.

15. Author interview with Charles Coletta.

16. Author interview with Charles Coletta.

17. Author interview with Bill Stephney.

18. Author interview with Kevin Goetz.

19. Author interview with Charles Coletta.

20. Author interview with Kevin Goetz.

21. Interview comments, 35th Anniversary, 2018 DVD Bonus Features.

22. Interview comments, 35th Anniversary, 2018 DVD Bonus Features.

23. Author interview with Kevin Goetz.

24. Rapper Brad Jordan, formerly of the Geto Boys, took the name "Scarface" as a performer. He is not without controversy within the rap community.

25. Author interview with Bill Stephney.

26. One phone box from Redbubble carries a quote attributed to Tony Montana, "I always tell the truth, even when I lie," that is actually from writer Harlan Ellison.

27. www.scarfacestore.com.

28. Author interview with Dennis Plaksin.

29. https://www.youtube.com/watch?v=3DI3uW97hRc&t=2811s.

30. Gabriella Paiella, *Gentlemen's Quarterly*, May 14, 2020.

31. Mike Fleming, Jr., "Universal Preps New 'Scarface' Movie," Deadline Hollywood, September 21, 2011.

32. *The Wrap*, March 24, 2014.

33. Ibid.

34. Tatian Siegel, "'Scarface' Remake Moving Forward with 'Straight Outta Compton' Writer," *Hollywood Reporter*, March 18, 2015.

35. Mike Fleming, Jr., "Antoine Fuqua Circling New 'Scarface' at Universal," *Deadline Hollywood*, August 10, 2016.

36. Ryan Scott, "Diego Luna Is the New Scarface, Director Antoine Fuqua Exits," *Movie Web*, January 31, 2017.

37. Max Evry, "Scarface Remake Gets Coen Brothers Script, Release Date," ComingSoon.net, February 10, 2017.

38. Lola Jacobs, "'Scarface' Reboot to Focus on Core Immigrant Narrative," *Vibe*, March 30, 2018.

39. Adam Chitwood, "'Scarface' Remake Director Luca Guadagnino Wants a 'Big R-Rating on His "Shocking" Film,'" BadTaste.it, September 8, 2020.

40. Mike Floorwalker, "Scarface Reboot–What We Know So Far," www.looper.com, January 21, 2022.

41. Although Universal acquired the rights to the Hughes/Hawks *Scarface* in 1979, this copyright search suggests that MGM/UA was planning an end-run around Universal to make their own version.

42. This is not meant as legal advice, only reportage based on documents in the *Scarface* file from the Margaret Herrick Library of the Academy of Motion Picture Arts and Sciences, the full citation of which appears on the Extended Credits page.

43. Author interview with Dennis Plaksin.

Afterword

1. DVD special features interview, *Scarface*.

2. Dan Moldea, *Dark Victory: Ronald Reagan, MCA, and the Mob* (New York: Viking Penguin, 1986).

3. Interview comments, 35th Anniversary, 2018 DVD Bonus Features.

4. Comments on 35th Anniversary, 2018 DVD Bonus Features.

5. DeMille, an über-patriot who extolled family values, had mistresses, among them actress Julia Faye and screenwriter Jeanie Macpherson.

6. Joshua Rovner, "Black Disparities in Racial Incarceration," The Sentencing Project, July 15, 2021, https://www.sentencingproject.org/fact-sheet/black-disparities-in-youth-incarceration/.

7. Interview comments, 35th Anniversary, 2018 DVD Bonus Features.

Index